Praise for

THE **ANTIDOTE** TO SUFFERING

This work is a gift of learning and awakening to all health professionals, informing, affirming, and inspiring our understanding of and sensitivity to suffering from the inside out and outside in. It also offers an effective practice model of Compassionate Connected Care™, which aligns compassionate care with safety, quality, and deep personal experiences. A must for all health practitioners!

—JEAN WATSON, PhD, RN, AHN-BC, FAAN,
Founder and Director, Watson Caring Science
Institute, and Distinguished Professor and Dean
Emerita, University of Colorado Denver

What begins as a painful reminder of the challenges facing patients and caregivers today unfolds with a framework for addressing these issues and a vision of a care model that delivers compassionate and connected care reliably and efficiently. This model relies on caregivers, teams, and institutions to deliver excellence in clinical outcomes and operational efficiency, through the intentional focus on reducing patient suffering, addressing caregiver burnout, and advancing team diversity and organizational culture.

—JESSICA C. DUDLEY, MD, Chief Medical Officer,
Brigham and Women's Physicians Organization,
and VP of Care Redesign, Brigham Health

In *The Antidote to Suffering*, Christina Dempsey tells the story of nursing in today's healthcare reality. This book is a must-read for nursing students, new graduates, and seasoned nurses, as well as other providers. It reminds us of our humanity, commitment, and most of all, the power of caring for others and how compassion can help transcend boundaries and barriers.

—KAREN S. HILL, DNP, RN, NEA-BC, FACHE, FAAN,
Editor-in-Chief, *Journal of Nursing Administration*;
and COO and CNO, Baptist Health Lexington

Healthcare is challenged on so many fronts for both patients and those privileged to participate in their care. This deeply personal work weaves stories with powerful analysis, providing us with a prescription to ease suffering for us all. Compassionate Connected Care reminds us of our sacred mission and offers practical guidance to enable us to fulfill our promise.

—MICHAEL BENNICK, MD, MA, AGAF, FACP,
Associate Chief of Medicine, Department of
Internal Medicine, and Medical Director of the
Patient Experience, Yale–New Haven Hospital

In this deeply moving account of her family's journey through the healthcare system, Dempsey has put a face on the very real suffering of patients and caregivers. The Compassionate Connected Care framework offers actionable strategies for everyone, from individuals to organizations, to address and reduce the hardships involved with this very real issue.

—LEE WOODRUFF, Cofounder, Bob Woodruff Foundation

Christy compassionately tells the story of suffering by weaving her passion, knowledge, experience, and data into proven solutions for improvement. She exposes suffering in patients and professionals to better enable team effectiveness and professional joy. This book is new required reading for our teams. Compassion is the right way to turn difficulties into opportunities.

—SHARON PAPPAS, PhD, RN, NEA-BC, FAAN,
Chief Nurse Executive, Emory Healthcare

This engaging, readable, practical, and highly personal book provides a valuable framework for concentrating our efforts to improve healthcare by reducing patient suffering. By doing so, it not only speaks to the best traditions of medicine and nursing—it offers a road map to better care.

—IRA NASH, MD, Senior Vice President and
Executive Director, Northwell Health

The Antidote to Suffering provides a compelling case to support the crucial importance of improving experiences for everyone who is involved in the sacred work of delivering care. Dempsey weaves in moving stories from personal experience to crystalize the importance of reconnecting to the authentic spirit of caring, while offering pragmatic suggestions for effective change management. Healthcare leaders and care providers across all levels will definitely benefit from this poignant book.

—LAURA COOLEY, PhD, Senior Director of Education and Outreach, Academy of Communication in Healthcare

Required reading for anyone who cares about quality, safety, and the overall experience in our healthcare system. Fascinating perspective that reframes the conversation and opens a new path to improvements in care delivery for patients, families, and the healthcare workforce.

—SUSAN M. REESE, DNP, MBA, RN, CPHIMS, Chief Nurse Executive and Director of Healthcare Practice, Kronos Incorporated

Christy Dempsey takes the idea of "compassionate, connected care" from rhetoric to reality, with thoughtful analyses, revealing vignettes, and practical suggestions for how all clinicians—doctors, nurses, and others—can pursue this noble goal.

—LARRY H. HOLLIER JR., MD, Associate Surgeon-in-Chief for Clinical Affairs, Department of Surgery, Texas Children's Hospital

Christy Dempsey has masterfully blended compelling personal stories, meaningful frontline experience, and actionable solutions in addressing patient and caregiver suffering in *The Antidote to Suffering*. She effectively supports her arguments for Compassionate Connected Care with a wealth of survey information and related insights. I appreciate the way she explicitly and forcefully takes on the need to recognize, discuss, and address suffering. This should be on the top of the reading list for nurses, physicians, and administrators who are looking to make a difference in their institutions regarding patient and caregiver experience.

—RICHARD SIEGRIST, Director of Innovation and Entrepreneurship, Co-Director of Health Care Management Program, and Lecturer of Health Care Management, Harvard T. H. Chan School of Public Health

If you've ever been a patient in a hospital, or had a family member sick or in pain, you will instantly recognize what Christy Dempsey is talking about in *The Antidote to Suffering*. The care you receive may be the best, but the experience is often fraught with pain, confusion, anxiety, and loneliness. As Ms. Dempsey points out, these are not minor inconveniences. They actually add to the suffering that we may already be experiencing as a result of sickness or injury. And suffering is not limited to patients—it extends to caregivers who are often asked to work multiple long shifts, under stressful conditions, with little support.

One of the unique aspects of *The Antidote to Suffering* is that it is a practical book as well as an inspirational one. Based on her own broad experience in healthcare as a caregiver and as a patient, and backed up by research, Ms. Dempsey presents a persuasive argument that healthcare can be improved for both patient and caregiver in very specific ways, which she calls Compassionate Connected Care. Designed for people who take care of people, the book goes beyond the usual definitions of what constitutes good care, patient satisfaction, and caregiver engagement. She pushes the reader to think more deeply about these issues and to envision a better way of providing care—and then dives below the surface of this vision to describe very specifically the actions that can be taken to achieve these improvements.

Clearly written and full of details that bring the author's experiences and ideas alive, *The Antidote to Suffering* is a thought-provoking, timely, and insightful addition to the debates going on in healthcare today.

—SUSAN L MADDEN, MS, Associate Director,
　　Case-Based Teaching and Learning Initiative Instructor,
　　Department of Health Policy and Management,
　　Harvard T. H. Chan School of Public Health; and
　　author of *The Preemie Parents' Companion*

This book is a wonderful testimonial of how patients and caregivers view the patient experience, especially at the critical point where caregivers intersect with patients.

—KELLY HANCOCK, DNP, RN, NE-BC,
　　Chief Nursing Officer, Cleveland Clinic

Seldom do we have the opportunity to learn from a nursing leader through their personal *and* professional experience. Christy Dempsey has provided the readers of this book with that opportunity. She shares from her own heart and mind the struggles of suffering experienced and observed and the ways to use our learnings to impact care and leadership. This is a wonderful contribution to the reflective learning for nurses in a multitude of roles."

—MARILYN DUBREE, MSN, RN, NE-BC, Executive Chief
　　Nursing Officer, Vanderbilt University Medical Center

THE
ANTIDOTE
TO SUFFERING

**HOW COMPASSIONATE CONNECTED CARE
CAN IMPROVE SAFETY, QUALITY, AND EXPERIENCE**

CHRISTINA DEMPSEY

New York   Chicago   San Francisco
Athens   London   Madrid   Mexico City
Milan   New Delhi   Singapore   Sydney   Toronto

1 2 3 4 5 6 7 8 9   LCR   22 21 20 19 18 17

ISBN   978-1-260-11655-7
MHID   1-260-11655-7

e-ISBN   978-1-260-11656-4
e-MHID   1-260-11656-5

Library of Congress Cataloging-in-Publication Data

Names: Dempsey, Christina, author.
Title: The antidote to suffering : how compassionate connected care can
    improve safety, quality, and experience / by Christina Dempsey.
Description: New York : McGraw-Hill, [2018]
Identifiers: LCCN 2017036827 | ISBN 9781260116557 (acid-free paper) |
    ISBN 1260116557 (acid-free paper)
Subjects: LCSH: Medical personnel and patient. | Hospital care. |
    Communication in medicine. | Medical ethics. | BISAC: BUSINESS &
    ECONOMICS / Customer Relations.
Classification: LCC R727.3 .D454 2018 | DDC 610.7306/9—dc23
LC record available at https://lccn.loc.gov/2017036827

McGraw-Hill Education books are available at special quantity discounts to use as premiums and sales promotions, or for use in corporate training programs. To contact a representative, please visit the Contact Us page at www.mhprofessional.com.

For Tom

Contents

Acknowledgments

IT IS MY great honor to recognize a number of family, friends, and colleagues who have made this book possible.

First, my colleagues at Press Ganey (who are also my friends) have been a wonderful support system through thick and thin. When Pat Ryan made me CNO in 2012, I had no idea what a wonderful journey it would be. I am forever in his debt. Joe Greskoviak, my friend and mentor, gave me the gift of security after my breast cancer diagnosis, a story I recount in this book. Tom Lee has been my biggest cheerleader since arriving at Press Ganey, and his support for this book has been no exception. Deirdre Mylod provided and continues to provide both the raw data and the additional insight that makes the numbers interesting and actionable. I wish to also thank Barbara Reilly, who has partnered with me in our study of engagement and resilience; Craig Clapper and Julie Samuelson, who shared personal stories; and Nell Buhlman, Patti Cmielewski, and Mary Jo Assi, who provided valuable feedback. To Gregg DiPietro, who offered a marketing and literary touchpoint throughout this endeavor: I couldn't have done it without you!

And to the many others at Press Ganey who contributed in some way to this project: I'm so honored to work with each and every one of you.

Brandy and Kylie, two individuals described in the book, are real people. Brandy continues to deal with thyroid cancer. As you consider the concepts of empathy, compassion, and suffering, please keep her in your thoughts. Kylie gave my family and me the gift of herself and, in doing so, helped me think about what compassionate and connected care truly is.

Seth Schulman, my collaborator, is the ultimate wordsmith. This is a better book because of him. Rachel Gostenhofer provided expertise with fact checking and citations. Thank you, Rachel, for your second (maybe third) pair of eyes! To Casey Ebro, my editor at McGraw-Hill, thank you for your commitment to this book.

To my family, I am in awe of you. To Aaron and Amanda who have been through so much and come out stronger: thank you for allowing me to share your story to demonstrate how important caregivers are to the people who need them. I extend my deep gratitude as well to Hilary, who now works for Press Ganey, and her wife, a paramedic, both of whom are carrying this message forward in healthcare. I wish to thank my sister, Wendy Harmon, who provided critical nonclinical feedback throughout the writing of this book; my mother, Cathy Schneider, a nurse, leader, and mentor—thank you, Mom; and my mother-in-law, Norma, who allowed me to share her story in hopes that it would help others stay healthy. Finally, to my husband, Tom, you've been my rock and my partner through it all. I couldn't have done any of this without you.

And to you, the faithful reader: I hope this book will give you food for thought, new tools and strategies to try, and, above all, a way to remember why you care.

Introduction

THE SOUND OF a door slamming awoke us. What was going on? I glanced at our bedside clock. It was 2:30 in the morning. "Mom, Dad," my younger daughter, Hilary, called from the front door. She sounded upset.

"Hilary," my husband, Tom, said groggily.

"Get up, quick!" Hilary shouted. "Aaron's been shot!"

Aaron was the husband of my older daughter, Amanda. He, Amanda, and their two young children—three-year-old Jackson and seven-month-old Jovie—had been at our house that evening for dinner. At 8 p.m., Aaron had left to work the night shift as a police officer in our town.

Tom and I jumped out of bed, threw on clothes, and ran to the living room. One look at Hilary, and I could tell that it was bad. She had run to our house and was alternately sobbing and gasping for breath. Standing next to her was our friend Ben, another police officer. Tom was a retired police officer, and Ben had worked for him on the narcotics squad.

"Where's he hit?" Tom asked the two of them. "Where have they taken him?"

Hilary knew very little. Ben put on a brave face, but he was shaken—you could tell by the look in his eyes. "It's pretty bad," he said. "Tom, Aaron was shot through the eye."

Having worked for decades as a nurse, I went into my clinical, problem-solving mode, calling the hospital to find out who the trauma surgeon was on duty. There wasn't much I could do, but making that call at least allowed me to combat the overwhelming feelings of panic and helplessness that were washing over me.

It was 3:30 when we arrived at the hospital. Amanda was there, and they had taken Aaron into surgery. Two police officers stood guard outside the room. From them, we learned that Aaron had been investigating a call in a high-crime neighborhood when he spotted a suspicious-looking man. As he approached, the man bolted, and Aaron pursued him. Without warning, the suspect turned and pointed a gun. We knew Aaron had drawn his own weapon because other officers later found it under his body. But he never had a chance to use it. Before he could, the suspect fired every round in his gun. Aaron went down. Other officers administered CPR until the ambulance arrived. The two officers were guarding Aaron because the suspect hadn't yet been apprehended; as it turned out, the perpetrator was a career criminal who had spent most of his life in prison and was out on parole after being incarcerated for assaulting a police officer.

Amanda sat sobbing. Her husband was probably dead. At the very least, he would be permanently disabled, possibly in a vegetative state. She had two babies to raise. How would she do it? What would happen to their family? As Tom and I hugged her and tried to console her, she sat clutching Aaron's wedding ring. A quick-thinking female officer had taken it off Aaron before they put him in the ambulance, mindful that if she didn't, Amanda would lose access to it—the police department would keep it as "evidence." As upset as Amanda was, it was such a comfort to her to have that ring. Somehow, it helped her get through the initial shock of what had happened.

Sometime later, a nurse came and brought us to a consultation room where we were to receive an update on Aaron's condition. This room was small and windowless, with seating for a family of eight. This is where the doctors and pastoral care staff come to give you bad news. Families sit there dreading the appearance of the hospital staff because they know that their lives are about to change forever. As the minutes ticked by one after the next, we stared at the door wondering what was in store for us. All we could do was wait.

Finally, Aaron's neurosurgeon came in. She sat down and took Amanda's hands. As she calmly recounted, the bullet had grazed Aaron's nose and entered through his left eye. It had broken apart upon impact. Half of it was lodged in the back of Aaron's brain, while the other half had fragmented in his left frontal lobe. Aaron had multiple facial fractures. "The best-case scenario," the doctor said, "is that Aaron will never speak again, and he'll have limited use of his right side."

I don't remember it myself, but other hospital staff later told me that when the doctor left the consultation room after speaking with us, she was crying.

An Epidemic of Suffering

I recount this story because so often in healthcare, we lose touch with what patients and their families experience when someone they love experiences a health crisis. But let me be more specific. So often we lose touch with the *suffering* that patients and their families feel. Imagine having something bad happen to a loved one—something that cannot be undone. Your loved one will never be the same and never achieve his or her dreams. In our case, Amanda was suffering, and so were Tom and I. Tom had encouraged Aaron to become a police officer—he had loved the job so much and believed (rightfully, it turned out) that Aaron would, too. Now Tom was overcome not merely with concern for his son-in-law and his daughter, but also with guilt. I felt sick to my stomach thinking of the suffering Amanda would soon experience. I thought about what it would feel like to look into my three-year-old grandson's eyes and try to explain why daddy wouldn't be taking him to preschool that morning.

As a nurse, I pride myself on taking charge and finding solutions. This time, however, there was nothing I could do. I couldn't make the situation better, I couldn't change what had happened, and I was completely powerless to fix anything, just like every other devastated family member of every other patient in the ICU.

I recount Aaron's story for another reason. We healthcare providers don't just lose touch with patient suffering. All too often, we unwittingly *cause* it or make it worse. After that initial consultation with the neurosurgeon, she went off call. Twenty-four hours later, Aaron was still in the ICU, and we still hadn't heard from anyone. To say we were worried doesn't begin to describe how we felt. We stayed in the waiting room with all the other families, sleeping on couches and chairs, using thin blankets and hard pillows. We tried to sleep, but of course, we couldn't. Every time a person in a white coat came by, we sucked in our breath and sat up straight, wondering if that person was coming to speak with us.

We wanted news, but the prospect of hearing it also terrified us. In the absence of information, we tended to dwell on worst-case scenarios. Truthfully, I wasn't sure what to pray for. As awful as it sounds, I knew that Aaron would not want to live in a persistent vegetative state on a ventilator and feeding tube for the rest of his life. I couldn't imagine what that would do to my daughter and my grandchildren. I wanted a positive outcome for Aaron, as positive as we could get. I wanted him to come back to us, but I wasn't sure that could happen. We had more questions than answers. Tom and I talked about what nurses we would choose to help take care of Aaron if he could live at home, and whether Amanda and the kids would need to come live with us. With each passing hour, we grew more anxious and despondent. I don't remember if I knew it all the years I worked as a nurse, but I sure knew it the night Aaron was shot: waiting, for family members of a patient, is suffering. It's excruciating, plain and simple.

More suffering was in store for us. When we couldn't take the waiting any longer, I called the chief of neurosurgery and asked him to have someone come and talk with us. He said he would send the neurosurgeon on call. An hour or two later, the doctor arrived, but he wouldn't talk to anyone but Amanda. In all fairness, there were a lot of us waiting by then, and the doctor probably felt intimidated. Still, as a nurse and our family's de facto clinical liaison, I felt aggravated that the doctor would not talk to me. Even as I asked questions, he never took his eyes off Amanda. That unnerved her, too. She was working hard just to get through life minute by minute, and she was looking to me to take care of the complexities of the healthcare system. This doctor didn't seem to get it.

He informed us that Aaron was not moving his left side at all due to the injury, and he was moving his right side very minimally. We were instantly concerned that Aaron's condition had taken a turn for the worse. "Oh, wait, no, no," the surgeon said. "I meant he's moving his left side, the side he had already been moving." I wasn't thrilled about the doctor's uncertainty, but I was willing to give him a break—he was, after all, the "on-call" surgeon. But then he said, "We've put him on antibiotics for his pneumonia."

"He has pneumonia??!!" I said.

"Well, no," he said, "but he's intubated . . ."

At this point, I stopped listening. This doctor clearly didn't know his patient, and I no longer trusted him to care for my son-in-law. For whatever reason, this doctor had failed in his most important responsibility to us: to make my son-in-law, and by extension, his family, feel safe. Without realizing or intending it, he caused us to suffer, worsening the trauma we were already experiencing.

Such suffering is endemic in healthcare. We don't like to talk about it, but it's there every day in hospital rooms, ICUs, waiting rooms, emergency departments, and exam rooms throughout the United States. In the course of dealing with a wide array of health issues, patients and their families get lost in our complex, fragmented, and chaotic healthcare system. They're treated in ways that cause or magnify fear, sadness, anguish, or other painful emotions. And it isn't just patients and their families who suffer. The people who care for them—doctors, nurses, therapists, technologists—suffer, too. With healthcare organizations trying to do more with less, bedside caregivers are left to navigate starkly competing priorities. They become tired, overwhelmed, and disconnected from the original passion that initially attracted them to healthcare. Work becomes painful drudgery and inconvenience rather than what it should be—a unique opportunity to find fulfillment and purpose in serving others.

Current systems, processes, and attitudes in healthcare prevent us from addressing the suffering of both patients and caregivers. So what's the answer? First, and most obviously, we should become more mindful of the suffering we cause, and make our colleagues more mindful of it, too. We should also measure both patient and caregiver suffering, in large part using data that already exist today. Going back to basics, we can better understand the care experience and determine if suffering is decreasing or increasing over time. But talking about and measuring suffering are not enough. We also have to *do* something about it—as individuals, as teams, as organizations, and as an industry. We need a concrete plan, one that helps us make meaningful progress and that allows all of us in healthcare to get closer to our basic purpose: caring for people and helping them to heal.

Solving for Suffering

Aimed primarily at readers who care for patients every day, *The Antidote for Suffering* is the first book to examine the problem of suffering and to offer practical solutions. In particular, this book presents a powerful, evidence-based plan for reducing suffering and optimizing the patient and caregiver experience. Over the past several years, my colleagues and I have conducted extensive qualitative and quantitative research into suffering and its opposite, compassionate and connected care. We asked hundreds of patients, clinicians, and nonclinicians what compassionate and connected care actually looked like to them. Analyzing their responses, we teased out common themes and patterns and eventually distilled our qualitative data into an affinity diagram consisting of twelve themes: six for patients and six for caregivers. This model, called Compassionate Connected Care™, covers the clinical, operational, cultural, and behavioral dimensions of care that all patients and caregivers experience in every setting.

As I show, the Compassionate Connected Care model points us to a variety of concrete tactics that individuals, teams, organizations, and the healthcare industry can implement to reduce suffering and dramatically enhance the quality of healthcare experiences. In the chapters that follow, I document the scourge of suffering, assess the various forces that have made it so prevalent in healthcare today, and present the Compassionate Connected Care model in detail. I devote the bulk of the book to describing tactics for reducing suffering. As you'll see, some of these tactics are so simple that you can begin to deploy them this very instant to make a meaningful difference in your work environment. Others require more collaboration and coordination. As a group, these tactics are practical and accessible, no matter what your specialty or the kind or size of your organization. These tactics also require very little to implement—no significant outlays of money, staff time, or other resources. In fact, taking steps to "solve for suffering" actually *saves money* and helps organizations to deliver higher-quality care. As research shows, caregivers who perceive a reliably better experience become more engaged and loyal employees. And patients who perceive a reliably better experience have lower readmission rates, shorter lengths of stay, and lower incidences of hospital-acquired conditions. Solving for suffering increases patient safety and decreases an array of costs for healthcare organizations.

A Unique Vantage Point

In addition to tactics, I'll present a number of stories from patients and their families, as well as caregivers, to help evoke the problem of suffering and the difference these tactics can make. Included among these are my own stories. For much of my career, I thought I understood well enough how patients and caregivers experience healthcare. I've been a nurse for over 30 years, working for 10 years at bedside before moving into a variety of leadership roles. Beginning in the late 1990s, I worked on redesigning the flow of patients from the emergency department to the operating room and downstream to the ICU, helping to improve overtime, efficiency, morale, and experience at an 800-bed community-based, level 1 trauma center. I eventually joined the consulting-firm startup PatientFlow Technology, and in 2009, when Press Ganey acquired PatientFlow, I was tapped to lead Press Ganey's clinical and operational consulting practice. In 2012, I became Press Ganey's first chief nursing officer. I also have taught Nursing

Leadership and Management at Missouri State University, my alma mater, for almost a decade.

As helpful as this varied experience has been, it didn't alert me to the epidemic of suffering in healthcare. What did was my own, personal encounters with healthcare. About a year before Aaron was shot, I was diagnosed with a serious illness and became a patient for the first time. All of a sudden, I understood the dozens or even hundreds of ways that patients can suffer, above and beyond the unavoidable physical and emotional pain accruing from the illnesses themselves. Then in January 2015, when my family and I struggled to process and cope with Aaron's trauma, I received a stark reminder of what suffering was. Thanks to both of these experiences, I came to understand the profound difference that compassionate and connected care can mean for patients. And I became resolved to *do* something about it—to spread the word in lectures, presentations, and now this book.

In the chapters that follow, I'll describe my experiences as a patient, family member of a patient, nurse, leader and administrator, and educator of nursing. The result, I hope, will be something relatively rare: a 360-degree perspective on healthcare and how it is experienced. This perspective in turn informs the scope and ambition of *The Antidote for Suffering*. Others have written about patient satisfaction, and indeed, my organization, Press Ganey, is known for it. But this book is not about patient satisfaction. It's about the *totality* of patient and caregiver experience, including clinical care, operational performance, behaviors, and culture. I'm not interested in helping people become happier or more satisfied. Nobody is happy about being sick or having a family member in the ICU or about waiting in a waiting room. If reducing suffering were only about smiling, making eye contact, and drawing the curtain for privacy, it would be easy. But it's not. I'm interested in exploring the experience of patients and caregivers from all angles, empathizing with them, and helping to reduce the tremendous suffering they experience every day.

While this book presents strategies and tactics, it isn't ultimately about these practical solutions or about achieving certain "scores" relating to patient experience. After all I've been through as a patient and the family member of a patient, I realize that a score is simply a number. When we went to college, we all majored in something: nursing, medicine, physical therapy, and so on. None of us majored in an "A." We didn't sit home until the wee hours of the morning writing "As." We didn't have study groups and talk about "As." We all wanted to make an A, but only because it alerted us to the progress we were making toward our ultimate goal: becoming a nurse, a doctor, a therapist . . . Likewise, I seek to challenge healthcare providers to consider why it is that we do what we do. I want us to remember each and every day that when we show up for work, we're not just treating patients clinically—*we're changing lives*. We need to understand the true impact we have on patients and their families and adjust our behavior accordingly. If we change our underlying mindset, all kinds of positive outcomes for patients, providers, organizations, and the industry become possible.

Kylie's Gift

About four days after his surgery, Aaron began to open his right eye and move his left side. He couldn't move it much—he was intubated and likely confused. Soon, he began to track movement with his eye. "Mom," my daughter Amanda said to me, "that means he's in there somewhere! I can deal with that. I can take care of him. It will be OK."

Over the next few days, Aaron began following basic commands, flashing a "thumbs up" when we asked him to, or wiggling his toes. "Mom, look!" Amanda said. "He can understand. We'll get through this. I'll take care of him."

The hospital brought in child life specialists to help the children, mainly three-year-old Jackson, prepare to see their daddy in the ICU. As a mother and grandmother, you never think that you'll have to prepare a three-year-old to see his daddy with bandages all over his head and face and with tubes coming out of his mouth and nose, hooked up to big and noisy machines. You never think you'll have to explain why his daddy can't talk to him or hold him or read to him.

We didn't want Jackson to be traumatized any more than he had to be, so the specialists took pictures of the machines and talked with Jackson about what Aaron would look like. When it seemed that Jackson was sufficiently prepared, Amanda took him into the ICU with her, with Tom and me following. She left seven-month-old Jovie behind, reasoning that she was too young and wouldn't remember anything.

The ICU is a scary place for adults, but imagine being a three-year-old and being told something is wrong with your daddy and everyone you love is sad. Jackson walked to the door, but he decided that he didn't want to go further. That's when the first of many miracles happened. In preparation for the visit, the nurses had elevated the head of Aaron's bed and loosened his restraints. Aaron lifted his eyebrow in a questioning manner and made his left arm into a cradle, clearly asking, "Where is Jovie?"

Amanda turned to me. "Look, Mom! He knows what's going on! I'm tired of crying. What's next?"

Months of painful recovery followed. After about two weeks in the hospital, when he was able to travel, Aaron was flown to a well-respected rehabilitation center known for its work with brain-injured patients. Amanda, the children, and I moved to the city where the rehab hospital was located. We expected to be there for nine months to a year. Afterward, Aaron could live with us and return for outpatient therapy. From the very beginning, the care at this facility was amazing. Aaron's team focused intently on getting him back.

This facility was not the only one to deliver incredible care. Back in the ICU, one of Aaron's nurses, Kylie, made a special impression on me. She was in her mid-twenties, petite, thin, blond, and very sweet. As time passed, she proved herself to be both a strong woman and a kind and confident clinician. It was Kylie who helped us understand Aaron's care and navigate the many medical specialists who interacted with him. It was Kylie and her colleagues who helped get the child life specialists involved to help my grandchildren. And it was Kylie who cried with us, prayed with us, and rejoiced with us at every milestone in Aaron's early recovery. But of her many acts of kindness, one stands out above the others.

At this hospital, patients were allowed only a few visitors at a time. Yet a great many people cared about Aaron. He had a "real" family—us—but he also had a law enforcement family that was just as important to him. His fellow officers needed to see him to know that he was alive, and Aaron needed to know that they were there supporting him. Kylie understood this. She didn't have to bend the rules for Aaron, but she did, allowing all his colleagues to come visit him. I will never forget this.

You see, Kylie recognized Aaron as a unique individual, not "the gunshot wound in bed four." Because she saw Aaron that way, she was able to offer him care that was truly compassionate and connected and that was tailored to *his* needs. Aaron's recovery was painful—he would suffer no matter what kind of care he received. But because of Kylie, his suffering was much reduced, and his ability to heal was enhanced. And because of Kylie, our suffering was reduced, too.

High-quality healthcare is about much more than just clinical success. It's about treating patients and caregivers alike with the utmost dignity, respect, and compassion. I will be the first to agree that this is much easier said than done. Sometimes we in healthcare get jaded. We wake up in the morning, have breakfast, go to work, come home, eat dinner, go to bed, and do it all over again the next day. But for all the patients in a bed, on a gurney, or in a waiting room, it isn't just another day. It's the day they hear they have diabetes. It's the day they learn they are pregnant. It's the day they receive a diagnosis of cancer and know they will be in a fight for their lives.

When we encounter patients, they are at their most vulnerable. They're scared and at the mercy of the people caring for them. As a result, everything we say and do matters. We may not remember patients and their families, but they will remember us. We have it in our power to change people's lives for the better, to give them gifts of kindness, like the ones Kylie gave to Aaron and our family. We can leave patients with more positive memories and fewer negative ones. Join me in rediscovering the true meaning of what we do as healthcare providers. And join me in taking new joy in our work. Together, we can improve the care we deliver, and we can help to end the costly and inhumane epidemic of suffering.

An Epidemic
of Suffering

IT WAS JULY 24, 2013, a Wednesday. My husband, Tom, and I were at the hospital, sitting in a small, windowless nurse's office before a desk laden with folders and papers. For years, I had worked in an office just like this one as a nurse administrator. But sitting here on this day was like no other experience I have ever had. This time, I wasn't the nurse, conveying the results of a cancer biopsy. I was the patient.

Many nurses see death up close. And thanks to this proximity, some of us come to feel less afraid of it. Not me. Rationally, I knew that I probably didn't have cancer. My doctor had told me that 80 percent of the time, the biopsies were benign for the kind of calcifications in my right breast—heterogeneous and BIRADS 4—that a routine screening mammogram had turned up. But frightening thoughts kept racing through my mind. What if I did have cancer? In that case, my life would change forever. I would be a cancer patient, a statistic. And the cancer might have spread to my bones or my brain. I might lose my hair from the chemo. I might die.

When I feel stressed, I don't cry. I get quiet and withdraw into myself. That's what I did here. "Well," the nurse finally said, looking me in the eye, "It's not what we had hoped for. You have cancer, both DCIS and invasive." DCIS—or ductal carcinoma in situ—is a form of breast cancer that has not spread beyond the duct in the breast. But I had both: the noninvasive kind and the kind that could spread and kill you.

I felt numb. The nurse proceeded to tell me about my disease and the prognosis, but I couldn't absorb any of it. I remained stoically silent, nodding my head at the appropriate times. Then, as my husband and I got up to go, the nurse complimented me on the gold bracelet I was wearing. When she said that, I began to sob. This piece of jewelry was very special to me: the year before, my husband had surprised me with it on Christmas. My husband held my hand as we walked out of the office and into the strange new world of cancer.

I wasn't the only one who was terrified. Later that day, Tom broke down and cried for maybe the fourth time in 30 years. My daughters, my mother, my sister: All of them were worried. Nobody in our immediate family had ever had breast cancer. Would I be OK? Would I need chemo, radiation, or some other therapy? What would happen with my job? And what would it mean for my family, especially my sister and daughters? I was supposed to be the rock in the family—strong, brave, the person who had all the answers. Now I had more questions than answers. I was feeling incredibly vulnerable and out of control.

As anxious as we all were, it could have been a lot worse. Because I had a medical background, the language that my nurses and doctors were using was familiar to me. I knew exactly what questions to ask and how to perform medical research, so I wasn't confused or uncertain about my treatment. I could convey my knowledge to the loved ones who worried about me. Imagine what people who don't know much about medicine must go through. I was also extremely fortunate to have a secure job at Press Ganey, with a boss, colleagues, and an organization that went out of their way to show their support. When I told our president, Joe Greskoviak, of my diagnosis, he said to me, "Christy, I want you to know that this is when you focus on you. You are our CNO, and you will continue to be our CNO. Don't worry about your job for another second." I can't tell you how much that relieved me, as did all the cards people sent me letting me know that they were thinking of me. Imagine what it must be like for the many patients who don't have this support. These patients are not merely frightened about their medical diagnoses, but about everything in their lives that now seems at risk. We wonder as caregivers why our patients are often angry, sad, distant, and distressed. Now I knew: it's scary to be a patient.

But my suffering as a breast cancer patient was by no means over. Once I had selected a surgeon who would remove the tumor, I had to undergo an MRI of both breasts so that we would know more about the scope of the surgery and the prognosis. The week after my biopsy, I found myself prone on an exam table and completely alone, save for a technologist on the other side of the MRI machinery. The MRI is loud and confining—equally scary for people who have never been in one and for those who know how they work and what they do. The preliminary results not only confirmed the cancer in my right breast; it showed four suspicious areas in the left breast as well. At this point, I was really scared. If the cancer was in both breasts, where else might it be? A follow-up ultrasound would provide some answers, but I had to wait two days for that. The waiting was excruciating. I just wanted the cancer out of me!

The ultrasound turned up nothing bad in the left breast, but I still had to decide whether to have a lumpectomy or a full mastectomy, and on one side or both. This was a very difficult decision for me. I had always thought that it wouldn't bother me to lose both my breasts if I ever had cancer, but now I wasn't so sure. When you have a lumpectomy, the breast is often misshapen but there is still breast tissue. When you have a mastectomy, all of your breast tissue is removed, including the nipple. You can have nipple-sparing surgery so that the surgeon can reattach your nipple after your mastectomy and during reconstruction, but the sensation is never the same. I talked with my family and my husband for hours trying to make this decision. And I had to think about all of this as I was still working hard at my job, dealing with my baseline anxiety about cancer, and trying to maintain some sense of normality for my family.

Other procedures leading up to my mastectomy brought torments big and small, some of which I'll recount later in this book. Perhaps my greatest misery occurred after surgery. Awakening in the recovery room, I was taken to a shared room, where I would spend the night with another patient as my roommate. I was in a great deal of pain, so I pushed the call light to ask the nurse for medication. She said that I could have something in 20 minutes and that I should remind her. I was somewhat taken aback. *I'm the patient*, I thought, *I have to remind you? I just had surgery. I can't even think straight!* My husband did remind her several times—still no pain medication.

I was hurting so much that I couldn't sleep. It didn't help that alarms were constantly going off, people were talking in the hallway just outside my room, and my roommate was shrieking with her own uncontrolled pain. Repeatedly I awoke thinking that an hour had passed, when it had only been a few minutes. I asked for earplugs, but the nurses didn't have any. My husband found some in the gift shop, and they helped a little. But then a nursing assistant came in and said I had to get up to go to the bathroom. After she made the necessary preparations, I walked slowly over to the toilet. She seemed in a hurry and somewhat frazzled, so I asked her how many patients she had that night.

"Eleven," she replied.

"How many does your nurse have?"

"Six."

"That's a lot," I said, entering the bathroom.

She shrugged. "It isn't that we have that many patients. It's just that everybody is so needy tonight."

That response confused me and made me feel a bit defensive. Did she mean me? I was trying not to be a pest or push my call light all the time. The last thing any patient wants is to be thought of as needy, especially a patient like me who also happens to be a nurse.

I happened to look down at that moment, and there on the toilet seat was blood—someone else's. How could the staff on duty have simply left that there when they knew I was going to the bathroom? It was their idea for me to go to the bathroom in the first place! If they weren't careful about keeping the bathroom clean for a scheduled visit, what else were they missing? The oversight didn't inspire much confidence that I was in a place that provided safe, high-quality care.

I went back to bed and continued to struggle to sleep. Sometime later, the night nurse came in. Without bothering to introduce herself, she looked at my armband, adjusted my IV, and lifted my gown to check my dressing. Finally, I asked her: Who *are* you? Again, this oversight on her part undercut one of the hospital's most basic functions: to help patients feel safe.

Morning finally came. I needed to get up, walk around, and stretch my legs. My husband helped me, holding me up by the elbow. I shuffled slowly around the unit. As we passed the nurse's station, I spotted a number of people chatting with one another and tapping at their computers. After the comment about being "needy," and after waiting endlessly for my pain medication, I was aggravated that they were all just sitting there. I knew that they were likely charting and reporting on patients to prepare for the next shift, but I still felt like I had gotten lost in the processes and paperwork. The people on the team hadn't performed a bedside shift report (although I could hear them talking about me out in the hallway as they changed shifts). It would have been nice as a patient to have participated in the report and to hear their thoughts about my care and condition. Although many parts of my care had gone well, I couldn't *wait* to get out of there.

Most caregivers don't think much about the impact of seemingly "small" miscues like a dirty toilet seat, delays in bringing painkillers, or noisy patient rooms. What matters, we think, are the clinical outcomes. Cure a patient's cancer, fix his or her fractured wrist, and you've done your job. This is horribly wrong. Clinical outcomes may be paramount, but the *experience* of healthcare is an outcome, too. When you're a patient, miscues such as those I witnessed are not small. They make the difference between healing experiences and those so inconvenient or uncomfortable or painful or downright awful that you can't wait to forget them. Of course, you can't forget them. Like scars on your skin, they heal but never really go away.

The concept of suffering in healthcare is not new. The word "patient" itself derives from the Latin word for "to suffer."[1] Today, patients truly embody this ancient meaning, as people who seemed destined to suffer.[2] Healthcare is seeing an epidemic of suffering, one that has only been increasing in recent years. You see it in every setting, from hospitals to clinics to doctors' offices. Patients are suffering physical pain, and they're tormented by emotions like anxiety, sadness, and loneliness. Rather than helping to ease this suffering, we in healthcare often worsen it. In too many cases, we're actually *causing* it. We're doing this not because we're evil, incompetent, or lazy. The staff that took care of me, from the moment of my diagnosis to my surgery through to my recovery, weren't trying to make my ordeal any worse than it had to be. And yet in a variety of ways, only some of which I've alluded to here, they were doing precisely that. Think about your own daily work. No doubt you show up every day trying to do your best. You work long hours, and you come home exhausted. But despite all that effort, are you sensitive to the suffering of your patients? Are you taking steps to ease it? Or are you, your team, your organization, and the industry as a whole serving unwittingly to worsen it?

Moving Past the Guilt

I say this not to lecture you from on high. Before getting sick myself, I had never really thought of my patients as suffering, either. I was caring for them, and they received great clinical care, so how could they be suffering? Yet they were. Early in my career, when I was working on a neuro step-down unit on the night shift, I cared for a woman in her thirties who had experienced a severe headache and lost consciousness. After giving her all the standard tests—blood work, CT scan, and an arteriogram of her brain to check blood flow—we discovered that she had had a subarachnoid hemorrhage from a cerebral aneurysm or weakness in the blood vessel. We had scheduled her for surgery the next day to fix the bubble in her blood vessel and reduce the risk of future bleeding. Brain surgery is very serious, and this woman had young children at home. I talked with her for about half an hour about what she could expect, and she described her fear of paralysis or a stroke during surgery. "I'm more worried about my family than anything," she said. "I'm afraid for myself, but I'm more afraid for them." I never thought of such fear as suffering, but of course it was precisely that.

This woman died on the operating table the next day. I have always asked myself what more I could have done to help her on that last night of her life. Could I have said something that might have eased her mind? Could I have attended better to her physical pain? Could I have listened better? Could I have been quicker handling her requests? Was there *anything* I could have done that would have made a difference? Thirty years later, I still think about this patient because I know she was suffering that night. She felt physical pain, she worried about herself and her family, and she was scared.

Why wasn't I thinking about this woman's suffering? And why do so few clinicians think of it today? I believe that the very word "suffering" makes clinicians feel guilty. We want to do right by our patients. And we feel that if our patients are suffering, we must be doing something to cause it, or we're not doing something to relieve it. We also feel overwhelmed in our jobs—powerless to do much more than we currently are. So we would rather not talk about suffering. In the 2013 *New England Journal of Medicine* article "The Word That Shall Not Be Spoken," Press Ganey's chief medical officer Tom Lee wrote that "we avoid the word 'suffering' even though we know it is real for our patients because the idea of taking responsibility for it overwhelms us as individuals—and we are already overwhelmed by our other duties and obligations."[3] We even go so far as to medicalize suffering as a psychiatric condition, "thereby transforming a moral category into a technical one." British historians William F. Bynum and Roy Porter have pointed out that we try to treat suffering with medications, and we don't pay attention to how we as caregivers contribute to it. "As a result, practitioners of biomedicine are in a situation unlike that of most other healers; they experience a therapeutic environment in which the traditional moral goals of healing have been replaced by narrow technical objectives."[4]

To help improve healthcare for patients, Press Ganey began using the word "suffering" in 2012 in connection with its work concerning the patient experience. Tom Lee, who joined Press Ganey in 2013 as chief medical officer, observed that the word was so traditionally verboten in healthcare that had it ever appeared in an article in the *New England Journal of Medicine*, it meant that the proofreaders hadn't caught it. He felt that we at Press Ganey had a role to play in bringing the needed change. I disagreed at first. Like so many others, I didn't like speaking of "suffering," and I asked that we use another word. Then I underwent my breast cancer treatment. Suddenly, everything I thought I knew appeared in a different light.

Defining Patient Suffering

My colleague at Press Ganey, Dr. Deirdre Mylod, postulated that we could distinguish between two kinds of suffering. The first kind, *inherent suffering*, is suffering that occurs inevitably as patients move through the healthcare system. The very diagnosis and treatment of a disease is guaranteed to cause a certain amount of suffering. Even if healthcare were perfect, the shock and uncertainty of a cancer diagnosis, and the physical and emotional discomfort associated with multiple diagnostic tests, surgeries, and treatments, would still exist. I know this firsthand. I suffered when I saw my husband cry upon learning of my diagnosis and when I saw the fear in my daughters' eyes. We all suffered. When I wondered initially if I would be able to keep my job, whether we would be able to afford the necessary treatments, or whether my hair would fall out, I suffered some more. These worries were constantly on my mind. They were so pronounced that the stress caused physical pain in my back. No healthcare provider could fix this stress. It came with the diagnosis. Providers could help by reassuring me and giving me medicine, but they couldn't take this suffering away entirely.

Do providers offer patients the help they need to ease inherent suffering? Quite often, we don't. We're slow with medication, or we provide insufficient pain relief. As one patient, in the study I described in the Introduction, told us, "I had difficulty with pain management and muscle spasms. This interfered with rest and recovery. I don't know how else I could have communicated my needs for improved pain management. I felt the need was not met." We must mitigate inherent suffering, knowing that we cannot eliminate it completely.

Avoidable suffering, meanwhile, is suffering that we as caregivers provoke or make worse because our systems are dysfunctional. Our actions give rise to avoidable suffering in a number of ways. When we leave patients waiting, we cause them to suffer. One respondent in our research related: "We had to wait nearly 1.5 hours to have a volunteer available to wheel me out—we were told 15 minutes." Another said: "Just had to wait six hours to be admitted to a room. Bed wasn't that comfortable while waiting." Imagine that you were facing a potentially devastating diagnosis and that you had to wait for a diagnosis, a test result, surgery, or a procedure. Think of the fear of the unknown that you would experience. If you're like many people, your mind would drift to worst-case scenarios in the absence of information. Your fight-or-flight response would kick in—your heart racing, your blood pressure rising, your pupils dilating. All you'd be able to think about would be the what-ifs. Every minute you wait would be a minute of extra suffering. It's not just that you wouldn't feel satisfied. You wouldn't feel safe. There is simply no light between clinical quality, safety, and the patient experience. It's all the same thing.

When we don't provide clean and quiet environments, we erode a sense of safety and cause suffering. We sometimes think of cleanliness as providing a nice environment, but it is much more serious than this. When I walked into the bathroom and spotted blood on the toilet seat that was not my own, I was not just revolted—I lost faith in the people taking care of me. When an environment is clean, patients trust that they will not get an infection. Cleanliness is a bellwether for patient safety.

Similarly, keeping rooms quiet at night isn't just a nice thing to do for patients. The literature is replete with evidence demonstrating the necessity of rest and sleep for healing. Caregivers must take care to assure that we are thinking about quiet in the same way that patients are. A large health system was struggling with its scores for the "quiet at night" survey question. Taking the issue seriously, the organization's administrators and staff applied many best practice solutions. They fixed all the squeaky wheels on carts and beds. They installed devices in nurses' stations that looked like traffic lights that would turn yellow and red when the noise in the area was too loud. Despite all this effort, the scores didn't budge. Finally, administrators convened their patient-family advisory council and asked members what they were missing. The answer was astonishing. For patients, quiet had less to do with the absence of noise than with the absence of *interruptions*. Patients offered feedback like "You wake us up to take our vital signs"; "You come in to do stuff every half an hour rather than doing more things when you come in"; "You wake me up at 4 a.m. to take my blood." Noise was important to control, but interruptions caused even more suffering.

Once administrators understood the true cause of suffering from the patients' perspective, they could take action. The hospital worked with staff to consolidate activity in the rooms, making sure staff weren't taking vital signs every four hours if it wasn't medically necessary. The chief of staff went to the residents and said, "I know those 4 a.m. blood draws are important for you to get the information about the patient that you need. So from now on, if you order a 4 a.m. blood draw, call me to discuss." Not surprisingly, those 4 a.m. blood draws were dramatically reduced. Once the hospital had made changes that mattered to patients, once it had reduced their suffering, the scores went up.

Another way that healthcare providers cause suffering is by treating patients without empathy. Healthcare providers sometimes talk about the need to be "nice." What I'm talking about here isn't being nice. It's about showing courtesy and compassion. Talk to patients and their families. Encourage them to ask questions and make decisions about their care. Be gentle toward patients and sensitive to *their* needs. Ask yourself, *How would I want to be treated?* When the nursing assistant remarked to me that her patients were all "needy" that night, I didn't feel respected. Instead of focusing on my recovery and future treatment, I became worried about what the staff thought of me. And I am certainly not alone in these feelings. As one patient in our study told us: "I had a good experience with all the nurses except one, and to this moment of discharge, I still feel that she was not fully professional and was judgmental in meeting with me." Why should a patient fearing for her health and her future have to deal with a nurse who seems to judge the patient for whom she is supposed to care?

In addition, we cause suffering by failing to connect with patients. As a caregiver, everything you do and everything you say matters. You may not remember your patients or their families, but rest assured, they will remember you forever. That's because you will have played a central role in one of the most frightening times of their lives. As we'll discuss later in this book, when caregivers connect personally or emotionally with patients, it completely changes the experience for both parties. And when caregivers fail to connect, they leave patients feeling lonely, unimportant, and uncared for. Healthcare, after all, is a pretty intimate experience. If we were patients, we would never wish to have an intimate experience with a provider who didn't try to find out a bit more about us *as people* apart from our needs as patients. Before someone touches us, performs a test on us, or sees us undressed, we would at least want to be acknowledged as fellow human beings who *matter*. Connecting with patients is as simple as understanding that the patient is a person with a family, a job, hobbies, friends, and a community who just happens to be a patient right now.

Healthcare providers also cause patients and their families to suffer when we don't work well as a team. Uncoordinated care leads to repetitive and unnecessary interactions with patients that confuse and disturb them. One 2012 study of activities at an urban medical center found that up to 28 people—and up to 18 *different* people—entered patients' rooms per hour.[5] Nurses made the most visits, but medical staff made up 17 percent, with other clinical and nonclinical staff constituting 11 percent. During a typical, three-day hospital stay, a patient who was awake 12 hours per day interacted with up to 60 people. Imagine meeting that many people when you're scared to death. How would you remember who they are, what they do, and why they're doing what they're doing? How would you be sure to follow all their instructions? You couldn't and wouldn't.

Clumsy or uncoordinated teamwork also erodes patient trust. When six different caregivers ask a patient the same question, the patient thinks either that we are inept or that we do not communicate with one another. They feel anxious about the people caring for them, and they suffer more. Healthcare is a team sport, and our patients need to know that we are all on *their* team communicating with each other about their care. Patients also need to know that their electronic medical records are accurate and that team members are using them well to coordinate the care they provide.

Of course, repetitive questioning often accrues not from poor teamwork but from a legitimate need to assure patient safety. Still, do we communicate that need to patients, framing the meaning of our interactions for them? Much of the time, we don't—and patients suffer as a result. Think of the difference it would make if a caregiver offered a simple explanation like "Mrs. Smith, our most important goal while you're in the hospital is to keep you safe, so you might hear us ask the same question multiple times in different ways. This is one of the ways that we make sure that we are keeping you safe." Later in the book, I'll present some other strategies that individual caregivers and teams can use to alleviate this kind of avoidable suffering.

Sometimes we use our team identity as an excuse not to treat patients as well as we might. We distinguish between "our" patients, and all those "other" patients who are not our immediate responsibility. When I worked as a nurse, I wanted to believe that my patients remembered that I was their nurse when they completed the surveys post-discharge. In truth, they might not have thought of it this way. When patients see a survey, "nurse" usually means everyone who took care of them, no matter what caregivers wore, how they introduced themselves, or what titles or other information appeared on their badges. From the standpoint of patient experience, we caregivers are all in this together. There is no "our patient" or "your patient." Every patient in a bed, on a gurney, or in a waiting room is our patient *and* your patient. Just as the gate attendant at NASA helps put astronauts into space, so every person working in your organization is a caregiver responsible for every patient in that organization.

Caregiver Suffering

It might seem like I've been hard on caregivers so far by enumerating the many ways we cause suffering. It's important to realize, however, that we caregivers ourselves experience suffering. Remember Kylie, the incredible ICU nurse my son-in-law, Aaron, encountered after he was shot? I asked her to come to the class I teach and to tell my students everything they needed to know to be just like her. She did come, and she confided that the work was hard—*really* hard. The hours, she said, were really long. Over time, the stress and exhaustion really wore on her. About a year after she took care of Aaron, I came across a message she had posted on Facebook. It read, "After working three jobs, driving more miles than I can count, and being away from my husband more than I ever want to be, I am officially retiring from nursing."

The long hours and stressful conditions had finally gotten to her. To this day, my heart grieves for the people Kylie would have cared for because she was such a wonderful nurse.

Kylie's experience is hardly unique. Nurses and other healthcare providers typically work shifts that go long past 12 hours. New nurses and some seasoned nurses sometimes want 12-hour shifts because they think that will give them 4 days off every week. Also, many of us have martyr mentalities. We say things like, "That's OK. I don't need a break today," or "We don't have enough staff. I'll skip lunch today." I used to do this myself. I remember thinking that skipping lunch or breaks showed that I was tough and busy and irreplaceable for my patients and my colleagues. I was the first to step up and take open shifts and work overtime. Little did I know that I was exhausting myself and limiting my ability to maintain my compassion bank for my patients, my family, and myself.

When nurses work three 13- or 14-hour shifts back to back, with 6 hours of sleep and little to no life outside work during those days, they pay a price—and so do their patients. Studies have demonstrated that extended work shifts will result in more errors, adverse events, and complications. Yet almost every hospital and medical facility has personnel working 12-hour shifts that easily turn into 13- or 14-hour shifts.[6] Consider a surgical technologist I happened to meet in the airport while traveling. I asked her if she worked 12-hour shifts, and she replied that she did. "Do you find that you are overly tired or make mistakes during those last four hours?" I asked. She told me that she really liked the 12-hour shifts, but that on the third day, she was, in truth, "not worth anything" at work. I certainly hope I'm not on the table on her third day!

Excessively long work shifts are only one source of caregiver suffering. Regulations, documentation, reimbursement pressure, physician and nurse shortages, patient complexity, and acuity are all facts of life for providers, and they all make connecting with the people who happen to be patients at the moment stressful and onerous. Over time, physicians, nurses, and other caregivers become overworked, exhausted, and unhappy. A job that had been fun, stimulating, and rewarding at first now causes daily suffering.

Consider a typical workday in the life of a nurse. She clocks in at 6:30 a.m. (or p.m.) and receives a report about how patients fared during the previous shift and what care patients will need. Ideally this report takes place at each patient's bedside, so that the patient is involved. The process for that nurse's patients takes at least an hour on a good day, longer if nurses have more or sicker patients for whom to care. The nurse must also assure that the patient care assistants (PCAs) also know patient needs, and the nurse must handle new orders from physicians that come in unpredictably as they make their rounds. Often, the patient knows more about the care plan than the nurse does, simply because the nurse couldn't join every physician on his or her rounds. Nurses have much to do: they must administer medications, change dressings, educate patients and families, transfer patients to diagnostic testing, and admit patients from ICUs, the emergency department, surgery, or elsewhere. Admissions and discharges typically take about half an hour, sometimes longer, as the nurse obtains detailed information about the patient's health, illness, medications, and history; assesses the patient from head to toe; and receives orders from the admitting physician. And all of this has to be documented.

Discharges also take time. Nurses must convey discharge instructions clearly so that patients will be safe and successful upon leaving the hospital. If patients require follow-up care, nurses must help them make appointments, locate equipment, or reserve rooms for skilled nursing or long-term care. In some busy units, every bed in every room might turn over during a 24-hour period, with an existing patient being discharged and a new one being admitted. This means that during a given shift, a nurse who normally cares for four to six patients might admit or discharge twice that number. Although many budgets are based on a midnight census (i.e., the number of "heads in beds" at midnight), the true amount of patient turnover and the true amount of work involved might be much higher. And of course, all of this doesn't include the task of documenting patient care. In a perfect world, nurses will perform documentation at the patient's bedside, but they often don't have the time. In these instances, they must perform documentation after their shift is over, leading to overtime and extended work shifts. Often nurses are so busy throughout their day that they don't even have time to leave the unit in order to eat lunch or grab a quick coffee. And tomorrow, they have to get up and do this all over again.

Every nurse's job is different—the scenario I've provided here is just a general sketch. But make no mistake—the caregiver suffering that results from a typical caregiver's job is real. You see it indirectly in the high rates of nurse turnover and engagement. A *Becker's Hospital Review* infographic from 2016 put the one-year turnover rate among all newly licensed RNs at 17.5 percent and the two-year turnover rate at 33.5 percent.[7] Citing other research, my colleague Dr. Barbara Reilly and I observed in the *Online Journal of Issues in Nursing (OJIN)* in 2016 that 15 out of every 100 nurses are disengaged based on the performance of nurse employees at one standard deviation below the mean in the largest healthcare employee engagement database.[8] "Conservative estimates suggest," we said, "that each disengaged nurse costs an organization $22,200 in lost revenue as a result of lack of productivity. For a hospital with 100 nurses, that equates to $333,000 per year in lost productivity. For a large system with 15,000 nurses, the potential loss skyrockets to $50 million." When we think about a lack of productivity, we might think of not working to our full capacity or not accomplishing as much as others. However, a lack of productivity can also manifest as a lack of teamwork, constant grumbling, poor attitudes, and absenteeism. Further, what we often attribute to staffing issues may in fact result from low engagement levels.

Retention of experienced nurses is also a significant issue leading to a perpetual cycle of lost productivity, lack of engagement, and turnover (see Figures 1.1 and 1.2). As we wrote in *OJIN*, the "National Healthcare Retention and RN Staffing Report" identified a 16.4 percent average turnover rate for nurses in 2014. The conservative estimate of the cost of turnover was listed at somewhere between $36,900 and $57,300. When you do the math, that means billions of dollars in nursing turnover costs alone.

Press Ganey data show that nurses score higher on the engagement scale, averaging 4.11 on a scale of 0–5. But while that may seem like good news, it has a dark side. The nurses that are most engaged are those that have only been with the organizations for less than six months. In other words, those with the least experience are the most engaged. Get more experience, and you become disillusioned with your job. Even worse, the data show that the further a nurse moves from the bedside, the more engaged that nurse is. The people at bedside are often the least engaged. How are we to engage patients if the people who are caring for them are not engaged?

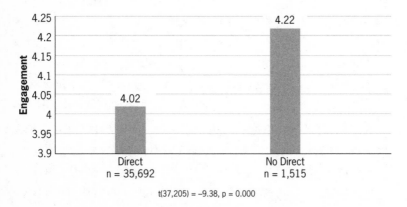

Figure 1.1   RN engagement by direct patient care

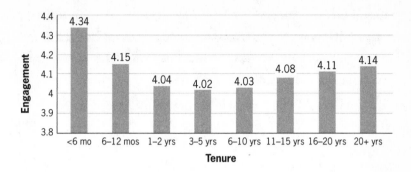

Figure 1.2   RN engagement by tenure

Nurses, like all other caregivers, want to provide optimal care, and it's difficult when they know they're not in a position to do it because of the processes, systems, and general work conditions that exist in their organizations. So they become disillusioned with their jobs and lose motivation to perform. They suffer.

High turnover due to caregiver suffering in turn directly impacts the performance of healthcare organizations. Many units facing staffing shortfalls require nurses to come in on their off days, and many hire traveling nurses to care for patients. Unfortunately, traveling nurses are at best an imperfect solution. Since they earn more, morale among permanent nurses sags when traveling nurses come on the job, and traveling nurses often don't feel the same levels of accountability and commitment. Over time, organizations sink into mediocrity. Lack of engagement by the nurses who remain on staff also proves costly to organizations, causing declines in the quality of care.

When speaking of caregiver suffering, we should distinguish between inherent and avoidable suffering, just as we did for patients. One might argue that in any profession or job, workplace conditions will cause a certain amount of suffering. Trial lawyers must deal with deadlines and the stress of courtroom appearances. Elementary school teachers must deal with the fatigue that comes with trying to corral six-year-olds for the better part of a day. Likewise, the basic conditions of healthcare cause a certain amount of suffering for caregivers. Healthcare is incredibly complex, and it's changing almost by the minute. Patients are very sick, and they sometimes die. Technology is exploding, and caregivers are expected to understand how to use it appropriately. These conditions cause stress for caregivers that is simply part of the job. Even if healthcare were perfect, this kind of caregiver suffering would persist. However, as I've suggested, caregivers also suffer a great deal of *avoidable* suffering—not just from overscheduling but from lack of trust in leadership, lack of respect shown by organizations, bullying by colleagues, verbal and physical abuse by patients and visitors, and lack of safe refuge for reporting. The causes of avoidable suffering are many, and organizations must address them if they are to improve both the caregiver experience and organizational performance.

Answers to Suffering

My struggle with breast cancer woke me up to a reality that had been around me all along but that I hadn't understood: the reality of suffering. We in healthcare don't like to think about it, but we're failing to alleviate the inherent suffering that patients feel, and we're also causing an incredible amount of avoidable suffering. Meanwhile, we're in pain, too, consigned to jobs that are exhausting, stressful, and all-too-often devoid of the fulfillment we expected when we left school and took our first healthcare jobs. Suffering represents a hidden plague that afflicts virtually everyone in healthcare. We talk about "patient satisfaction" or "employee satisfaction," and we think that this suffices to capture the way people experience healthcare environments. It doesn't.

Whether we like it or not, suffering is real, and we need to deal with it. We can't satisfy ourselves with delivering excellent clinical care. As a cancer patient, I took clinical excellence for granted. It was the compassion and connectedness with caregivers that I needed, the absence of which created suffering for me. The care I received saved my life, and for that I was and remain profoundly grateful. Yet the elements of my care that weren't right left a scar every bit as real as the ones on my chest. No patient should suffer such scars more than absolutely necessary.

Much of the time, we have it in our power to alleviate suffering. Later in this book, I'll provide many solutions to this problem that are readily available to us. But we also need the will to carry them out. Sometimes that will exists. A few days after my breast surgery, I called the president of the hospital where I'd received treatment as well as the director of service excellence. I told them everything about my experience and the suffering I'd felt. To their credit, they invited me to come and describe my experience to members of their patient and family advisory board, which was composed of both internal staff and community members. Several weeks later, I met with the board and found its members eager to hear my story and to correct the issues presented. I commend them for that, and I hope that administrators and boards everywhere demonstrate the same zeal to improve what they do and reduce the suffering that patients and caregivers experience.

To address suffering, we ultimately must get back in touch with our purpose as healthcare providers—why it is that we got into this business to begin with. We need to remember that we're here to serve patients and help them to heal. But it also helps to understand just a bit about *why* suffering has become such a problem in healthcare today. As my analysis so far has suggested, the vast majority of suffering doesn't result from "bad" or unfeeling caregivers, but from systemic factors that limit how we approach and perform our jobs. It is to this topic we now turn.

CHAPTER 2 | The Roots of Suffering in Healthcare

SOME PEOPLE KNOW from a very young age that they want to be a nurse. As children or adolescents, they yearn to help people heal. They feel it in their bones.

I am not one of these people. When I was growing up, I wanted to be a journalist, not a nurse. I loved seeing bylines in newspapers and magazines, and I felt titillated at the thought that hundreds, thousands, even millions of people would see those words on the page and respond to them. Writing seemed powerful, a way of changing people's thinking. In the best-case scenario, it changed lives.

It looked for a time that I would realize my dream of becoming a journalist. As I prepared to graduate from high school, I learned that I had won a college scholarship at Southeast Missouri State University—all four years, including room, board, books, and tuition. The university had a strong journalism program. I was excited to leave my small town of Poplar Bluff, Missouri, and attend. What an amazing opportunity!

I never went. It was a hopelessly romantic decision (and if either of my daughters had acted similarly,

I would have strangled them!). My boyfriend planned to stay in our small town, and I didn't want to leave him. So, to the chagrin of many, I turned down the scholarship. In the end, it worked out: that boyfriend became my husband and the father of our daughters. As of this writing, we've been together for 36 years and are still going strong! Sometimes, you do need to go with your gut and do the "crazy" thing.

But my decision to stay in Poplar Bluff confronted me with a question: What would I do with my life? One option—nursing—appealed to me over all others. When I was nine years old, my single mother went to nursing school. She was working full-time to support my sister and me, and her school required that students who worked had to maintain a 4.0 average if they were to remain enrolled. Somehow, my mom managed to do that. She went to school during the days, spent time with us during the evenings, and at night went to work at her job. I don't know how she did it. But I do know that going to nursing school not only changed my mom's life—it saved it. Thanks to nursing, she found not just a better job but a career, a calling. She discovered that she was a nurse's nurse to the core, that she absolutely loved caring for people. As sleep deprived as she was, she could come home and tell us story after story about the people whom she had met and cared for. If she had loved nursing so much, maybe I would, too.

I started in an associate degree program, and in short order I discovered that my mother's calling truly was my own. My first real clinical role, undertaken while I was still in school, was working the night shift in a hospital's burn unit. I debrided burns, helped the nurses change dressings, and talked to patients who were in indescribable amounts of pain. It was an incredible experience—truly eye-opening. Once I cared for a two-year-old girl who had toddled over to see her grandpa as he cleaned out the fireplace. She stuck her little hand in a bucket of ashes and suffered full-thickness burns up to her elbow from the hot coals mixed in. She didn't understand what was happening to her and why her mommy and daddy had to wear gowns and gloves when they held her. I played games with her, read books to her, and helped her color to distract her from her pain and confusion. It felt thrilling to be able to help another person in the most difficult of circumstances. This little girl stayed with me in my mind, as did other patients and colleagues I encountered early in my career. I'll never forget the 74-year-old man I cared for who had poured lighter fluid on a bonfire to make it catch quicker, or the 40-old truck driver in the neuro trauma intensive care unit who would be a quadriplegic for the rest of his life, or the people who worked for me in my early days of managing the OR.

Many educators and chief nursing officers worry that young people today no longer go into nursing in order to help people, but rather because they want a stable job in tough economic times. Certainly, many young people today still perceive healthcare as a calling. But even if they don't, many *find* a calling there over time, like I did. It's no exaggeration, I think, to say that the vast majority of nurses stay in nursing at least in part for noble reasons—because they want to help people and they think of healthcare as a way to make a powerful difference. Doctors, technicians, and other staff no doubt harbor similar motivations. But all that raises a question: If so many people want to do good, why are we seeing so much suffering in healthcare? Certainly, we're not *deliberately* trying to cause suffering, nor are we intentionally ignoring it when we encounter it. The physicians, nurses, and techs who cared for me during my breast cancer surgery didn't wake up that morning thinking they were going to make me wait, do procedures without sedation, and fail to communicate with one another. And yet that's precisely what happened. Why?

Deprioritizing the Patient Experience

Many factors contribute to the prevalence of suffering in health-care, but we can look first to the priorities that dominate within most healthcare organizations today. As our healthcare system has transitioned from the older pay for reporting system to pay for performance (P4P) quality metrics, and now to value based purchasing (VBP), leaders have tended to emphasize clinical excellence far more than they have the emotional and psycholog-ical aspects of care for both patients and caregivers. Back in 2009, when I was serving as a consultant, CEOs of healthcare orga-nizations would tell me that they knew patient experience was important, but their Medicare reimbursement hinged on their clinical excellence measures. To maximize those reimbursements, and thus secure their organizations' financial health, these leaders had to focus on assuring that the staff executed clinical processes properly and consistently. Processes and behaviors that bore on the patient experience took second place—a distant second, I might add—in the minds of many leaders.

These executives were correct: during the 2000s, the "core measures" the government would use to calculate healthcare qual-ity were indeed evidence-based measures of clinical care that, when implemented and performed consistently over time, had been shown to yield better outcomes for patients. These measures included elements such as how often a hospital provided aspirin on arrival for patients who presented to the emergency depart-ment with chest pain, or what percentage of time a hospital would get patients from the emergency department to the cath lab in 90 minutes, or what percentage of time a hospital provided discharge instructions to congestive heart failure patients, or what percent-age of time the hospital provided antibiotics 30 minutes prior to a surgical incision. What mattered was simply that the staff per-formed these tasks, not *how* they performed them or how patients perceived the handling of their care. As one CEO told me, perhaps without realizing what he was saying, "We provide the best clinical care possible, and if we can be nice in the process, that's a bonus."

The Affordable Care Act promulgated important changes in the way that the government calculated healthcare's value. When the law was enacted in 2010, it dictated that hospitals would be reimbursed based on scores that measured both clinical care processes *and* the patient experience. Although this system paid much more attention to the experience of patients, most of a hospital's reimbursement still reflected measures that did not relate to patient experience. When VBP scores began to drive reimbursement, 70 percent of VBP points were based on clinical processes of care, with patient experience accounting for the remaining 30 percent (Figure 2.1 demonstrates how this is structured through 2018). Although the Affordable Care Act is under intense scrutiny as of this writing, the movement away from volume and toward

Fiscal Year	Applicable Domains and Weights
2016	Clinical Process of Care (10%) Patient Experience of Care (25%) Outcome (40%) Efficiency (25%)

2017*	Patient and Caregiver-Centered Experience of Care/Care Coordination (25%)
	Safety (20%)
	Clinical Care (30%)
	    – Clinical Care—Outcomes (25%)
	    – Clinical Care—Process (5%)
	Efficiency and Cost Reduction (25%)

2018	Patient and Caregiver-Centered Experience of Care/Care Coordination (25%) Safety (25%) Clinical Care (25%) Efficiency and Cost Reduction (25%)

*Beginning with FY 2017, CMS reclassified the quality domains to align more closely with CMS' National Quality Strategy (NQS). NQS serves as a blueprint for health care stakeholders across the country and helps prioritize quality improvement efforts, share lessons and measure collective success.

Source:
https://www.cms.gov/Outreach-and-Education/Medicare-Learning-Network-MLN/MLNProducts/downloads/Hospital_VBPurchasing_Fact_Sheet_ICN907664.pdf

Figure 2.1   Applicable CMS domains and weights, by year

value, with quality and outcomes driving healthcare reimbursement, will likely persist, no matter what happens with a particular piece of legislation. That's because widespread consensus exists inside and outside the industry that it's the right thing to do. As Figure 2.1 demonstrates, patient and caregiver experiences are slated to account for 25 percent of the score, while clinical processes of care will be superseded by outcomes, safety, and efficiency metrics.

Fortunately, leaders at healthcare organizations and in government are coming to understand that the patient experience plays a critical role in the provision of value. They are looking to provide "patient-centered care" that takes into account how patients actually *feel* about the care experience.[1] The evidence that focusing on patients delivers more value is also becoming increasingly clear. As we'll see in the next chapter, when patients perceive a reliably better experience, organizations experience lower readmission rates, lower lengths of stay, lower rates of hospital-acquired conditions, and higher PSI safety scores.[2] Costs decline and outcomes improve, leading to higher overall value (according to Harvard economist Michael Porter's well-known equation: Value = outcomes/cost).[3] And yet while the evidence supporting patient-centered care is growing, organizations don't always define this care appropriately, nor do they truly deliver it. We are still rewarding volume over value, trying to maximize reimbursements even as we try to optimize quality of care so as to assure positive outcomes. Leaders struggle—they have to have a foot in both worlds, volume and value—and it's difficult for them as well as for the people taking care of patients every day.

One of my goals in this book is to highlight the importance of delivering fully on the promise of patient-centered care. I hope to convince you that by focusing more on patients' needs, we will reduce their suffering and that of caregivers, and that organizations will benefit, too. Improving patient experience—and reducing rates of suffering—is not only a moral imperative. It makes profound business sense. But until organizations, teams, and individuals fully internalize this reality, we won't make the changes required to reduce the causes of suffering. Patients will continue to deal with healthcare experiences that are far more painful than they need to be.

Teaching the Technical Skills, Not Compassionate Care

The financial incentives that fuel organizational priorities are hardly the only reason we see an epidemic of suffering today. Other causes, such as changes in the way we educate caregivers, are equally important.

During the early 1980s, when I first attended nursing school, students spent part of their time sitting in classrooms and learning about subjects such as pharmacology, chemistry, biology, anatomy, and physiology. To practice our skills, we also spent a good part of our time in our clinical rotations. We gave one another shots, started IVs on one another, provided head-to-toe assessments, and gave bed baths and backrubs. We also had a chance to perform these tasks on real live patients—an experience I and many of my peers found invaluable.

In recent years, we've stopped putting young caregivers in real-life situations with patients during their training as much as we used to. Instead, we rely on technology, training students in electronic documentation and providing simulations with sophisticated, lifelike mannequins. Let's be clear: Although these mannequins come with computer programs that confront students with vital sign changes and manifestations of clinical symptoms that are similar to those of patients, working with mannequins is not *nearly* the same as working with a live human patient.

Mannequins are not real, and they do not have the full range of emotions, family dynamics, disease processes, and needs that real people have. Mannequins don't get scared, angry, or belligerent. They don't cry, and they don't try to hit you. Most of all, mannequins don't have lives, jobs, families, and hobbies. They are, simply, mannequins. While great for teaching code blue algorithms and procedures like intubations and IV insertions, mannequins do not teach students how to communicate or connect with patients.

As a result, the reliance on training with mannequins often produces students who are less able to communicate with patients and attend to their complex emotional needs. Bear in mind, most students today don't have much experience of their own communicating interpersonally in healthcare settings. Many of them have never actually been patients in the healthcare system, other than for preventive care. Without that experience and without the practice of interpersonal communication under stressful conditions, we set these caregivers up to fail. In the process, we set the stage for patient and caregiver suffering to continue.

Back when I was a student, interacting with other human beings helped us learn how to *connect* with patients on a deep level. Trust me, when you practice skills that are as intimate as a bed bath, not only do you learn to introduce yourself, you also learn how to ask open-ended questions so as to solicit information. You learn to identify body language and cues that help you care for the whole person, not simply treat the disease or condition. The very first patient I ever treated was a behavioral health patient at a Veterans Administration hospital. He was in his seventies, and I was all of 20 years old. We had nothing in common—and yet I had to talk to him. That was my clinical objective for that rotation. Putting to use all the communication techniques I had learned, I began to talk to him about his family, gently feeling my way to assure that this topic relaxed him and didn't agitate him further. I had to evaluate his body language and listen for verbal cues, gleaning important details that would allow me to provide the best possible care.

A year later, I cared for a woman with end-stage breast cancer. The clinical objective for that week was patient teaching—my instructor wanted me to teach this patient about breast health. To this day, I'm embarrassed to say that I did what I was told. I went to this kind, bald, incredibly sick woman and talked with her about performing breast self-exams. This patient listened intently, nodding in all the right places, and she took the pamphlets that I gave her. When I came back the next day, I found her room empty. When I asked the nurses where she was, they told me that she had died overnight. I often think about how I served this patient. What could I have done to ease her suffering? Would today's students tune the television in the room to the education channel and instruct this patient to watch a video on breast health? Would they do any better than I did at discerning that this woman needed help dying, not performing breast self-exams? I wonder. I, at least, got a lesson over those two days—one I'll never forget. Many students today are spared such lessons, to their detriment as well as their patients'.

Interacting directly with patients taught us many skills that we nurses would need to reduce suffering. As a senior nursing student, I performed rotations in the operating room and in the intensive care unit, places that in most cases no longer offer full rotations. We learned how to read an EKG monitor and perform manual central venous pressure monitoring, skills that aren't normally taught today since the monitors do the work for you. I performed nasogastric tube insertions, suctioned ET tubes, suctioned the lungs through the nose, and inserted urinary catheters into both men and women, tasks that today are practiced on mannequins. No question—learning these skills first on a mannequin is safer for our patients. Still, the mannequins only teach students the technical skills. They don't wince when you insert the catheter.

They don't cough uncontrollably when you insert the tube into the lungs. They don't cry when they hear their diagnosis. As a nursing student encountering these responses, I learned about suffering as a human condition. It's this learning that we're often simply not delivering anymore.

As a nursing professor over the past decade, I have watched as we've graduated nurses who are amazing with simulations using mannequins, who are incredibly proficient at electronic documentation, and who are wizards when it comes to social media. And yet these students flounder when confronted with the needs of real live patients. When these 20-something students are ministering to an 80-year-old sick person, they have no idea how to connect. This is not simply my observation. Nursing educators, chief nursing officers, and nurses across the country have echoed it in conversations with me. As one nurse educator remarked: "We are so intent on making sure that our students can pass [board exams] that we focus on the skills and the tasks that they need to understand. We do not provide the same kind of focused attention for the intricacies of connection and practice for communication between diverse populations that will make our students successful in practice, not just on the test."

You don't have to be an 80-year-old patient to encounter a caregiver who seems disconnected. As a 40-something breast cancer patient, I experienced it myself. Take the nurse who came into my room that night after my surgery. She performed the necessary tasks, checking off all the boxes on her to-do list but neglecting to introduce herself. She forgot that she was caring for a real live person, and consequently she didn't make the human connection that would have changed the experience for me. I should add that this connection would also have created a trusting relationship between us. Research has shown that trusting relationships tend to render patients more apt to open up about their concerns about their disease and their care and to be more compliant with treatment. Besides other benefits, the presence of trusting relationships will reduce the amount of emotional and inherent suffering that patients experience.[4]

Of course, shifts in the training of nurses—and the costs attendant to them—are not unique to nursing. As Dr. Tom Lee related in his seminal book *An Epidemic of Empathy in Healthcare*, the clinical rounds he performed during medical school emphasized "acquiring diagnostic and procedure skill, not a compassionate bedside manner."[5] The whole system of medical education prompted students to focus on doing what it took to "get into the best residency program for their specialty." Medical students suffered—they were "under extreme pressure, constantly sleep-deprived, and occasionally feeling abused by senior staff."[6] As Lee notes, such conditions prompt a decline in empathy among medical students. They simply don't have the energy or time, and they distance themselves from patients as an act of self-preservation.

The Deepening Challenge of Compassion

If healthcare practice has deemphasized the reduction or amelioration of suffering, and if training is no longer preparing nurses, doctors, and others to handle patients' emotional needs, a variety of trends are also conspiring to make taking care of patients much more challenging.

First, society is becoming more atomized, making personal connections of all kinds more difficult to form. As Harvard sociologist Robert Putnam has observed, the amount of social capital (defined as "connections among individuals—social networks and the norms of reciprocity and trustworthiness that arise from them") in American communities has plummeted in recent decades.[7] Attendance at public meetings, participation in civic organizations, and trust in strangers are all down. Ours is an age of isolation—we rarely connect with each other personally anymore, and we become habituated to this disconnection. To some degree, our isolation owes to our reliance on personal technology. One 2013 study of Facebook users found that online interactions did not provide the social connectedness that one might think. Social networking, while seemingly engaging and productive of community, actually undermined a sense of well-being and human connectedness.[8] Everyone in healthcare settings, both patients and caregivers, must negotiate a social space in which awkwardness, aloofness, inattention, and carelessness are more frequent.

At the same time, our society has become more diverse, leaving caregivers to navigate relationships with patients not merely of different ages, genders, or ethnicities but of different socioeconomic statuses, lifestyles, and sexual orientations.[9] These differences can cause rifts that make patient suffering more likely and harder to address. If a nurse of Christian upbringing is asked to care for a 50-year-old Muslim patient, opportunities for misunderstandings and disconnection exist. In many Muslim cultures, care is delivered in a gendered way, with male doctors and nurses treating male patients, and female doctors and nurses treating females. What if the unit only has female nurses available? Have these nurses received training about patients' religious traditions? Are they aware of patients' concerns? If not, they might intensify the emotional suffering that a Muslim patient feels.

Or consider the role that generational differences play. If 20-somethings cared for other 20-somethings, communication with text messaging, Snapchat, or Instagram might help. Yet most patients in most acute care hospitals are not 20-somethings,[10] a fact that leads frequently to communication challenges between younger staff and the older patient population.

Generational differences can also impact the suffering felt by caregivers. A 2014 doctoral dissertation examining generational differences in healthcare workers found that baby boomers are typically hard workers and very competitive, shaped by events like the Vietnam War and the civil rights movement.[11] As healthcare workers, they are questioning, passionate, and not always patient. They expect and demand respect and are motivated by money, title, and acclaim. Generation Xers, the study related, view lifestyle as more important than work and have been shaped by the age of computers and easier access to people and information. Xers want education and want to work because it can mean a better life for themselves and their families. They are flexible and, in turn, demand this flexibility of others.[12] Millennials have been shaped by the Internet, instant access to information and people, and terrorism. This group is much more socially conscious and team oriented. They have had instant access virtually their entire lives and are not accustomed to waiting for anything, including promotions. They tend to be more service-learning oriented.

With all these generations in the workplace, and with training about differences often scarce, leaders of healthcare organizations face the daunting task of understanding not only what motivates each of these generations but, more important, what motivates each individual in order to maximize engagement and performance. "We've tried all of these reward and recognition programs in my hospital," one leader told me, "and nothing really worked. We finally figured out that was because [these programs] didn't really motivate everybody and, in some cases, it really upset some people because they didn't see it as a reward at all!" Without adequate incentives, caregivers typically languish, resenting their job and the burdens it places on them. They perceive a lack of respect, and they come to distrust their coworkers and organizations. Their suffering increases.

If patient populations are becoming more complex, so, too, are the health problems facing patients. Obesity, diabetes, congestive heart failure, and hypertension are just some of the chronic conditions that providers today commonly see. These conditions are challenging, requiring polypharmacy, multiple visits, and interventions to keep patients out of the hospital. Once in the hospital, patients have multiple needs related to their disease processes as well as their lifestyles. Technology, polypharmacology, and new therapeutic techniques related to these chronic illnesses change almost by the day. Providers and caregivers must keep pace with this stunning amount of information and change. And they must do so in a care environment that is frequently fragmented and poorly coordinated.

Sixty-eight-year-old Kevin is a patient with type 2 diabetes with the comorbidities of heart disease, hypertension, and kidney involvement. He eats poorly and maintains a sedentary lifestyle. Kevin doesn't just have a primary care physician caring for him, but also has a cardiologist and a nephrologist, each prescribing medications and providing Kevin with information. Kevin has to go to the outpatient clinic or hospital for diagnostic testing, therapy, or procedures, further complicating an already complex care plan. In addition, physical therapists and nutritionists help him to improve his lifestyle so as to minimize the complications associated with his disease processes.

Currently, most hospitals and health networks are not built around addressing patient needs seamlessly. So Kevin must go to each of these locations to get testing or treatment or to consult with his providers. He has to navigate this fragmented system and interact with providers who might not know about other parts of his care. As we discussed in Chapter 1, inpatients may see between 60 and 100 different people during a hospital stay. Patients worry that their providers won't have their acts together and that they, the patients, will fall through the cracks. It isn't because caregivers don't care about patient suffering. There is simply too much to do, too many people involved, and not enough communication and collaboration between us.

Beyond increasing complexity, a final trend that leads to more suffering—for both patients and caregivers—is the problem with caregiver shortages, turnover, and engagement. More people are entering nursing, but more are also leaving, creating a persistent shortage of faculty and experienced nurses in the profession. As the American Nurses Association (ANA) has determined, the nursing population is aging. Between 2000 and 2010, the average age of employed RNs rose from 42.7 years to 44.6 years.[13] As ANA president Pam Cipriano stated in a 2016 *Atlantic* magazine profile, "The biggest cohort of registered nurses joined the workforce before the 1970s." She added that "many nurses held off retiring during the downturn in the economy, but now the retirements are starting."[14] In the future, healthcare organizations are likely to face a greater shortage of nurses,[15] and of doctors as well. The Association of American Medical Colleges projects that by 2025, our country will face "a shortfall of between 14,900 and 35,600 primary care physicians" and approximately 37,400 to 60,300 physicians in other specialty domains.[16] This trend appears especially concerning given that more care for prevention and treatment of chronic conditions is now provided outside the hospital. To tackle this problem, the AAMC supports an increase in residency positions, greater innovation, and enhanced deployment of technology. In the near term, many states are also expanding the responsibilities and duties of advanced practice nurses to help offset the primary care physician shortage.

Staff shortages present obvious challenges for patient care and caregiver engagement, but they also increase the potential for patient and caregiver suffering. Both direct care nurses and leaders cite staffing shortages as a primary reason why nurses cannot spend more time with patients, and they also view it as a cause of caregiver errors. If a unit is short three nurses during a shift, patients might well face longer waits for medications, rushed conversations with caregivers, or caregivers who seem stressed out or inattentive—all sources of suffering. Innovative staffing practices—working 12-hour shifts or working 24 hours in a weekend in exchange for full-time pay—are no solution. As a 2004 study of over 5,000 work shifts found: "Hospital staff nurses worked longer than scheduled daily, and generally worked more than forty hours per week. Half of the shifts worked exceeded ten and a half hours."[17] Statistical analysis linked longer shifts to caregiver mistakes, which will of course lead to more patient suffering. We don't let pilots or truck drivers work extended shifts because they might make devastating mistakes, so why do we let caregivers do it? And if you've ever worked a 14-hour shift, you know that caregivers are suffering, too—from exhaustion and stress. As a 2012 study further affirmed, "Nurses' shifts of more than thirteen hours were also associated with greater likelihood of nurse burnout, job dissatisfaction, and intention to leave the job. The current literature cites twelve-hour shifts as a way to recruit and retain nurses because it is the preferred shift length among nurses. We found that most nurses said they were satisfied with their schedule and that the majority of our sample worked shifts of at least twelve hours. But we also found that the nurses who worked shifts of 12–13 hours were more likely to intend to leave the job than nurses who worked shorter shifts, contrary to what the literature suggests."[18]

I asked a class of 56 graduating nursing students how many of them were planning to work 12-hour shifts when they graduated. They all raised their hands. I then asked how many of them had worked 12-hour shifts prior to graduating. Only a few of them raised their hands to that. Then I asked, "What if I told you that a 12-hour shift is not really 12 hours? They are really more like 13 or 14 hours by the time you finish with everything and are able to leave the hospital. So you'll work back-to-back 13- or 14-hour shifts. You'll get maybe 6 hours of sleep, and you really won't have much of a life." They told me, "That's OK. We'll get four days off!" I reminded them that their managers might be calling them on their days off asking them if they can work overtime to fill vacancies. "Now you're not only exhausted," I tell them. "You're dangerous!"

Some nurse leaders have reminded me that it's often not quite that simple to say that 12-hour shifts and extended work shifts are "bad." They may have nurses who travel up to 2 hours to work in their hospital or healthcare organization. To work less than 12 hours would make it almost impossible for these nurses to travel to and from their jobs. While this may be true, the data are clear. Extended work shifts lead to errors, adverse events, and complications. They also lead to issues with the patient and caregiver experience. Patients are not typically admitted and discharged on a 12-hour cycle. We must change our schedules to meet patient needs in terms of their acuity, admission, and discharge, taking into account nurse education, specialty certification and training, and skill mix. In healthcare today, we know how many patients are admitted and discharged along with their acuity and staff skill mix by the hour of the day and the day of the week. Yet we are not using the data to make schedules that meet the needs of patients and staff. In this way, we cause suffering. Nurses might prefer 12-hour shifts, but unless we can mandate breaks and time away from patient care during extended work shifts, and unless we can improve our scheduling practices, we will continue to achieve the suboptimal results we see in today's healthcare system.

A Conundrum

A friend of mine—I'll call him Mark—was living with his wife in a medium-sized city in New England. Mark's wife had recently given birth to a baby boy and had experienced heavy bleeding several days after returning home. Doctors performed an emergency dilatation and curettage (D&C) to scrape out her uterus so as to dislodge any pieces of the placenta that had not been discharged during the birth and that might become infected. When they sent Mark's wife home, they had advised her to come back if she experienced any of a number of symptoms, including abdominal pain. A couple of days later, she did experience abdominal pain. She wasn't sure if it was anything serious, but she wasn't about to take any chances. The heavy bleeding and emergency procedure had been traumatic—she had feared for her life. She was terrified all over again as she and her husband rushed to the emergency room.

It was four o'clock on a weekday afternoon, and the waiting area didn't seem especially busy. After a quick assessment from a triage nurse, it took almost an hour for Mark's wife to be seen by another nurse. She told his wife that a doctor would see her and probably order some tests. Mark and his wife went back to the waiting room. And wait they did. An hour passed. Then another. And another. Finally, they were ushered in to see a doctor, who seemed rushed. He ordered an ultrasound test, but she would have to go to a different area of the hospital for that. Mark and his wife trudged over and waited for an hour more for the ultrasound, and then they waited another hour to obtain the results. All along, the staff seemed pleasant enough, but not terribly attentive or helpful. The ultrasound turned up nothing, and the doctor said (after another wait of over 30 minutes) that either the hospital could do another test that evening, or she could go home and come back the next day if the pain persisted, and she could have the test then. By this time, it was almost 11 p.m., and the pain seemed to be diminishing. Mark's wife elected to go home and come back the next day if necessary.

On the way home, Mark's wife shook her head. "I can't believe we just spent almost seven hours of our life in that hospital. For what?"

Mark agreed with her frustration. Why had everything taken so long? Didn't staff at the hospital know that people were waiting? Didn't they care? "I really don't get it," he said. "They're supposed to be working there because they want to help people."

Suffering is indeed mysterious. It remains endemic even though hospitals are full of people who want to do good, and indeed have devoted their careers to that purpose. But as we've seen in this chapter, the underlying causes of suffering are many and easy to discern, if you know where to look. Patients and caregivers suffer, in the first instance, because organizations don't pay as much attention as they should to the patient experience and because the healthcare industry doesn't provide the right kinds of training. Even as caregivers become more handicapped in their ability to prevent and address suffering, the demands on them have increased: More diverse medical populations, more complex medical conditions, more fragmentation. Shortages and other staff issues only make a bad situation worse. Rest assured, patients are also paying more attention. They are comparing doctors and hospitals on quality and are posting accounts of their experiences on social media.

There is some good news: the scourge of suffering isn't untreatable. We can do something about it, addressing some of the underlying trends that cause the problem and making adjustments to lessen the impact of these trends on patients and caregivers. But how do we know that suffering is real, and not just something we've dreamed up? And if we can confirm that it is real, how do we know exactly where and how to intervene? Further, how do we know with confidence that we're making progress because of these interventions, and not wasting resources? Doctors and nurses treating patients don't just rely on subjective impressions. They rely on *data*. And to address suffering, we must, too. Suffering, so long ignored and unspoken, can be quantified, just like clinical performance can. In the next chapter, we examine sophisticated methods that we can use to measure the suffering of both caregivers and patients.

3 | Quantifying Suffering

NANCY, 72 YEARS old, was at an amusement park with her 8-year-old grandson when she began to have trouble breathing. Standing in line, she found that she just couldn't get enough air in. She tried sitting down, but that didn't help much. An hour or two earlier, she had noticed that her ankles were swollen, and she had attributed it to all the walking she had been doing and the salty junk food she had eaten for lunch. Now she wasn't so sure. A park attendant noticed her and was worried enough to call an ambulance.

At the local hospital emergency room, a nurse looked her over carefully, asking questions, listening to her chest, taking blood, and squeezing her ankles to gauge the extent of the swelling. Nancy's grandson sat quietly in the corner of the room, watching intently. Nancy smiled at him. "Don't worry," she said, "I'll be fine!"

"Are you sure, Grandma?" he asked.

"Of course, I'm sure."

The nurses left, telling Nancy that someone from radiology would be down to take her for a chest x-ray. While she waited, she did her best to reassure her grandson. He was watching a TV mounted on the wall, but he still seemed frightened. Nancy really wasn't feeling very well, and she found it hard to talk. Needing to relieve herself, she pressed the call light. A nurse peeked her head in, but only to say that the team was "short-staffed" today and that someone would come as quickly as possible to take her to the bathroom.

Five minutes passed, ten minutes—nobody came. Outside the room, the nurses were running back and forth, attending to patients, typing into computers, and coordinating with one another—they were obviously very busy. Finally, almost a half-hour later, a nurse came to take her. When she got to the bathroom, she found that the trash was overflowing and that the floor was covered with muddy footprints, probably from boots worn by a previous occupant. She felt queasy just looking at the mess, but she had no choice—she had to go.

When she returned to the examination room, a young man from radiology came down and put her on a gurney. He wheeled her into the hallway and said, "Hold on, I'll be right back to take you up." But he didn't come right back. A half hour later, she was still lying on that gurney in the hallway, while her grandson remained in the room watching TV. Finally, 45 minutes later, the attendant returned to take her for the x-ray. His explanation for the wait: "Oh, I'm really sorry. We're just so behind today."

Back in the emergency room after the x-ray, Nancy continued to wait. Finally, a man entered and introduced himself as Dr. Samuelson. He proceeded to examine her, asking many of the same questions as the nurse in the treatment room. Nancy wondered whether her answers had been documented someplace, and the doctor somehow hadn't been able to find them. Or maybe the nurse hadn't shared the information with the doctor. Either way, it was strange.

Dr. Samuelson left but returned a half hour later to tell her that she was likely experiencing congestive heart failure. Nancy went pale and muttered, "Oh, my God." She heard "heart failure" and thought this meant she was going to die. She collected herself as best she could, trying not to let her grandson see her so afraid. But it was hard to be brave not knowing what was going to happen. Dr. Samuelson told her she would be admitted to 4South.

When Nancy arrived at 4South with her grandson in tow, the admissions nurse, Sandra, listened to a report on Nancy's condition delivered by the emergency department nurse accompanying her. Then Sandra assessed Nancy herself, and to Nancy's astonishment, Sandra asked her the very same questions! Still, Sandra seemed nice. She put the head of Nancy's bed up a bit to help her breathe, got her a warm blanket, and looked at her IV. Hearing Nancy's grandson say through tears, "My grandma is going to die," she reassured him that his grandma wouldn't die anytime soon and offered him some cookies and juice from the staff lounge. What Nancy couldn't know—because Sandra hid it so well—was that Sandra herself was tired, frustrated, and disillusioned about her job and her career. This was Sandra's third 12-hour shift this week. Of course, none of them had actually been 12 hours—more like 13 or 14 by the time she had finished report and charting. Sandra had a toddler at home whom her mother helped care for while she was at work. Sandra wanted nothing more than to go to home, see her baby, and go to sleep.

This scenario is fictional, but it happens every day in hospitals across America and the world. Nancy, her grandson, and Sandra are all suffering: Nancy from anxiety about her future, fear of her diagnosis and treatment, confusion at having to answer the same questions over and over, concern that the bathroom was disgusting, frustration at the need to wait so long, and discomfort that stemmed from her physical condition; her grandson from anxiety about his grandmother and boredom from all the waiting; and Sandra from being fatigued and feeling overwhelmed by her job. Now that we understand all this, as well as some of the reasons why suffering is so prevalent in healthcare, it's tempting to just jump in and confront the most important question: What should hospital administrators and caregivers *do* about common situations like this? But there is a preliminary step we must attempt before we can take action. We must first *measure* suffering. If we can't measure it, we can't target our response, and we certainly can't track our progress over time. But how can we possibly hope to measure something as subjective as suffering?

Rediscovering Data About Customer Experience

It turns out that we *can* measure suffering. In fact, we already do. The healthcare industry has been measuring suffering all along in its quantitative and qualitative patient surveys. We just didn't call it suffering, nor did we think that we were measuring anything so profound. But we were. To see how this is true, let's briefly review how healthcare organizations have queried their patients.

Drs. Irwin Press and Rod Ganey founded Press Ganey in 1985 hoping to understand and measure how patients perceived the care they received in the hospital. They developed a survey that posed a number of quantitative questions about the care experience, with patients responding using a Likert scale. Questions included items such as "Degree to which hospital staff addressed your emotional needs—very poor, poor, fair, good, or very good" and "Staff concern for our privacy—very poor, poor, fair, good, or very good." As scientists, Drs. Press and Ganey sought to assure that their survey questions were appropriate and psychometrically sound. They worded questions precisely so as not to influence answers, and they sequenced them so as to provide insights without leading or prompting certain responses. During the 1990s and 2000s, hospitals across the United States widely adopted Press Ganey's patient satisfaction survey, generating unprecedented data about patients' experiences. Hospitals became interested in Press

Ganey's data, with leaders wishing to benchmark this information among their peers for marketing and other purposes.

In 2006, hospitals began fielding a second instrument, the Hospital Consumer Assessment of Healthcare Providers and Systems survey, better known as HCAHPS (pronounced "H-caps"). This survey was developed as part of a larger Consumer Assessment of Healthcare Providers and Systems (CAHPS) program sponsored by the Agency for Healthcare Research and Quality (AHRQ). Another organization, the Centers for Medicare and Medicaid Services (CMS), had requested a survey that supported the evaluation of patients' perspectives on hospital care, one that uniformly measured and publicly reported patients' perspectives. In 2012, CMS began to require that all hospitals nationwide implement the HCAHPS survey under its Inpatient Quality Reporting. To boost hospital accountability and create incentives for improving quality, CMS tied Medicare reimbursements to survey scores. CMS also stated that HCAHPS should complement rather than compete with quality improvement instruments such as Press Ganey's that hospitals were already using. CMS also approved Press Ganey as a vendor able to administer HCAHPS for clients.[1]

HCAHPS differs in important ways from the original Press Ganey survey. As mandated by CMS, HCAHPS contains 21 patient perspectives on care and patient rating items, encompassing the following topics: "communication with doctors, communication with nurses, responsiveness of hospital staff, pain management, communication about medicines, discharge information, cleanliness of the hospital environment, quietness of the hospital environment, and transition of care." "The survey," furthermore, "also includes four screener questions and seven demographic items, which are used for adjusting the mix of patients across hospitals and for analytical purposes."[2] The Press Ganey proprietary survey, meanwhile, offers additional questions around patient perceptions of care so as to identify underlying issues with greater precision. Also, whereas Press Ganey's survey uses a Likert scale, HCAHPS uses what is called a "frequency scale," asking patients *how often* they observe particular behaviors (see Figure 3.1). For example, HCAHPS asks: "During this hospital stay, how often did nurses treat you with courtesy and respect?" Patients can respond with "Never," "Sometimes," "Usually," or "Always." Instead of just probing a bit further and asking, say, how often nurses explained things in a way you can understand, the additional Press Ganey questions also ask what the nurses' attitude was toward your requests, how much attention was paid to your special or personal needs, and how well the nurses kept you informed. This additional information allows leaders to target improvement efforts on the real problem. Another way to look at it is this: if we ask patients how often the nurse was in the room to check on them, the patients may say the nurse was in every hour. That sounds great! But what if every time the nurse came in the room, she or he seemed distant or even rude? It's not enough to

---

Please answer the questions in this survey about your stay at the hospital named on the cover letter. Do not include any other hospital stays in your answers.

YOUR CARE FROM NURSES

1. During this hospital stay, how often did nurses treat you with <u>courtesy and respect</u>?
    1 ❑ Never
    2 ❑ Sometimes
    3 ❑ Usually
    4 ❑ Always

2. During this hospital stay, how often did nurses <u>listen carefully to you</u>?
    1 ❑ Never
    2 ❑ Sometimes
    3 ❑ Usually
    4 ❑ Always

3. During this hospital stay, how often did nurses <u>explain things</u> in a way you could understand?
    1 ❑ Never
    2 ❑ Sometimes
    3 ❑ Usually
    4 ❑ Always

4. During this hospital stay, after you pressed the call button, how often did you get help as soon as you wanted it?
    1 ❑ Never
    2 ❑ Sometimes
    3 ❑ Usually
    4 ❑ Always
    5 ❑ I never pressed the call button

Figure 3.1 Sample questions from the HCAHPS survey

know how often something happened; you have to know how well it happened, too.

Hospitals have a choice in how they survey patients. They can use only HCAHPS to measure the frequency with which patients observe behavior, or they can use an integrated survey that incorporates Press Ganey questions to evaluate *how well* behaviors were performed, not just how often patients observed them. With either survey, we can question what the questions really measure. Both surveys were designed to evaluate individual patients' perception of how *satisfied* they were with their care. Press Ganey advisors talked about and counseled clients on how to get better scores. If hospitals improved their scores, we all thought, they would deliver better quality care, leaving patients more satisfied. But by 2012, our organization came to a radically different conclusion. We realized that these surveys didn't just measure satisfaction, in the sense of how "happy" patients were or how "nice" caregivers were. Rather, they served as a proxy for something deeper and more important: patient suffering.

Dr. Deirdre Mylod, executive director of Press Ganey's Institute for Innovation, was instrumental in this change in thinking. Having experienced both healthcare regulatory changes and changes in leadership and philosophy during her 20 years with Press Ganey, Deirdre had come to recognize that we in healthcare were trying to meet clinical needs, but we were conceiving of patient experience as separate, something extra to attend to if we had enough time or staff (which we never do!). To Deirdre, this was no longer good enough. We had an obligation to take caregivers' deep motivation to heal patients physically and apply it as well to patients' psychological experiences. Tragically, our traditional focus on patient satisfaction was missing the significant physical and emotional suffering that patients were bringing with them to the treatment experience. Given the long history of service recovery initiatives, Deirdre felt that we were giving up too easily, accepting that the patient experience would be subpar and then trying to become proficient at apologizing. We weren't challenging ourselves to fix the root problems.

Deirdre's intellectual shift altered Press Ganey's perception of the healthcare industry and our opportunity to improve it. It also changed how we saw the existing patient surveys. We knew that both surveys provided data on important needs of patients that hospitals either met or failed to meet—the need for clean facilities, for instance, or prompt attention from staff. But now we realized that when patients reported that their needs were not being met, it was reasonable to assume that they were experiencing suffering—both inherent and avoidable, as described in the last chapter—as a result. The surveys thus enabled us to assess how much suffering exists, which patients are most affected, and in precisely what areas of behaviors—operations, clinical care, or culture.

Let's take a closer look at the connection between unmet patient needs as measured in the surveys and suffering. Press Ganey and HCAHPS both measure the extent to which patients feel included in their care (see Figure 3.2). If my caregivers don't consult me in making decisions about my care, I will feel a loss of autonomy and feel disrespected. An already frightening situation will seem even worse. I will suffer more emotional pain. But of

Respond to Inherent Patient Needs	Prevent Avoidable Suffering
Promote Confidence in **Skill**	Improve **Teamwork**
Manage **Pain**	Deliver Care with **Courtesy**
Ensure **Safety**	Be **Helpful**
Inform/Prepare	Avoid Unnecessary **Wait**
Personalize Care	Make **Processes** Efficient/Easy
Reduce **Fear/Anxiety**	Maintain Clean/Quiet **Environment**
Protect **Privacy**	Provide Adequate **Amenities**
Include in Decisions/Choice	Ensure Appropriate **Service Recovery**
Demonstrate **Empathy**	

Figure 3.2 Behaviors charted by the Press Ganey and HCAHPS surveys that relate to inherent and avoidable suffering

course, I won't just feel the loss of control. I will also feel that the people taking care of me are missing important information about my health and my care and that I may not receive the proper treatments or tests. My sense of trust will diminish, and I won't feel safe. I'll suffer emotionally even more. And when I fill out the survey, my answers will reflect that my caregivers failed in their most important responsibility to me: to make me feel safe.

Likewise, the Press Ganey and HCAHPS surveys measure how well caregivers discharge their patients. If you hand me a piece of paper with my discharge instructions 20 minutes before I leave, I will be so occupied intellectually and emotionally with the process of going home that I won't be able to retain this information, and I won't have a chance to ask thoughtful questions. In addition, I'm probably feeling scared about my illness and uncertain about how I'll take care of myself at home. This fear and the associated fight-or-flight syndrome will prevent me from remembering details about my care, and in turn, from following directions well. If caregivers have not talked to me about my discharge and explained my medications throughout my stay, I may well become confused and noncompliant, eventually returning to the hospital as an unplanned readmission. All this makes for more suffering—in some cases, much more.

Finally, the Press Ganey and HCAHPS surveys measure how well caregivers respond to calls from patients. Our research shows that when a patient presses the call light, over 70 percent of the time it is for one of four reasons: patients are sick, are in pain, need to go to the bathroom, or are bothered by malfunctioning equipment in the room. Often, a patient presses the call light and someone at the nurses station picks up the phone and asks, "May I help you?" Yet nurses can't fix any of these four problems over the phone or from the nurses station. These patients need help, and they need someone to come to them to deliver it. Patients who are sick, are in pain, need to go to the bathroom, or are bothered by equipment malfunctions and who don't receive prompt attention are experiencing unnecessary suffering.

You might wonder why caregivers can't simply *ask* patients in the moment whether or not they're suffering. Wouldn't that be simpler? For one thing, CMS has ruled that "interviewing or distributing surveys to patients while they are still in the hospital is not permitted."[3] But there is a more important reason. Think about what might happen when you go out to dinner. You get dressed up and are excited to go someplace new. But when you arrive at the restaurant, you have to wait for a table. No problem—the restaurant has a great reputation, so you're willing to wait for a little while. After 20 minutes, a host appears to escort you to your table. The waiter comes and takes your drink order, returning a few minutes later with your iced tea. Five or ten minutes after that, he comes back and takes your food order. Then he's gone. You finish your iced tea, but for 30 minutes you can't even flag your server down to ask for a refill. You have no idea what's going on. But he's taken your food order, so you assume that the kitchen is preparing it.

Let's say the restaurant manager comes around right about now to ask how things are going. How do you respond? Some people will reply that the service is terrible—their iced tea glasses have been empty for 20 minutes, and the waiter has disappeared. But most patrons *won't* say that. They'll fear that someone will spit in their food or that their service will get worse. Instead of telling the manager the truth, providing her with useful feedback, they'll smile and say, "Oh, everything is fine," when really, they're seething. It's the same in healthcare. In hospital settings, patients feel—quite understandably—that they are at the mercy of the people taking care of them. They fear that if they communicate honestly about negative experiences, the people taking care of them might retaliate by neglecting them or otherwise providing subpar care. Patients don't want to do anything that might impact or jeopardize their care. If they receive a survey after an encounter, they will probably answer more honestly because they now feel that it is safe to do so. The HCAHPS and Press Ganey surveys thus provide more accurate information about suffering than direct queries by healthcare providers, particularly those that take place in the moment.

What Really Causes Suffering—and What Patients Really Want

The Press Ganey and HCAHPS surveys give patients a voice, a rare chance to talk about their care and the pain they experience. The surveys provide a surprisingly rich and nuanced view of suffering, because in completing them, patients or their families don't just give numerical responses. Quite often, they include detailed comments about their care, both validating the notion that failure to meet needs causes suffering and providing directional information that caregivers and organizations can use to make meaningful improvements. Every one of these comments, good and bad, tells a story about the patient experience. As we'll see later, we can deploy technology to evaluate these qualitative data and group the data thematically into "sentiments." Such analysis further expands how organizations can understand and improve on the patient experience.

Of course, organizations must choose to listen to patient voices, and they must know *how* to listen in thoughtful, even sophisticated ways. Intuitively, we know that patient perceptions that serve us as proxies for suffering differ depending on factors like age, sex, ethnicity, and education level. How quickly a geriatric patient needs a nurse to respond to a call light might differ from how quickly a millennial needs a nurse to respond. As the graph in Figure 3.3 shows, needs vary by not only age but also by the patient's perception of their health. For example, for patients 65–79 years old, medical patients who said that they were in excellent health, 88 percent of them would give a 9 or 10

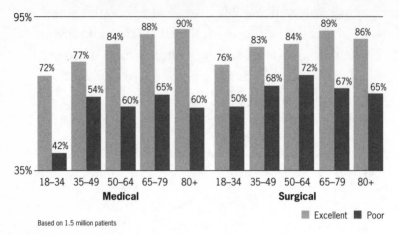

Based on 1.5 million patients

Figure 3.3   HCAHPS rating by age and health. Graph adapted from "Patient Experience in the Very Elderly: An Emerging Strategic Focus," Press Ganey, research note.

on HCAHPS. Conversely, in the same age range, if the patient reported they were in poor health, only 65 percent would give an HCAHPS top box rating.

Understanding different patient *segments* thus affords a way to listen better so as to target improvement efforts. Breaking down patient data demographically, organizations can go beyond blanket solutions and instead tailor measures to individual patient populations.

Patient diagnosis also affords a basis for more tailored improvement measures. As Figure 3.4 suggests, survey questions identify met and unmet patient needs for information, discharge preparation, responsiveness to call lights, environment of care, and so on. The bars to the left of zero reflect items in which patients with congestive heart failure have a greater unmet need than other medical patients, like those with pneumonia. The bars to the right demonstrate areas in which the needs of congestive heart failure patients have been met better than those of other medical patients. We can conclude from these data that congestive heart failure patients require more information about their illness, their medications, and the side effects of their medications in order to avoid

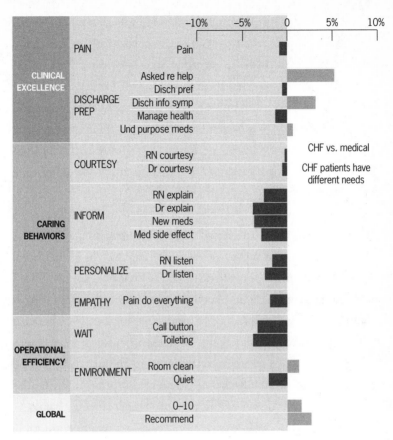

Figure 3.4 A comparison of met and unmet needs between patients with congestive heart failure and other patients

suffering and stay out of the hospital. They need more help with toileting, and they need a prompter response to call lights. When hospitals don't segment data in this way, they might assess suffering of patients generally, missing the nuances of experience among particular patients. With segmentation, organizations may focus their improvement in ways that will allow them to alleviate suffering most effectively.

If the hospital reduces suffering by meeting the specific needs of different patient groups, these patients won't simply feel more satisfied. They'll become more loyal and be more willing to recommend the organization to others. If I as a patient feel that I have suffered, either because my inherent needs were not mitigated (for instance, you didn't help me understand my care or bring pain medication when I needed it) or because you imposed suffering upon me by not listening to me or not working well together as a team, I am unlikely to return to you for care, and I certainly won't recommend you to my family or friends. Our analysis of data from 937,000 patients in outpatient care confirms this, as do analyses of large data sets performed by others.

In our analysis, we identified the key drivers of "Recommendation Failure Rate," or the percentage of patients that did not give a top rating on a five-point scale for their likelihood to recommend either the provider or the practice. Overall, 15.7 percent of patients were "not very likely" to recommend their physicians or their medical practice to others (see Figure 3.5). The most important single variable driving "Likelihood to Recommend" was the confidence that a patient had in his or her clinician. The second most important variable was the patient's perception that the care team worked well together, followed by the perception that caregivers showed concern for the patient's worries. Issues commonly thought to drive loyalty, such as waiting time, convenience, and amenities, did not significantly impact loyalty. Patients prefered to wait less and enjoy amenities, and they suffered when these needs weren't met; but they suffered more when other needs weren't met, and they were less willing to recommend providers. In essence, patients wanted good clinicians who worked well together and who listened to them—clinicians who delivered compassionate and connected care. Even when patients had confidence in clinicians, 11 percent refused to recommend them if they perceived their care team didn't work well together, and 22.3 percent refused if they felt that caregivers weren't profoundly concerned about their issues.

Similar themes emerged from our analysis of patient experience data from hospitalized patients. In the analysis in Figure 3.6, based

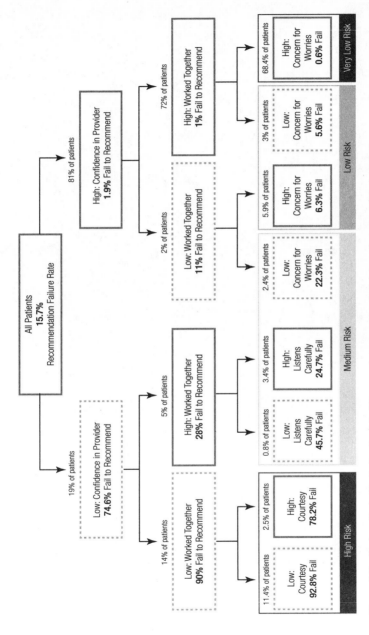

Figure 3.5   Factors that affected patients' willingness to recommend clinicians, in order of their impact

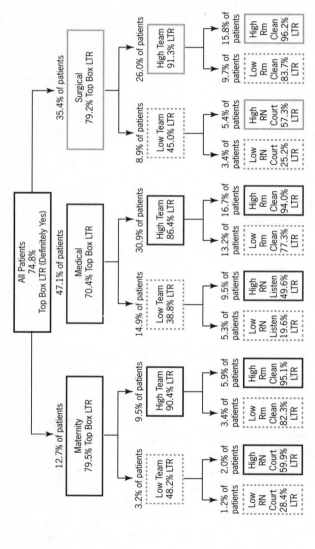

Low = Non Top Box Response   High = Top Box Response   Team = "Staff worked together to care for you"

Analyses reflect more than 1.5 million responses to Inpatient surveys returned during the calendar year of 2013 that included HCAHPS and Press Ganey measures.
© 2016 Institute for Innovation

Figure 3.6   Key drivers of top HCAHPS ratings for hospitals across all service lines

on HCAHPS data, we identified the key drivers of top HCAHPS ratings for hospitals across all service lines. Across every service, the perception that staff worked well together was critical to recommending the hospital. Specifically, 87.1 percent of patients who felt that staff worked well together gave the hospital high overall ratings. In contrast, among patients who felt that teamwork was lacking, only 36.7 percent gave the hospital top ratings. Room cleanliness and empathy on the part of caregivers only drove patients' willingness to recommend hospitals after care coordination expectations were met. While an unclean room and disrespectful staff caused patients to suffer, this apparently meant little compared with the suffering caused by poorly coordinated staff.

Looking closely, we can understand why all three of these factors matter in the first place. When patients feel that the people taking care of them are working well together as a team, collaborating on a clear plan of care and managing each other "up" well, patients feel safe. When caregivers talk to patients about their care and involve them in decisions about their care, patients also feel safe. When their room and bathroom are clean, patients perceive that the entire organization is clean and that they will not get infected—so they feel safe. In all three cases, suffering is averted. There is no light between clinical quality, patient safety, and patient experience and minimization of suffering. It's all the same thing.

That an absence of safety would lead to the greatest levels of suffering among patients makes sense in light of a famous psychological construct, Maslow's hierarchy of needs (see Figure 3.7). In his 1943 paper "A Theory of Human Motivation," Abraham Maslow represented human development and motivation as a pyramid. At the base of the pyramid he placed the needs he regarded as most fundamental. Upon this base, he layered a series of additional needs, each of which could only be satisfied after meeting lower-level needs. In Maslow's reckoning, the human need for safety was quite basic, subordinate only to physiologic needs such

Figure 3.7   Maslow's hierarchy of needs

as food, water, and sex. People could only satisfy other, higher needs such as love, esteem, and self-actualization if they felt safe. In depriving patients of safety, we're causing suffering by failing to account for one of their most basic requirements in order to thrive as human beings.

Safety itself is a multifaced thing. CMS and the Joint Commission require caregivers to take measures to assure patient safety, such as adhering to building regulations, sterilizing medical instruments, following universal protocols, and so on. However, patients need to *feel* safe, and this, in turn, requires that many other parts of the care experience go well, including parts that, at first glance, don't seem related to safety. When I was receiving treatment for breast cancer and that nursing assistant came into my room to take me to the bathroom, it was a scheduled visit. However, when I walked into the bathroom, looked down at the toilet seat, and saw blood that wasn't my own, I was not merely thinking that the seat was disgusting or dirty. I now wondered, "If they can't get this right on a scheduled visit to the bathroom, what else are they getting wrong?" I no longer felt safe, and so, based on Maslow, I was stuck at the bottom of the pyramid. I no longer trusted the people taking care of me. And I experienced suffering.

Measuring Caregiver Suffering

Just as we can measure patient suffering by proxy using instruments already at our disposal, so we can do the same for caregivers. Here, the quantitative tool of choice is engagement surveys. According to common definitions, engaged workers are committed to their employers, satisfied with their work, and willing to work harder to achieve the organization's goals. When workers feel more highly engaged, they stay longer in their jobs, perform better, and call in sick less often. Hospitals and health systems with highly engaged employees perform better on safety, quality, and experience measures, and they find it easier to recruit top talent. In particular, organizations in the top quintile of engagement perform significantly better on HCAHPS than those in the bottom quintile (see Figure 3.8).[4]

Press Ganey has been fielding surveys of employees at work since the mid-1990s. Initially, we focused on assessing employee "satisfaction," concentrating on understanding how employees felt about dimensions such as their work environment, their job characteristics, the management style, compensation, and so

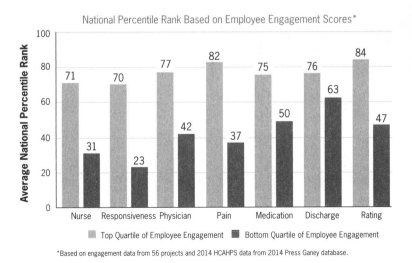

Figure 3.8   Relationship between engagement and experience

on. In 2002, we launched an "Employee Perspectives" question-naire that included questions on employee satisfaction as well as questions that measured overall levels of engagmeent. By 2008, that survey gave way to a new survey that measured the extent to which employees felt like "partners" with their employers to pro-vide healthcare. This survey contained questions specifically about engagement, including job engagement (how fulfilled caregivers felt about the work they performed on the job), work engagement (the extent to which caregivers felt they were participating in a work group focused on providing quality care and meeting patient needs), and organizational engagement (how much pride care-givers took in their organization and how much loyalty they felt).

In January 2013, Press Ganey announced the acquisition of Morehead Associates, a well-respected organization that main-tained close affiliations with integrated healthcare systems, academic medical centers, and children's and specialty healthcare organizations. Following the Morehead acquisition, we launched our Employee Voice survey, which queried employees about their feelings about their work, their manager, and their organization, yielding an engagement score as an outcome metric. As part of the survey, a key driver analysis identified the most critical issues that influenced employee engagement inside an organization.

Engagement surveys such as these prove especially helpful in allowing us to understand and access the *suffering* that caregivers experience. Let's pause for a moment to consider the particular kind of emotional toll on caregivers in healthcare settings. The sociologist Arlie Hochschild defined "emotional labor" as "the management of feeling to create a publicly observable facial and bodily display; emotional labor is sold for a wage and therefore has exhange value."[5] In relation to emotional labor in healthcare, peo-ple tend to "turn off" the emotions they feel because they judge that these emotions are not conducive to their work. They also "turn on" emotions that they don't really feel because they perceive that these emotions *are* conducive. Think about what happens when caregivers walk into a room to find that a patient couldn't get to the bathroom in time and has had an accident in bed. From the caregivers' perspective, the smell is awful, the patient's bed will have to be changed, the patient will have to be helped out of bed, and all of this will take precious time that caregivers don't have. Many caregivers will become frustrated in this situation, not because they are "bad" or uncaring people but simply because they are human. They are likely juggling many priorities, whether related to their patient load, other work expectations, or their personal lives. But caregivers cannot show their frustration or their disgust. They must switch off those emotions so that the patient can maintain his or her dignity. Likewise, caregivers must "turn on" optimism when interacting with terminally ill patients so that these patients feel as hopeful and safe as possible. The daily control of emotions isn't easy, and over time, it takes a toll.

We can measure this kind of suffering indirectly through engagement surveys that ask about topics like caregivers' trust in leadership, their ability to disconnect when not at work, their perception of the quality of care delivered in their organization, or their staffing, scheduling, and ability to take breaks away from patient care. Just like patient surveys, these surveys help us understand the caregivers' met and unmet needs and the totality of *their* experience, with the unmet needs serving as proxies for suffering.

So what needs are most important to caregivers, causing the most suffering when they're not met? A key driver analysis we performed confirmed that seven items correlated most with engagement compared with other factors:[6]

1. A feeling of belonging ("I feel like I belong in this organization.")

2. A sense of pride in what the organization does ("This organization provides high-quality care and service.")

3. A belief in senior management ("I have confidence in senior management's leadership.")

4. A sense that the organization treats employees well ("This organization treats employees with respect.")

5. A sense that job stress isn't overwhelming ("The amount of job stress I feel is reasonable.")

6. A sense that pay is adequate ("My pay is fair compared with that of other healthcare employers in this area.")

7. A sense that the job offers opportunities for personal growth ("My work provides me an opportunity to be creative and innovative.")

When these needs are marginally met or when they're not met at all, caregivers feel frustrated, stressed, disillusioned—they experience suffering. Of course, many other factors influence whether employees are engaged in their jobs, including those related to job requirements, the work environment, management behaviors, and organizational conditions. In particular, staffing, retention, and the feeling of being appreciated impact not only the patient experience, but also the caregiver experience and clinical quality. We can equate poor metrics in these areas with increased caregiver suffering.

In Table 3.1, we find that the number of hours of nursing provided per patient day was correlated with how nurses viewed their jobs and the quality of care their organization provided. The table demonstrates statistically significant positive correlations between nursing hours per patient day, nurses' experience of their job, and their perception of the quality of care provided by their organization or unit. It demonstrates a positive correlation between nursing hours per patient day and how the patients perceived their care, and it demonstrates a negative correlation or presumably fewer

Table 3.1 Analysis of the Effects of Nursing Hours per Day Relative to Other Factors

	Total Staffing HPPD	Intent to Remain	Status of Nursing
RN Perception			
Job Satisfaction	.370**	.784**	.763**
Quality in General	.354**	.682**	.779**
Patient Experience			
Rate Hospital 0–10	.261**	.330**	.678**
Nurses Listen	.190**	.342**	.634**
Prompt Response	.199**	.392**	.609**
Patient Outcomes			
Unassisted Falls	–.202**	–.248**	–.558**
CLABSI	–.168**	–.142**	–.383**
HAPU II	–.189**	–.202**	–.500**

**Statistically significant

hospital-acquired conditions. So while staffing is definitely correlated with the nurses' experience, the patient's experience, and hospital-acquired conditions, the correlations, while statistically significant, are not strong ones, since the correlations are below .5. The "Intent to Remain" column demonstrates the correlations with the nurses' intent to stay on the unit or in the organization. In many cases, the correlations are stronger, particularly for nurses' perception of their jobs and their perception of the quality of care delivered. But it is the status of nursing that demonstrates the strongest positive and negative correlations across the board. So while staffing is important, the work environment may play an even larger role in not only shaping nurses' perceptions but influencing the patient experience and clinical quality. If we agree that surveys help us understand met and unmet needs for both patients and caregivers, and that the existence of these needs serves as a proxy for suffering, these data provide meaningful insight into where we might target improvement efforts to better meet caregiver needs and to reduce their suffering.

To take our analysis further, we used data from the National Database of Nursing Quality Indicators (NDNQI) to examine elements of the work environment, including workplace safety and the ability of nurses to be proactive in care (their surveillance capacity). An analysis across domains found that safer workplaces led nurses to feel better about their jobs and the care they were delivering to patients. Compared with organizations ranking in the bottom quartile for nurse workplace safety, those in the top quartile saw a 27 percent higher rate of job enjoyment among nurses and a 52 percent lower rate of missed care as perceived by nurses. We've seen that safety reduces patient suffering, and this study confirmed it as well. To reduce both caregiver and patient suffering, organizations need to focus on improving safety. Again, we can look to Maslow's hierarchy of needs to help us with this understanding. If nurses don't feel safe in their practice of nursing, they can't move beyond that level in the pyramid. Organizations shouldn't expect to be at the ninetieth percentile of engagement or have caregivers that feel like they belong or make a meaningful contribution until they first meet those safety needs.

In general, our focus on engagement data suggests that lower levels of caregiver suffering correlate with lower levels of patient suffering—and higher levels of clinical quality. According to data from NDNQI (and as shown in Figure 3.9), when the nurse, as an employee of the organization, is likely to recommend the organization (and who experience less suffering) patients will also typically be more likely to recommend the organization when care is needed (and who, as we've seen, are suffering less). Likewise, across every domain of HCAHPS, patients score a hospital higher when employees are most engaged (i.e., suffering the least). When caregivers are engaged, they feel that they belong, that they provide good care, and that they contribute meaningfully. If they aren't engaged, they may be disillusioned, feel burned out, and lack resilience—in other words, they're suffering. Organizations with the highest caregiver rating have overall patient experience scores that are 37 percentile points higher (see Figures 3.10–3.12). For organizations, the implications are clear: reduce caregiver suffering, and you reduce patient suffering directly and indirectly as well.

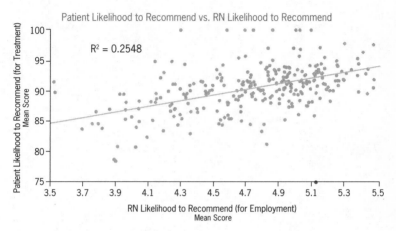

Figure 3.9   Patient loyalty and nurse loyalty

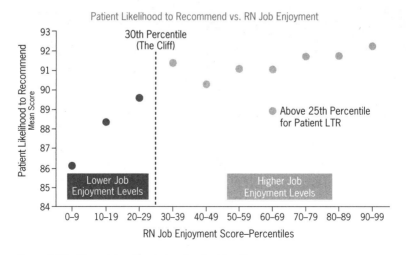

Figure 3.10   Nurse job enjoyment and patient loyalty

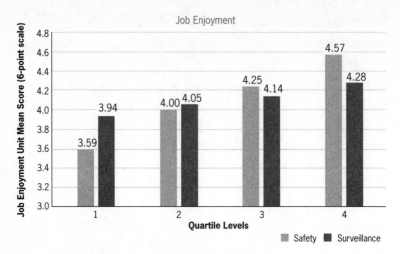

1 = unit RNs strongly disagree they enjoy their job, 2 = disagree, 3 = tend to disagree, 4 = tend to agree, 5 = agree, 6 = unit RNs strongly agree they enjoy their job

Figure 3.11   Safety and job enjoyment

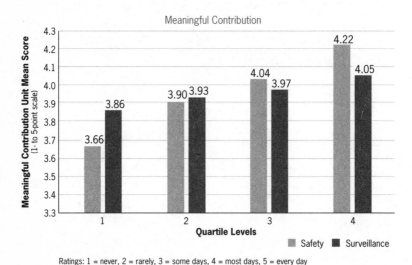

Ratings: 1 = never, 2 = rarely, 3 = some days, 4 = most days, 5 = every day

Figure 3.12   Safety and meaningful work

Measuring Matters

We've examined how we can measure patient and caregiver suffering using quantitative and qualitative tools already at our disposal. Yet such measurement isn't simply a matter of academic interest. It allows us to make tangible changes within healthcare organizations and to reduce the suffering of both patients and caregivers. Some organizations are already beginning to do exactly that. Consider Duke Women's Cancer Care Raleigh.[7] In 2016, Duke Raleigh Hospital opened a new center dedicated to the care of women with cancer, combining many specialties in one location, including radiation, oncology, breast surgeons in private practice, and cancer center support staff. Patients could now go to this center for everything from genetic testing to surgery to dietary consultations. But would the dozens of medical professionals manage to come together seamlessly as a team during the many months of transition?

As we've seen, poorly coordinated care contributes mightily to patient suffering. Mindful of this reality, team members took steps to talk openly with patients about the shift to a single, unified center and to address patient concerns. Every month, the team charted its performance on both clinical and patient experience measures. The members of the team could monitor their progress, so they knew that their efforts to stay coordinated and communicate well with patients were paying off. In fact, the team's patient experience scores were coming in *higher* than the average score for the entire hospital, as was its score for the item "staff worked together to care for you." Patients were experiencing less of the suffering they did elsewhere due to lack of staff coordination. So, too, were caregivers. As leaders were pleased to see, the new center scored the highest possible rating for engagement just before it opened—an intense time that was perhaps most challenging for caregivers.

Duke Raleigh is just one of many organizations today reducing suffering—and incidentally, improving safety and clinical outcomes. It's doing it by addressing the full spectrum of patient and caregiver needs, not just needs for strong teamwork and coordination. But given the complexity of those needs and the relationships among them, how might organizations address suffering in a systematic way, from top to bottom? Is there a comprehensive solution to the problem of suffering, one that any team or organization can embrace and progressively implement? Indeed, there is, and as we'll see in the next chapter, it revolves around delivering not just excellent clinical care but care that is both compassionate and connected.

CHAPTER

4

Compassionate Connected Care

IN 2013, BRANDY, a 36-year-old medical sales rep, was diagnosed with thyroid cancer. The fear of the diagnosis was bad enough for her and her young family, but it was made all the worse by the unnecessary anxiety and stress Brandy suffered while trying to advocate for herself when it seemed like no one in healthcare would.

Some 18 months earlier, Brandy had started to feel run down. She was just overworked, she thought. But was she? She was feeling cold all the time, sleepy, angry—just plain *bad*. To cope, she drank energy drinks and took naps in her car between surgical cases (her job was to sell interventional spine implants and help with them during surgery).

Pretty sure that something wasn't right, she went to her primary care physician, but he told her she was likely just experiencing the normal symptoms of aging. Brandy wanted to believe him, but six months later, her symptoms still hadn't improved. She talked with other providers, hoping that they might take her symptoms more seriously. Yet they, too, dismissed her problems and wouldn't order any blood tests.

Brandy trudged on with her life as best she could, hoping that her caregivers were right but afraid that they weren't. The turning point came in February 2013 when she fell asleep while driving to a surgical case in broad daylight after a full night's sleep. Waking up on the side of the road, and thankful that she hadn't hurt herself or anyone else, she went back to the doctor that very day. Her symptoms hadn't abated, and her neck hurt all the time. She wanted a blood test.

He still wouldn't do it. "What you need," he said, "is a pain management physician." So that's where he sent her.

Brandy happened to know the pain management doctor from her work in the OR, so she texted him and asked if he'd order labs for her. The physician did so, and her labs came back abnormal—and not just a little. They were way off. Noting that she'd had a double-shot espresso right before the test, the primary care physician told her that the results probably reflected the caffeine in the drink. She was fine, he assured her. A medical student who happened to be in her physician's office that day felt her thyroid, which was swollen. "You definitely need an ultrasound," he told her. After much discussion, the primary care physician finally agreed to order one. The ultrasound confirmed what Brandy in her heart already knew: there was something big and solid in her neck that wasn't supposed to be there—a larger nodule on the right side of her thyroid and a smaller one on her left.

Even at this point, she couldn't get her doctors to take her seriously. The endocrinologist told her that he wasn't going to biopsy the nodules. As a sales rep in the operating room, Brandy had been exposed to a certain amount of background radiation from the two C-arm imaging machines and live fluoroscopy. She knew that she was supposed to wear a thyroid shield, but the shields weren't always available. "Everyone has nodules if they're exposed to radiation," the endocrinologist told her. "Nothing to worry about." Brandy insisted on a biopsy, and a good thing. Twenty-four hours later, the endocrinologist called her with the news: differentiated papillary thyroid cancer.

Some weeks later, Brandy had her thyroid removed. She followed up with radioactive iodine to kill any remaining thyroid cells. For almost four years, stretching into 2017, she was largely symptom-free. Then in April of that year, she began to feel tired again. More lab work and an ultrasound revealed bad news: she had a tumor on the left side of her neck. This time, it was metastatic in her lymph nodes. Her doctors didn't feel a biopsy was necessary. The tumor was likely slow-growing, so they could just keep an eye on it for now.

Brandy wasn't so sure. All this time, her care providers hadn't listened to her. She called friends who knew friends at MD Anderson Cancer Center, and she quickly booked an appointment with a thyroid cancer specialist. As of this writing, she is still undergoing tests and will likely have more surgery soon. Brandy is scared for herself and her family—and frustrated that it has taken so long and required so much effort on her part for her doctors to take her concerns seriously. Why were caregivers seemingly so disconnected from her needs, fears, and perspectives as a patient? Why hadn't they cared enough about her to put aside their assumptions about "patients like her" and listen to what *she* was feeling in her body?

Experiences like Brandy's are frighteningly common. They continue to occur not just because of the causes of suffering described in Chapter 2, but because individual providers, teams, healthcare organizations, and the industry as a whole haven't quite known what to do to improve patient and caregiver experience. They've understood that healthcare is chaotic and patient experience subpar, so they've tried mightily in recent years to improve that experience (without framing it as suffering per se). *How* they've focused, however, has missed the mark. Much of the time, organizations, teams, and individual caregivers work on improving specific scores relating to patient experience. That makes sense—the scores drive reimbursement. But a constant focus on scores obscures the greater challenge: to create an entire *system*, a culture, in which patients are at the center of care. If Brandy's providers had oriented their work in fundamental ways and at every level around *her*, they would have listened to her and showed compassion instead of dismissing her concerns time and again. Quite possibly, they would have caught her cancer earlier. At the very least, they would have reduced unnecessary suffering.

We can't just address particular metrics on a piecemeal basis and hope to make progress on suffering. If it were that easy, healthcare organizations wouldn't see the many patient problems, the negative comments, the poor scores, the turnover, and the burnout they see today. To make progress, we must embrace a *comprehensive approach* toward patient experience, one that locks our attention on the *real* meaning of what we do and why it's important.

Individuals and organizations *want* to improve healthcare for patients and caregivers. They feel like they've tried everything, and nothing has worked. I speak daily with healthcare providers and administrators who are perplexed about their scores and who feel demoralized. "We've done service training," they say. "We've implemented hourly rounding and bedside shift reports, we're doing leader rounding, but the scores are not reflecting it." Or they'll say, "You know, we've got great engagement scores for our employees, and our patients say they'd recommend us, but the rest of our patient experience scores don't really reflect that." These comments always follow with, "What do we need to do now?"

Any performance improvement or quality initiative needs an overarching framework to help bind goals and strategy together. And any organization likewise needs an overarching mission, vision, and values to organize people and bring them together behind a common purpose. Patient experience is no different.

We need a methodology that brings disparate groups of people together around the goal of reducing suffering, that helps them remember why they wanted to become caregivers in the first place, and that provides a structured approach for actually accomplishing that goal. But where can we find such a methodology?

Building a Model to Tackle Suffering

For the past several years, we at Press Ganey have been researching, developing, and deploying a model that we call Compassionate Connected Care. I began creating Compassionate Connected Care back in 2013, when Dr. Tom Lee first joined our organization as chief medical officer. Tom and I spoke on a number of occasions about how we would provide a consolidated vision for clinical thought leadership at Press Ganey. Early in his career, he told me, he had a mentor, Lee Goldman, who helped Tom develop his own "brand" as a thought leader. Tom said that conceiving of thought leadership in terms of branding had helped him to focus his efforts around topics that mattered to him, with an eye toward his legacy. "What will your legacy be?" he asked me. "How will you define *your* brand?"

These were good questions, and I had to take time to reflect on them. I first told Tom that my brand was the totality of the patient experience and all things nursing. But he encouraged me to think about making a difference in a more specific way. So I pondered some more. What was really most important to the patients I served as a nurse and to the caregivers I served as a healthcare leader?

Thinking back to my colleague Deirdre's notion of met and unmet needs as a way to measure suffering, I had an epiphany. Healthcare organizations had been collecting data about patient experience, engagement, and clinical quality for years. Often, we had monitored it to the point of "analysis paralysis." We looked at the data all the time but never actually *did* anything with it. Or if we did take action, we never managed to sustain the gains. What we needed, I realized, was a new way of looking at the problem of suffering that would enable us to take more effective and sustainable action. We needed a *framework*—an action model. With Tom's support, I set about creating one.

I spent a great deal of time researching the concepts of empathy and compassion, watching Cleveland Clinic's 2013 empathy video, which I felt poignantly demonstrated the need for empathy and compassion,[1] and contemplating the definition of words like "sympathy," "empathy," and "compassion." According to the *Oxford English Dictionary*, "sympathy" is a feeling that one might have "of pity and sorrow for someone else's misfortune."[2] When you can understand that misfortune *from the inside,* and when you can actually communicate what it feels like to someone else, you've achieved the ability to empathize.[3] Meanwhile, the *Cambridge Dictionary* defines "compassion" as "a strong feeling of sympathy and sadness for other people's suffering or bad luck and a desire to help."[4] That "desire to help" is crucial, leading us to think of compassion not as a noun but as a verb. Compassion is the *action* you take when you feel sympathy or empathy.

Earlier in this book, when I told you about how my son-in-law, Aaron, was shot, you might have felt sympathy for me. You could imagine what it must have felt like to have been in that situation. But perhaps you not only understand that police violence proliferates in society today—you also know *firsthand* the devastation caused by a bullet to the brain. Or perhaps you can also imagine the devastation that the patient's family is experiencing because you've seen or experienced that yourself as a caregiver. In fact, perhaps you can imagine it so well that you can communicate that understanding to me. You might have even cried at hearing Aaron's story or wanted to reach out and hug my daughter. What you experienced was empathy. And let's take that one step further. Perhaps in your state of empathy you wanted to *do* something to ease my daughter's or Aaron's pain. That action is compassion.

Following this logic, I concluded that all of us in healthcare require compassion to reduce suffering. But I realized that compassion alone wasn't enough. Obviously, our clinical skills and expertise mattered as well in order to provide the best possible outcomes and safety. Empathy and compassion don't make much of a difference if patients suffer from hospital-acquired pressure injuries, falls, and infections. But thinking about suffering further, I concluded that even compassion and good clinical care weren't enough to reduce suffering. Somehow, we needed to *connect* compassion with high-quality clinical care, and we had to focus on connection in general and in its own right.

Conceptualizing Connection

As I had seen firsthand during my cancer treatment, care was frequently fragmented and disconnected, on every level and in every sense of the word. To reduce suffering, I felt, we had to remedy this systemic and almost existential quality of healthcare. Yes, the model we were creating had to connect compassion with clinical excellence. But we also had to connect many other elements with one another. In particular, based on my past experiences in healthcare, we had to make four specific connections in order to mitigate suffering: those relating to the clinical side, the operational side, the behavioral side, and the cultural side of healthcare (see Figure 4.1).

First, our model had to connect *clinical excellence* with *outcomes*. I may put in the best central line around, but if patients get infected, it doesn't matter how well I placed the line or how many I put in. It's the *outcome* that matters. Increasingly, patient-reported

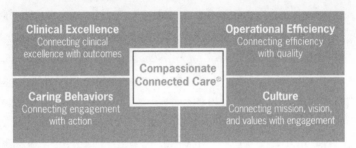

Figure 4.1   The Compassionate Connected Care model

outcomes measures (PROMs) are helping to measure not only the clinical outcome but the functional outcome as well. If I have a total knee replacement and leave the hospital without an infection, fall, or pressure injury, but I am not able to walk 20 feet unassisted after two weeks, then my outcome is not what it should be. Again, who cares how excellent my surgeon and nurses were? The net result is I can't walk 20 feet. Since every person involved in my care has an impact on my outcome, attending to outcomes as well as clinical excellence and process measures means taking steps to help teams work better together. We need to remember that we're all in this together, and so we all need to help to facilitate the desired outcome.

Second, our model had to connect *healthcare quality* with the *efficiency of operations*. A healthcare organization that spends 10 times more than its competitors on high-quality care may well deliver it, but it does so at an unsustainable cost. No business owner would accept a 3 percent margin year-over-year, and yet hospitals and healthcare organizations do. They thus have no choice but to deliver *both* quality *and* efficiency. As the sisters said to me many times in my career at a large, faith-based organization, we must understand the reality of "no margin, no mission!"

Think of it this way: those who pay for and partake of healthcare expect clinical excellence. But operational excellence (efficiency) assures that hospitals have the financial, material, and collaborative resources they need to make exceptional clinical care happen. When I worked with organizations to improve flow, many hospitals wanted to focus on the emergency department (ED), where the operational issues seemed most obvious. I couldn't blame them: the ED was exhibiting long wait times, poor patient satisfaction, high turnover of talent, and many other problems. However, when I examined clinical and operational data relating to triage, door-to-provider times, total time spent in ED, disposition to inpatient bed placement or discharge, interaction between staff and physicians in other areas of the hospital, and diagnostic testing turnaround times, it became obvious that focusing solely on the emergency department would not suffice. The hospital faced *systemic* issues, and it needed to address them systemically.

Why, for instance, *were* patients waiting? Well, in some cases, the emergency department couldn't obtain needed results from the lab or imaging department in a timely fashion. In other cases, hospitals required that a hospitalist see a patient in the ED prior to inpatient admission, but it took an hour or more for the hospitalist to make it to the ED. In still other cases, a social worker or case manager wasn't available, or no staff was available to accept the patient when he or she arrived on the inpatient floor. In all these situations, the patient waited. And waited. And waited.

So often, EDs felt isolated and at the mercy of inpatient units, and in many ways, they were. But in order to achieve operational excellence, these emergency departments had to recognize that they and the rest of the hospital were in this together. In my work, I helped form flow teams in the ED that consisted of ED physicians, nurses, techs, lab representatives, pharmacy personnel, hospitalists, cardiologists, surgeons, imaging specialists, and administrators. The broad representation of specialties assured that recommendations coming out of this group were realistic and within its purview. We examined data around key process indicators and defined common goals. The operational changes that resulted led to significantly shorter wait times in the waiting room, higher patient experience scores, and better engagement. Working collaboratively, we confirmed that operational excellence, clinical excellence, and patient experience went hand in hand.

If our model to address suffering forged links between efficiency and quality of care, it also had to make a third connection: between *engagement* and the *behaviors* that contribute to it. Having surveyed the behavioral aspects of patient experience, Press Ganey was keenly aware of the connection between caregiver engagement and the behaviors caregivers needed to render in order to provide an optimal patient experience. Employees in organizations that ranked in the top quintile for engagement scored higher in patient experience on every domain of HCAHPS. As we discussed in Chapter 3, HCAHPS evaluates behaviors on a frequency scale—how often teams exhibited desirable behaviors—while the Press Ganey survey evaluates behaviors on a Likert scale, charting how well those behaviors were exhibited.

Of course, the *consistency* with which these behaviors are exhibited also matters. If 90 percent of employees demonstrate 90 percent of the necessary behaviors 90 percent of the time, that seems pretty good, right? Almost everyone is performing most of the desired behaviors pretty much all the time. That's A-grade performance. But hold on. Multiply 90 percent by 90 percent by 90 percent. You arrive at 73 percent—meaning that the hospital is only satisfying patients 73 percent of the time. That will put you in the tenth percentile of hospitals, and nowhere close to maximizing your value-based purchasing reimbursement. A 73 percent is a "C" grade—average at best and definitely not "very good." The reality is that patients deserve caregivers who perform 100 percent of behaviors 100 percent of the time. Would you want *your* family members to experience the 10 percent of care encounters in which providers missed opportunities to minimize or mitigate your suffering?

As we saw in Chapter 2, young caregivers often don't learn the behaviors required to mitigate or avoid suffering in school, nor do they receive the coaching they need to make those behaviors automatic. "Seasoned" caregivers may forget these necessary behaviors when they become jaded after years of work. So what does "showing courtesy and respect" really look like? We feel its absence, and we know it when we see it, but do we teach it and demonstrate it to one another and to our patients *every time?* Do we *always* provide information that makes our patients feel safe and successful when they leave us for additional care? Do we often give patients a chance to influence care decisions, helping them to feel at least some autonomy in a process that seems totally out of control? Again, what do these behaviors look like? We need to proffer the training, coaching, and moment-to-moment affirmation that allow *all* caregivers everywhere to understand and adopt these behaviors.

A fourth and final connection that our model for reducing suffering made was that between *engagement* and *the organization's mission, vision, and values—its culture.* When I was a new nurse, I walked to the elevators every day on my way to my unit, and I stared at the framed document on the wall next to the elevator button—our mission, vision, and values. I never really gave the plaque much thought, and I didn't connect it to my own purpose as a nurse. Today, I realize that mission, vision, and values constitute *the most important information to pass on to employees, not to mention patients and visitors.* Without that shared purpose, individuals, teams, and organizations can never achieve their strategic goals. We will all work myopically to do the right thing *as we see it,* and we won't understand how our little area of work fits into the larger organization and its mission. We'll address suffering in a piecemeal fashion, and perhaps in ways that conflict with how other individuals and teams are addressing it.

One of the best CEOs I ever worked with carried a pocket-sized version of the strategic plan for our health system. At the top of this document, the mission, vision, and values were printed. Whenever someone made a request of him or suggested a change in a policy or practice, he would take out this little document and ask the person how the request or suggestion was integral to the organization's larger mission and mandate. Every meeting included a discussion about how the agenda connected to the mission, vision, and values. My colleagues and I all understood that the mission, vision, and values weren't just words on a plaque—they truly drove the strategic direction and decisions for our organization. Over time, this CEO and his team succeeded in creating a *culture* that reflected the mission, vision, and values of the organization. To this day, when I pass the hospital over which this CEO presided, I feel proud of that culture and the organization it sustained.

In 2014, I encountered a great example of how a strong culture can improve patient experience and reduce suffering when I visited the University of North Carolina at Chapel Hill's hospital. Its CNO, Dr. Mary Tonges, and her team had implemented a program there, based on Kristin Swanson's Caring Theory,[5] to spread a culture of caring called "Carolina Care."[6] When I stepped into the hospital (without a name badge or identifying clothing), I was amazed at what I found. The greeter helped me out of my taxi and showed me to the check-in and information desks. Although not lavish or especially beautiful, the lobby was clean and comfortable, and everyone I encountered greeted me warmly and made eye contact. In a medical-surgical inpatient unit, a patient suffering from a chronic illness told me of the outstanding care he was receiving. In fact, since he often had to be admitted to the hospital, he made a habit of requesting this unit because the people there took such good care of him. The nurses on duty not only were able to tell me about Carolina Care but could explain how it informed everything they did. A unit secretary told me how much of a difference Carolina Care made for her, saying, "I *own* Carolina Care." What an incredible statement! This woman was so proud of her work and her organization that she not only committed herself to it— she identified with it.

I asked Tonges how UNC had managed to instill such a strong sense of cultural ownership in her workforce. She told me that the organization had first worked hard to understand Swanson's theory. Then the organization educated all staff, assuring that they knew what the cultural principles it had adopted meant both in general and as applied to their work. Finally, and perhaps most important, UNC branded the culture "Carolina Care," affirming that the culture belonged to everyone who worked at UNC because *everyone*, even the janitors and food services staff, was a caregiver. After all, if you don't provide direct patient care, you support someone who does.

I was impressed. Every organization, I thought, needed to do what UNC was doing, *connecting* engagement with the organization's mission, vision, and values such that it was palpable for everyone at all times.

More generally, I concluded that healthcare organizations large and small needed to forge all four of the big connections I have surveyed. All these connections working together would give rise to the total patient experience, and careful attention to all these dimensions, combined with compassion, would reduce suffering. In sum, I concluded that the pathway to reducing suffering was the following: *the provision of exceptionally skilled clinical care, in an environment that is efficient and effective, by engaged and resilient caregivers, in a culture that was driven by a shared purpose to achieve the optimal outcome for all involved.*

Detailing Compassionate Connected Care

Once I had determined our framework's basic structure, I gave it a name—Compassionate Connected Care—and began to develop the model further in its specifics. I decided to research how a large and diverse group of people conceived of the notion of Compassionate Connected Care. I asked hundreds of patients, clinicians, and nonclinicians to provide me with very clear descriptions of what this kind of care looked like to them. I wanted detailed mental images of behaviors involved—not "Compassionate Connected Care means that doctors and nurses communicate better with patients," but "When the nurse comes in to take my blood pressure, he puts his hand on my shoulder to comfort me." Those were the only instructions I provided to people when I asked them for images.

In all, 117 image statements came back, and I analyzed them using the affinity diagram method. Originating as a business tool, affinity diagrams allow you to sort a large number of ideas into groups in order to review, categorize, and assess them. With Tom Lee's help, I sorted individual image statements into groups of three or more, eliminating duplicate or overlapping statements and discarding statements that conveyed abstract ideas (for instance, "The nurse was kind and empathetic"). From the remaining statements, six basic themes emerged as definitions of Compassionate Connected Care:[7]

- **Acknowledge suffering.** We should acknowledge that our patients are suffering and show them that we understand.

- **Body language matters.** Nonverbal communication skills are as important as the words we use.

- **Anxiety is suffering.** Anxiety and uncertainty are negative outcomes that must be addressed.

- **Coordinate care.** We should show patients that their care is coordinated and continuous and that "we" are always there for them.

- **Autonomy reduces suffering.** Autonomy helps preserve dignity for patients.

- **Caring transcends diagnosis.** Real caring goes beyond delivery of medical interventions to the patient.

In addition to these themes, the statements allowed me to identify specific actions that alleviate suffering in a variety of healthcare settings. Under "Acknowledge Suffering," for instance, I uncovered actions such as bearing witness to the suffering (saying "I'm sorry" to a patient who wasn't able to sleep), asking patients about their concerns, and anticipating and mitigating the patient's discomfort. Under "Body Language Matters," actions identified by my study participants included making eye contact, physically touching the patient (for example, gently holding the patient's shoulder while obtaining blood pressure), and attending to one's body position when in the presence of a patient (for example, not turning your back disrespectfully). Tables 4.1A–F in the following sections show behaviors for each of the Compassionate Connected Care themes.

Let's now run through these themes and their associated actions in a bit more detail.

Acknowledge Suffering

In Chapter 2, we detailed how healthcare education today limits the amount of time that students spend actually connecting with other human beings. As a result, students have a harder time acknowledging suffering and providing empathic and compassionate responses. In fact, many of them—and us—would rather

Table 4.1A   The Compassionate Connected Care
Themes and Behaviors: Acknowlege Suffering

We should acknowledge that our patients are suffering and show them that we understand.	
Actions	**Images**
Bearing witness to their suffering shows patients that we care.	A physician says,"I'm sorry," to a patient who said she didn't sleep well the night before.
	A doctor who has just told a daughter that her mother is terminally ill sits with her to console her.
	When care does not go as planned, staff apologize, acknowledge the impact on the patient, and engage the patient in exploring options.
Asking the patients what they are worried about allows them to be a person rather than a disease.	The clinician asks what concerns he or she may address.
	The clinician asks the patient what he or she is most concerned about.
	While caring for a patient, the clinician discovers something personal about the patient that establishes a connection to make a positive, memorable moment for future interactions with the care team.
	The clinician asks how the patient would prefer to be addressed.
	The clinician notes a patients' greatest concern on the communication board so all caregivers are aware.
Anticipating and mitigating the patients' discomfort shows concern for their suffering.	The nurse applies EMLA cream to the patient's hand before starting the IV.
	Staff members update the patient and family of delays at least every 30 minutes.
	Staff members inform the patient and family of what to expect prior to beginning any procedure or test.

send a text or tweet than physically speak with another person. To reduce suffering, therefore, we must consider closely what acknowledging suffering really looks like and how we can teach it to caregivers.

As a model for teaching it, we might adopt the SCOPE model of communication. SCOPE stands for "Solve the problem," "Criticize," "One-up," "Probe," and "Empathize." Suppose Sally is a patient in your ambulatory practice. She presents today with a massive headache. As the provider, you ask, "What brings you in today?"

"I have the worst headache I've ever had in my life!" Sally says.

You can respond to this statement by doing one of the following:

1. **Solve the problem.** You might give Sally medicine for her headache, wash your hands, and leave the room. You feel great because you think you have solved Sally's issue, so you move on to your next patient.

2. **Criticize.** You might say to Sally, "I doubt that your headache is really that bad. After all, you drove yourself here, and you were reading a magazine when I came in the room." You might also scold Sally for taking up time that patients with "real" issues could have used. Clearly, criticizing is rarely, if ever, a good response.

3. **One-up.** You might say to Sally, "I get it! I've had a migraine for the last week!" Sally now feels understood, but she also likely perceives that you have minimized her concerns.

4. **Probe.** You might ask Sally more questions. "How long have you had this headache? What is the intensity? Where exactly does it hurt? Sometimes when you have a headache, it's because you're dehydrated. Have you had enough water to drink?" All of these are good questions that require answers, but they are not, ideally, the first thing you say to patients. Any idea what that is? Read on!

5. **Empathize.** You might say to Sally, "I'm so sorry you're having to deal with this headache. It must be hard when you have things you want to do." If you say something like this, Sally will feel both heard and validated by her provider.

In today's fast-paced, technology-loaded, reimbursement-cognizant, and still largely volume-driven healthcare world, we all tend to behave primarily as solvers and probers. We want to solve the problem quickly, or ask more questions to solve the problem quickly. That way, we can move on to the next crisis or patient. It's *natural* to want to do this. However, is it the wisest, most efficient, most compassionate course of action? What if after you empathized with Sally and validated her pain, she told you, "Yes, I've been under a lot of pressure lately. I'm going through a really nasty divorce." Tylenol and water are not going to fix *this* problem. Sally is in crisis, and it has given rise, in all likelihood, to an intense headache. By empathizing, you have reached the root cause of her visit. Had you simply given Sally a Tylenol or asked about her symptoms, you would not have validated her concerns nor gotten at the root of her issue. You would have been addressing the wrong problem.

Body Language Matters

In my role teaching at Missouri State University, I typically have about 55 students in Nursing Leadership and Management, the last course in the university's baccalaureate nursing program. Every semester, I send students to their preceptors, telling the students, "Follow your preceptors. Do everything they tell you to do, but I want you to do one thing differently. Sit down. You don't have to spend any more time in the room or talk about anything differently; just sit down while you're there. Come back and tell me how it went."

Every semester, students come back and say things like, "That was amazing! The patients said we were better nurses than the nurses!"

One semester, a student came back to me and said, "So I tried your little experiment."

"And how did it go?" I asked.

She responded, "Well, I sat down, and we started talking about fishing. I spent maybe a couple more minutes in the room, but not many. The weird thing was that the rest of the day, he never used his call light. And he never asked for pain medicine.

Table 4.1B   The Compassionate Connected Care
Themes and Behaviors: Body Language Matters

Nonverbal communication skills are as important as the words we use.	
Actions	**Images**
Eye contact matters.	The clinician sits at eye level and looks the patient in the eye during the conversation.
	The front desk caregiver looks up from the computer to establish eye contact.
	As the patient begins to say what is really on his or her mind, the caregiver pushes work aside, leans forward, and listens attentively.
	The caregiver explains to a patient that he/she is listening and is fully engaged with the patient while documenting on the computer.
Physically touching the patient closes distance.	The nurse gently holds the patient's shoulder while obtaining blood pressure.
	The physician sits down and holds the patient's hand while explaining tests and treatments.
	The clinician takes a seat and holds the patient's hand when the patient starts to cry.
	The physician makes a point of shaking hands with patients and visitors when introducing himself/herself.
Body position matters.	The physician sits face to face with the patient while talking with him or her.
	The caregiver sits down at eye level with the patient.
	The caregiver does not turn his/her back to the patient until the interaction is over and the caregiver leaves the room.

And the next day, I wasn't taking care of him, but his family sought me out to give me a hug and tell me thank you."

Body language matters. When a provider sits down face-to-face with the patient and makes eye contact, the patient perceives the interaction to be both longer and more meaningful than if the provider spent the same amount of time but spoke to the patient while standing up.[8] When our chief medical officer, Dr. Tom Lee, goes into a patient exam room, he sits down first, acknowledging the patient and empathizing with him or her. Only then does he begin to perform his exam. The process of acknowledging and empathizing doesn't take long, and even when the chairs in the exam room are all filled, Tom says, "Sally, I really want to talk to you about your headache, so I'm going to go get a chair." As Tom tells me, a family member in the room will invariably stand up and say, "No, no, take mine." And he does. Or he goes and gets a chair. Because it matters.

Anxiety Is Suffering

Here's something you should know: Every patient on a gurney, in a waiting room, in an exam room, or in a bed *is scared to death*. And their families are often just as stressed. Even when you go to the doctor for a routine exam, you have those niggling questions in the back of your mind: "I wonder what they'll find? Will I be healthy, or will they find something wrong with me? How bad will it be?" If you're there with a specific concern, the visit can feel even more harrowing. And let's suppose you're in the waiting room of the emergency department with your child, who has been coughing uncontrollably and running a high fever. You want relief for your child, and you also want the doctor to tell you that your

Table 4.1C   The Compassionate Connected Care Themes and Behaviors: Anxiety Is Suffering

Anxiety and uncertainty are negative outcomes that must be addressed.	
Actions	**Images**
Reducing uncertainty and anxiety for patients and families acknowledges that they are in a stressful situation.	Caregivers round on patients frequently in a way that is purposeful and meaningful to the patient—inquiring about pain, positioning, toileting, and at least one nondisease/treatment-oriented discussion topic.
	The employee notices a "lost guest" and personally escorts the person to his or her destination.
	Staff members describe what will happen next when the patient arrives at the exam room.
	Clinicians tell patients when they will be in to see them again.
	Caregivers greet patients warmly (e.g., "We've been expecting you, Mrs. Smith").
	Caregivers provide reassuring phrases (e.g., "Mrs. Smith, I am going to be with you every step of the way"; "Mrs. Smith, we are going to take very good care of you"; "Mrs. Smith, we are going to do this together").
	Volunteers escort patients and families to their destinations (e.g., surgery area, tests, and treatment areas).
Reducing waits shows we understand patients' suffering and respect their time.	There is no lag time in response when a patient presses the call light.
	Staff members provide an estimate of wait times.
	Staff members do not pass call lights without inquiring if they can help.
	Staff members work together to reduce waiting time for bed placement, transfers, and testing.

child's health problem is no big deal. But of course, your mind is also running through every awful scenario you've ever heard about or seen on TV. And you feel completely vulnerable and out of control, at the mercy of the people taking care of you.

None of us like these feelings; yet as caregivers we often forget that every patient we encounter experiences them. When human beings become frightened, we experience a physiologic response that dates from times when we had to contend with threats like saber-tooth tigers. It's an autonomic response, and it kicks in when we're confronted with something scary. Our heart rate accelerates. Our blood pressure rises. Our pupils dilate. We have to decide: Are we going to flee from the danger, or are we going to fight? This response is both normal and real. Unfortunately, when it kicks in, we don't remember instructions very well, and we don't follow them. We focus solely on the threat.

My own breast cancer diagnosis terrified me, even though I had been a nurse for 30 years, worked in multiple areas of the hospital, and taken care of thousands of patients. Of course, as an "old" OR nurse, the last thing I was going to do was let someone else pick my surgeon. So I interviewed my surgeons, narrowing my choice to two. The first surgeon was a great guy and had a wonderful reputation. I had known him for years, and he had even coached my younger daughter's T-ball team. But when I went to my first appointment, his nurse was gruff, rushed, and a bit surly. I knew that I would interact with her more often than with my surgeon. Did I really want to have to deal with her sour demeanor on top of everything else? No, I did not. So I didn't choose that surgeon.

I had hired the second surgeon as a patient care assistant in the OR before he went to medical school—it was his first job in the OR. That was 15 years earlier. I arrived early for my appointment and waited until my appointment time. Then I waited 45 minutes after that. I was growing frustrated and was thinking about leaving, but I waited another 15 minutes and the medical assistant finally called me to the exam room.

Once I got there, the staff members did everything right. They pulled the curtain to protect my privacy. They sat down when talking to me. They shook my hand. They asked not just about my diagnosis but about my family and my job. After the surgeon, Dr. Brian Biggers, performed his exam, he invited my husband and me to join him in his conference room. There, he answered every single question and did a genetic test for the BRCA gene right then, even though I told him that I hadn't settled on a surgeon yet.

"Christy," Dr. Biggers said, "I am the best there is at this. I'm fellowship trained. I have a low infection rate. I have great outcomes. No one can take care of you as well as I can. I'm the best." Today, I chuckle thinking about what I would have done if he had said that when we were working together in the OR. I imagine that "arrogant" would have been the least of the adjectives I would have used! But as a patient, this was exactly what I needed to hear. I needed to hear that I was in the best place, with the best people, who were going to take the best care of me. In my moment of fearfulness, Dr. Biggers and his team made me feel safe. I no longer felt like I had to fight or run away from the threat. My stress level and fear decreased, and I could focus on becoming a full participant in my care.

I still feel good every six months when I go to see Dr. Biggers. I know that he is with me and that he's going to take good care of me. I had the same experience with the plastic surgeon, Dr. Robert Shaw, who performed my reconstruction. These young surgeons were honest about what to expect and how much the procedures would hurt (and cost). They informed me about the risks and benefits of the procedures as well as of alternative care options. They were great clinicians, but the reason I will always be loyal to them is not their clinical ability per se. It's that they reduced my anxiety by making me feel safe. All our patients and their families need that feeling of safety, too. And when they get it, the benefits rebound to caregivers.

In a well-known study conducted at Vanderbilt, researchers found that when physicians maintained a good relationship with their patients, the patients were less likely to sue the physician even if adverse events occurred.[9] An analysis of plaintiff depositions revealed that over two-thirds of malpractice claims (71 percent) stemmed from difficult relationships between physicians and patients, with patients perceiving that physicians were uncaring. A quarter of malpractice plaintiffs faulted physicians for conveying medical information poorly, and 13 percent cited physicians' poor listening skills.[10]

Coordinate Care

Healthcare is delivered in a wide array of settings, including the provider practice, outpatient clinics and therapies, acute care hospitals, surgery centers, rehabilitation hospitals and outpatient clinics, long-term acute care hospitals, hospice, home healthcare, skilled nursing facilities, and long-term care. As care continues to move toward a paradigm of population health management, organizations will increasingly have to assure that care is coordinated, provided in the best venue, and provided in the most efficient and effective manner. In Chapter 2, I referenced studies that show that patients may see between 60 and 100 different caregivers in a single hospital stay. Those numbers don't take into account patients' primary care providers, home health nurses, physical therapists, and others who may help with their care both before and after their hospital stay. Patients need to know that all these caregivers are talking with one another. Patients understand that we have to use electronic medical records, but are we actually using those records to coordinate? Does the primary care

Table 4.1D   The Compassionate Connected Care
Themes and Behaviors: Coordinate Care

We should show patients that their care is coordinated and continuous and that we are always there for them.	
Actions	**Images**
Showing patients that the relationship doesn't end when they are not directly in contact deepens the relationship.	The clinician calls the patient for follow-up within 48 hours.
	Clinicians follow up appropriately when information is received on the discharge phone call.
	Clinicians show that they are concerned about what will happen when the patients go home and provide instructions to make them successful in their recovery.
	Caregivers "manage up" each other, complimenting the caregivers on the care team.
	The nurse explains who will be taking care of the patient after shift change.
	The clinician uses good handoff techniques and is accountable for communicating the patient's condition and needs.
	Caregivers use the teach-back method to ensure patients understand discharge instructions.
	Patients are provided with written instructions for home care prior to the day of discharge with an opportunity to read and ask questions.
	Clinicians use data to improve patient care processes.

physician refer to what happened when the home health nurse visited? Do caregivers have to rely solely on the patient to learn about the plan of care?

As caregivers, we must show patients that we communicate with one another. We need to "manage each other up," letting patients know that the next person who will be caring for them is going to take great care of them. And we truly need to collaborate with one another because it makes our patients feel safe.

Now, I will admit that when I was a staff nurse, I did like to blame issues like excessive wait times on the anesthesia or radiology department rather than on my own failings. "I'm sorry, Mrs. Smith," I used to say. "I don't know when you're going to surgery. Anesthesia is behind again, and I'm not sure when someone will be out to get you." It was easy to fall back on blaming anesthesia, because that department did always seem to be backed up. Besides, I wanted Mrs. Smith to know that it wasn't *my* fault she was waiting—I was simply the messenger.

This response on my part might have served my purposes, but did it help Mrs. Smith? Not at all. Instead of making her feel safe, I was only worrying her more. Now she was thinking, Why is the anesthesia department backed up? Do they have enough staff? Will I get to go to surgery tonight? Will the staff be tired when they get to me? Will they take good care of me?" Thanks to my response, Mrs. Smith didn't feel any safer than she had before. She felt *less safe*. I should have said, "Mrs. Smith, I'm sorry you've waited longer than you expected to. I want you to know that your anesthesiologist is Dr. Stewart, and he is a fantastic physician. He is going to take great care of you, and he'll come and see you before you go back to the operating room. You're going to be in great hands." In responding in this manner, I wouldn't necessarily seek to boost Dr. Stewart's ego. Rather, I would seek to reduce Mrs. Smith's fear, which, after all, is a very significant form of suffering.

Autonomy Preserves Dignity

When patients visit a provider practice or the hospital, they are told to put on a gown and store their clothes in a bag or closet. They are told when they can have visitors and how many. They are told when and what they can eat, when they can walk around, and how far. They are told when they can leave the facility and what they can do when they leave. They are told when the doctor or other caregivers will see them, operate on them, or perform a test on them. In short, patients lose all control. Sometimes they can't even go to the bathroom when they want to or relieve themselves in private. This loss of control is often demoralizing, and it causes anxiety because patients feel vulnerable and at the mercy of those caring for them. I've heard many patients say, "I wish I could do it myself, but I know I'm not supposed to. I know how busy you are, and I hate to bother you. I'd much rather do it myself."

**Table 4.1E   The Compassionate Connected Care
Themes and Behaviors: Autonomy Preserves Dignity**

Autonomy helps preserve dignity for patients.	
Actions	**Images**
The patient is a full participant in guiding his or her care.	The clinician asks patients and family members about their preferences in care issues lying ahead.
	The clinician asks the patient for his or her preferences on even minor issues, such as the preferred hand for an IV.
	The clinician provides a full range of care options when discussing diagnosis and treatment plans.
	Caregivers involve the patient in bedside shift reports.

Many times, patients *can't* perform tasks themselves. But we caregivers often forget that some choices don't really matter to us, and they might make all the difference for patients feeling deprived of choice. Here's what it sounds like to offer more choice to patients when we can:

"Mrs. Smith, which arm would you like me to take your blood pressure on?"

"Mrs. Smith, would you like to take a walk in the morning or the afternoon? And when we walk, where would you like to go?"

"Mrs. Smith, you know that we have to document your information in the computer. Would you like to see what I'm charting right now, so you can tell me if I got it right?"

Affording patients a voice in issues such as these doesn't require more time or resources. But by simply encouraging Mrs. Smith to make these decisions, we can ease her fears and help her to feel a greater sense of autonomy.

Real Caring Transcends the Medical Diagnosis

When I was in the hospital receiving treatment for breast cancer, the people caring for me didn't see me as Christy Dempsey, a person with a family, job, hobbies, and dreams. Rather, I was "the mastectomy in 902." I had lost my identity, as patients everywhere so often do. Sometimes they become their diagnosis, or their doctor's name—"the Dr. Smith patient in 405." Although this depersonalization may be entirely unintentional, it still happens, and it prevents *us* from connecting with patients, too.

Once when I was consulting in a large academic medical center, I was standing in the room of a patient who had open heart surgery the day before. The nurse practitioner entered, and there was no chair for her to sit in. Without hesitation, she knelt on the floor so that she could address the patient at eye level. She held his hand and talked about his family and his needs after discharge. She not only allowed him but encouraged him to make decisions about his care and how he would manage with his elderly wife at home. He was not the CABG in Room 408. He was Mr. Jones with a family, who needed to feel safe and who needed to be successful in recovery after discharge. Caregivers provide this kind of care every day, but we sometimes forget that we need to

Table 4.1F   The Compassionate Connected Care Themes and Behaviors: Real Caring Transcends the Medical Diagnosis

Real caring goes beyond delivery of medical interventions to the patient.	
Actions	**Images**
Personal touches outside medical care strengthen relationships.	The nursing assistant brings a patient his or her favorite dish from the cafeteria as he or she awakens from surgery.
	The director of service excellence walks a patient's service dog outside the hospital to give a stressed family member time to grab lunch.
	The nurse talks with a patient about his or her children.
	The nurse is simply silent while touching the patient or family during a difficult time.
Caring for the patient means caring for the family.	The nurse gives a warm blanket to a family member who is cold.
	On a nightly basis, the nurse holds the phone to the ear of a terminally ill patient, so his daughter can say goodnight.
	Caregivers provide instructions to the family prior to discharge to ensure they are comfortable with caring for the patient at home.

Source: Tables 4.1A–F directly adapted from "Compassionate Connected Care: A Care Model to Reduce Patient Suffering," Press Ganey, January 19, 2015.

personalize what we do and connect with the people who happen to be patients at the moment.

On another occasion, when I was director of perioperative services for a large, level 1 trauma center, I used to watch a nurse named Sheila who took her role in the patient experience to heart. Sometimes Sheila spotted patients in the OR's holding room who were trembling with fright. She took their hands and talked with them about their families, jobs, or hobbies. Then she spoke with them about the procedure they were about to have and what they could expect in the OR. She would help to transport these patients to the OR and help them onto the table, talking to them the whole time—not about the procedure, but about what she had learned was important to them in the holding room.

Just before the anesthesiologists would put these patients under anesthesia, Sheila would whisper in their ears: "I am going to be with you during the whole procedure. We will take good care of you. You are safe, and we are really good at what we do." You could see these patients relax and then drift off into a peaceful sleep for the procedure. At these moments of peak vulnerability, when patients feared not waking up after surgery or waking up and feeling intense pain, Sheila was there. You see, she understood that providing care isn't just a job. In the heartbreaking and inspirational memoir *When Breath Becomes Air*, Dr. Paul Kalanithi writes that our "duty is not to stave off death or return patients to their old lives, but to take into our arms a patient and family whose lives have disintegrated and work until they can stand back up and face, and make sense of, their own existence."[11] This is what we do. We heal. We comfort. We care.

Compassionate Connected Care for the Caregiver

As we discussed in Chapter 1, the people who care for patients are under tremendous stress and pressure. In many ways, they suffer, too. As we at Press Ganey began to talk about Compassionate Connected Care with clients and in conferences and publications, caregivers told us that the model helped them get back to the basics and rediscover the passion they had for their work. A number of these caregivers conveyed their wish that we create a framework for reducing their suffering as well. They knew that it was tricky to apply the term "suffering" to them. Unlike sick patients, they had known what they were getting themselves into when they became caregivers. Still, they felt the need to be heard and helped as well.

I thought about how we might utilize the same kind of action framework for the kind of suffering that caregivers experience, primarily stress, fatigue, and distress at work. Working again with

Figure 4.2   How caregivers experience care

Deirdre Mylod and Dr. Barbara Reilly, I reviewed a number of engagement surveys and methods for identifying, measuring, and distinguishing the experience of caregivers. We noted that the caregiver experience had several distinct dimensions (see Figure 4.2). First, *clinical* knowledge was a key part of caregivers' work and professional identity. Second, caregiver experience had an *operational* component. Efficiency and effectiveness profoundly influenced the caregivers' ability to succeed in their work. Third, caregiver experience was inflected by *culture* and the organization's mission, vision, and values. In particular, culture enabled both engagement and good care for both patients and the people who care for them. Finally, we perceived that caregiver experience depended on a *connection to purpose and the organization*. In this last respect, the caregiver experience differed, in our estimation, from the patient experience, which hinged on caregiver behavior rather than connection with purpose. In all these areas, caregivers had needs that could be either met or unmet. To the extent that these needs were unmet, caregivers experienced suffering (see Chapter 3).

Following a methodology similar to the one we used to generate the patient-oriented Compassionate Connected Care model, we asked thousands of caregivers—both clinicians and nonclinicians—to describe caregiving experiences that they regarded as compassionate and connected. Receiving 184 unique responses, we analyzed them using the affinity diagram method. Once again, we arrived at six themes:

- All of healthcare should acknowledge the complexity and gravity of the work provided by caregivers.

- Management has a duty to provide support in the form of material, human, and emotional resources.

- Teamwork is a vital component for success.

- Empathy and trust must be fostered and modeled.

- Caregivers' perception of a positive work-life balance reduces compassion fatigue.

- Communication at all levels is foundational.

All caregivers want to perform well, but sometimes they feel hindered by the healthcare system, just like patients do. Many caregivers told us that they often hear about problems or issues that arise when they do something wrong—and that is fine. But they also need to hear that they do a good job when they perform well, and they need to hear that their work means something to patients and colleagues. As psychologists have long understood, positive reinforcement yields more sustainable changes in behavior than negative reinforcement. All too often, though, colleagues and managers only call attention to behavior when they wish to criticize it.

Managers in healthcare settings might think that they provide positive feedback, but do their team members perceive it this way? Consider how managers typically deal with adverse safety events. When such an event happens, they bring together the team involved to identify what went wrong. They take the event as their starting point and work backward, asking everyone involved to be honest and open. They identify what caused the failure and arrive at steps to take for avoiding it in the future. All this is as it should be.

Now, consider the last time you had a really good day at work or a time when a patient had a really good outcome, thanks to care in your unit, department, or practice. Did you take the time to understand the contributing factors? Did you pull the team together to deconstruct why the outcome turned out so well? Probably not.

The next time you have a really good day or you identify a really good outcome for your team, convene everyone around a conference table. Start by describing the good day or outcome and work backward. Ask team members *why* things went well. Was it the patient population? The team members who worked that day? The fact that the physicians participated in rounds? The way that the manager came out of her office to provide lunch relief? When you analyze the success and break it down into its component parts, your team can draw new insights about how to change practice, process, or policy going forward so as to replicate that success. And when team members perceive that such meetings *do* enable progress, they'll feel acknowledged, and they'll feel like they are active participants in the team's success.

Analyzing the links between patient experience, nurse engagement, and clinical quality, we've confirmed that staffing is important, but we have also found that work environments might be even more so. In particular, work environments must enable caregivers to feel safe and to provide proactive care or surveillance capacity. These features of work environments depend in turn upon management's ability to provide human, material, and emotional support to caregivers. To my surprise, none of the caregivers we surveyed told us that they wanted more money or better benefits. Rather, they asked for more emotional support in stressful situations, safe staffing, more equipment, and better maintenance or more frequent replacement of equipment. One caregiver wished for "an environment that is safe, nonjudgmental, supportive, empathetic, and healthy, so that the caregiver feels comfortable and encouraged to share concerns, questions, and suggestions for improvement and so that the caregiver can thrive in his/her role as caregiver to others."

Significantly, the needs identified by these caregivers all reside near the bottom of Maslow's hierarchy of needs. They are physiologic needs, safety needs, and emotional needs. As Press Ganey's research has demonstrated, managers cannot expect to achieve top engagement scores, low turnover, or top box patient experience scores until first satisfying these kinds of needs. Our first state-of-nursing report, released in 2015, identified the crucial role that work environment plays in the patient experience, nurse experience, and clinical quality, paying attention to falls, pressure injuries, and hospital-acquired conditions. Afterward, Press Ganey delved further into which aspects of the work environment drove key outcomes like intent to stay, overall rating, and clinical quality in terms of falls and pressure injuries. The results clearly demonstrated that the safety of nurses' work environment, above and beyond surveillance capacity, greatly influenced how nurses felt about their jobs. It also impacted how they felt about their ability to contribute to patient care and intention to stay. All three of these considerations contributed to nurse engagement, which correlated directly with critical safety, quality, and patient experience outcomes and which influenced an organization's financial health.[12]

As I began talking to healthcare audiences and clients about the six themes of Compassionate Connected Care for the Caregiver, I wanted to understand how each of the six themes ranked in the minds of people who care for patients. During a large, multidisciplinary conference, I used polling software to ask my audience of 500 caregivers to prioritize the themes. This audience chose "teamwork" as the most important theme of all the themes of Compassionate Connected Care for the Caregiver. While this is not a statistically valid study, clearly teamwork matters. We need professionals across the continuum of care to collaborate closely with one another, not just work alongside one another. One caregiver put it this way: "We engage in mutual relationships with patients, with families, and with colleagues, to foster physical and spiritual healing, while honoring human dignity, values, and beliefs." In Chapter 6, we'll discuss ways in which we can form and sustain teams in order to optimize both patient and caregiver care and engagement.

The emotional dimensions of teamwork are especially important. In order to display empathy and compassion to patients, caregivers must receive it as well. Colleagues and supervisors must model the behaviors, teaching and coaching empathically and also showing empathy and compassion to one another. When leaders demonstrate empathy with patients, colleagues, and subordinates, they model the behaviors that matter to the organization. I have worked with organizations whose leadership is convinced that they provide care with empathy and compassion. The organizations talk about their mission, vision, and values, and they provide exemplary clinical care. But these leaders cannot understand why their patient experience and engagement scores remain subpar.

When I talk to managers on the units and in the ambulatory practices, they know the right things to say. They perform rounds and can produce the rounding logs documenting that their staff is in the room. The leaders tell me that they round as well, with the logs to prove it. On these rounds, patients tell them that everything is "fine." When I go with leaders on their rounds, they stand in the doorway to greet patients—they don't sit with them. Often, they read a scripted group of yes-or-no questions. I like to call this "flyby" rounding. Leaders go through the motions of rounding but make no real connections with patients and glean no real information. Feeling trapped and put on the spot, patients provide information that they think the leader wants to hear so that they don't get their caregivers "in trouble." They're afraid to give honest feedback, aware that caregivers watching the leader round would be put on the defensive to explain negative comments. Those caregivers in turn emulate the leaders' rounding behaviors, becoming "flyby" rounders themselves. Leaders in this situation perform rounding as a "check the box" exercise. They haven't demonstrated real empathy or compassion to either the patients or caregivers.

When caregivers don't receive empathy or compassion from team members and leaders, they themselves become burned out or exhibit compassion fatigue. The term "compassion fatigue" was first coined to describe the phenomenon of secondary trauma from being bombarded by complex physical and emotional challenges on the job.[13] Others have identified the antithesis of compassion fatigue, a phenomenon called "compassion satisfaction." Caregivers who experience compassion satisfaction experience "attitudinal values such as absorption, vigour and dynamism" while undertaking work-related endeavors.[14] Nurses who experience compassion satisfaction generally burn out less, possibly because such satisfaction helps them avoid feeling lonely, disenfranchised, marginalized, and bereft of meaning or purpose.

Besides compassion satisfaction, resilience might allow caregivers to decrease compassion fatigue and avoid burnout. It's not that the stressors, distress, and suffering experienced on the job goes away. Rather, resilient caregivers can bounce back from these stressors because intrinsic and extrinsic motivators exist that continue to add to that person's resilience bank. The caregivers in our qualitative study identified some of these motivators as "work-life balance," with one telling us that that she "protects [her] own health and healing as a whole being of body, mind and spirit with as much enthusiasm and dexterity as [she gives] to others." Another remarked, "Having quality downtime on days off, spent doing something the healthcare provider enjoys, which is important for the recharging of one's batteries."

In addition to discussing their own health, caregivers told us they needed more flexibility in scheduling as well as more work incentive choices to become more resilient. Many caregiver schedules reflect organizational and provider needs, not the hour-by-hour and day-to-day volume and acuity needs of the patients we serve. To build resilience, we must build schedules that assure that we put the right caregivers in the right roles for the right amount of time focused on the patients and their goals. Press Ganey is working with Kronos, a workforce management company, to marry time, attendance, and role data with caregiver and clinical data from NDNQI. Client organizations in our study will change caregiver schedules in order to understand how the schedules impact the nurse and patient experience. That analysis will help organizations identify scheduling changes capable of improving the experience of caregivers and patients.

A final theme we uncovered, one that underpins all the other themes of Compassionate Connected Care for the Caregiver, is communication. Teams work best when we break out of our silos to assure accurate, transparent, and meaningful dialogue among team members and between them and other teams. As research has shown, "Nurses who receive supportive communication from their peers and supervisors are more likely to experience lower rates of burnout."[15] They also feel better about their employers, so much so that they think twice about leaving to work elsewhere. Unfortunately, many factors impeded communication among healthcare professionals.

Michelle O'Daniel and Alan H. Rosenstein argue that communication and teamwork camaraderie are vital to effective healthcare outcomes. Common paths to better communication, they believe, include a "nonpunitive environment," "shared responsibility for team success," "clear and known decisionmaking procedures," "regular and routine communication," and access to necessary resources.[16] Our study recipients identified behaviors along similar lines: "Listening to my patients and other staff members to understand their needs"; "Managers and coworkers listen and hear your worries and physical needs"; "Clear, direct, timely communication of clinical impressions and plans between all members of the team, to align our focus and messaging to OUR patient." As our participants' responses make clear, we need to attend to communication at all levels to improve resilience, engagement, and patient care.

Brandy's Story Revisited

Remember Brandy, the thyroid cancer patient who had trouble advocating for her care? Imagine what might have happened had practitioners caring for her closely applied the Compassionate Connected Care model. Brandy's PCP would have provided up-to-date, evidence-based clinical care driven not only by Brandy's clinical signs and symptoms but also by her own concerns about bodily changes she had seen. The PCP would have assured Brandy that her team would continue to follow up and figure out what was happening. Brandy's physician would have felt supported in practicing research- and evidence-based, zero-harm care. He would have communicated with his colleagues across disciplines and specialties, recognizing their expertise and asking questions without fear of being marginalized.

But that's only the beginning—the clinical piece of Brandy's care. As regards the operational dimension, Brandy would have only needed two primary care visits and would not have incurred at least three unnecessary visits. The provider, the insurer, and Brandy all would have saved money. The interprofessional team caring for Brandy would have sought opportunities to reduce waiting time for appointments and testing and would have communicated her results through an electronic health record portal as well as by phone. The members of the team would have had the resources available to reduce redundancy in their work and streamline processes, automating them whenever possible. The operations of the practice and the organization would have been optimized, so that when caregivers did the right thing for Brandy, they also would have been operating most smoothly and efficiently.

How might Brandy's caregivers have behaved in her presence? Well, the PCP would have sat with her to discuss her care, listening to her concerns and taking 56 seconds to connect with her on a personal level, thus assuring that Brandy felt safe in his care. Members of the team would have narrated their care for Brandy, so that she would know what was happening at all times during her diagnostic testing and treatment. The team would have answered Brandy's questions and asked for her to participate in decisions about her care. Team members would have ensured that Brandy's husband also felt supported, answering his questions and involving him in her care as well. Finally, team members would have provided education and information to Brandy and her husband proactively, helping them to avoid feeling anxious.

As for the dimensions of connectivity and culture, the people caring for Brandy would have worked together as a *true* team, communicating transparently and appreciatively, eliminating silos, and sharing decision making. Each provider would have felt a part of something bigger than his or her individual efforts, and each would have felt that the organization supported him or her and that he or she had the resources needed to do a great job. Team members would have understood how their work aligned with the mission, vision, and values of the organization. A culture of safety would have existed that rewarded good catches and near misses, with teams conducting positive root cause analyses and appreciative inquiry to prompt questions and improve care delivery. That way, when Brandy questioned her diagnosis, treatment, and care, team members would have followed up with their colleagues in due course to address her concerns.

All of this sounds good, right? Maybe a little idealistic? I absolutely agree. Achieving care like this is anything but easy. And yet some organizations have taken the Compassionate Connected Care frameworks to heart, "owning" the concepts and achieving positive change in their organizations. At Conway Regional Medical Center (CRMC), a nonprofit, 154-bed acute care medical center located in Conway, Arkansas, caregivers and administrators felt frustrated by stagnant HCAHPS scores. Nothing they did seemed to push the scores higher in a sustainable way. Working with Press Ganey on a pilot basis using the Compassionate Connected Care framework, the members of a unit at the hospital selected a priority key driver change initiative—in their case, frequent patient rounds. They focused on embedding certain key driver behaviors into the entire organization.

To help with behavior change, the unit created broad and ongoing messaging explaining the need for change. The unit trained and engaged executive leaders to behave as sponsors of the initiative, and it trained unit leaders and staff on how to conduct patient-centric hourly rounds. To support caregivers, the unit emphasized coaching as well as positive, appreciative coaching techniques. The results were impressive. Patients rated the hospital higher, and they gave nurses higher scores for treating them with respect, for listening to them, for explaining aspects of their care to them, and for delivering prompt care. Patient experience improved, and suffering declined (see Figure 4.3).

This unit worked comprehensively on improving a particular feature of the care it delivered. The initiative operated on multiple levels at once, addressing individual caregivers, the workings of teams, and organizational aspects. In the chapters that follow,

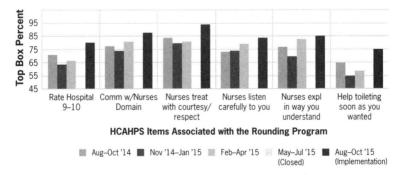

Figure 4.3   HCAHPS rating by age and health

we'll examine in greater detail how you and your colleagues might apply the model on all these levels, and we'll also look at how the healthcare industry as a whole might adapt Compassionate Connected Care. In the next chapter, we zoom in on the most basic level, the individual caregiver delivering care face-to-face with patients. Healthcare doesn't get any more direct than this. As we'll see, each of us as caregivers can take a series of steps on a daily basis to deliver care that is more compassionate and connected, both for patients and for the colleagues who support us.

The Compassionate
5 Connected Caregiver

In June 2017, my daughter-in-law, Olivia, experienced excruciating abdominal pain that came on unexpectedly and wouldn't go away. She went to the emergency room twice over the course of a week. Each time, she waited for well over an hour to see a doctor and then longer for diagnostic testing, wasting the better part of a day. All the diagnostic tests—including CT with contrast, ultrasounds, and lab work—came back negative. And yet she still felt tremendous pain, an 8 out of 10. The doctors gave her the narcotic hydrocodone, but Olivia didn't want to take it. She was a paramedic and couldn't work shifts while the drug was in her system. Unfortunately, she had no choice. The pain was that bad.

A couple of nights after her second ER visit, Olivia and her wife (my daughter Hilary) came to our house for dinner. Before we could sit down to eat, Olivia had to go home to lie down because her stomach hurt so bad. She called a bit later saying she couldn't stand it anymore and had to get some kind of relief. Olivia had scheduled an appointment with a GI specialist, so Hilary called the nurse on call for the GI provider. As it was after hours on a Sunday, the nurse told them to go back to the ER. So they did, with me in tow.

When we arrived, it was 8:55 in the evening, and Olivia was clutching her abdomen and rocking back and forth in pain. She had gone pale, and she was scared. Hilary was angry—it was Olivia's third time in the ER in less than a week, and nobody had taken care of her wife's pain or given them any answers. Over a half hour later, the triage nurse finally saw Olivia. Taking her vital signs, he apologized and announced that he would have to send them back out to the waiting area. "How much longer before we can see a doctor?" she asked.

"Between now and the end of time," the nurse responded. "We just never know what's coming in."

I'm sure the nurse was feeling stressed out and overwhelmed by the workload. Hour after hour, he had to deal with any number of frustrated patients. Still, we didn't appreciate his flippant remark, and in a small way, it caused suffering. The nurse may have been technically correct in saying that the ER staff "never knew what was coming in," and he might have felt better letting us know that our long wait wasn't his fault. But the comment and the way it was delivered only engendered further fear, anxiety, and anger at a process that was beyond our control.

For the next two hours, we sat in the waiting room without so much as an update. People around us were in severe pain, moaning and crying out. Some were angry, and at least one patient was accompanied by two security guards. The ladies' restroom was filthy—I'll spare you the details—and the soap dispensers were all empty.

Finally, just before midnight, a nurse whom I'll call Cathy came in to interview and assess Olivia. She tried taking her blood pressure, but the machine wasn't working, so she went to get another. It took another 20 minutes for her to reappear (without a new machine) and announce that a Dr. Edelman (not his real name) would see her.

Five minutes after that, Dr. Edelman came in. He was a young physician, very personable. Holding out his hand, he introduced himself by his first name, Jim. He empathized with Olivia about the long wait and apologized for it. Then he conveyed that he understood Olivia's frustration at having come to the ER three times without receiving any answers or pain relief. He leveled with Olivia, saying, "I can do more tests, and I'll be sure that we haven't missed anything. Unfortunately, I can't get you answers tonight. But we'll do everything we can to make sure you're comfortable." He went away for a few moments, and upon returning, he admitted that Olivia probably should have been put on Protonix for potential gastritis. He ordered an IV for her and sent her home later with a prescription to fill. Overall, we all found Dr. Edelman extremely kind. He had made us feel safe in his care, and in the course of a very short interaction, he had connected with us. As we left the hospital, I found myself thinking, *Why don't all caregivers do this?*

The Reduction of Suffering Starts with *Us*

All caregivers can reduce suffering, and with the Compassionate Connected Care model in hand, my hope is that more of us will. The patients and caregivers in our study provided us with a wealth of insight into specific *behaviors* that caregivers can practice, master, and deploy in their work to help avoid or mitigate patients' suffering. These behaviors—which as we saw in the last chapter include connecting with them, acknowledging suffering, providing autonomy, and so on—are not rocket science. Any of us can perform them. In fact, many of us already are. The problem is that we're not adopting these behaviors *consistently* or effectively enough to improve patient and caregiver experience as reflected in the quantitative and qualitative surveys.

In many ways, our failure to achieve consistency and excellence in these behaviors reflects the broader context in which caregivers work. As we'll explore in later chapters, our cultures don't always support these behaviors, and our organizations don't "operationalize" them by providing adequate staffing, resources, and encouragement. But there's another reason we don't always behave in ways that prevent or alleviate suffering. Existing change initiatives designed to foster these behaviors tend to falter due to a misplaced emphasis on tactics rather than purpose.[1] At staff meetings, leaders often stand before teams and say: "Our scores on responsiveness are terrible! We're in the thirtieth percentile, and corporate has given us a goal of the eightieth percentile. We have to step it up!" Team members hear that the team has to improve to meet a goal that corporate has set. Is that really a compelling rallying cry?

Imagine if leaders were to say, "Listen, our patients are telling us that they don't feel like we are responsive enough and that we might be making them wait too long before we respond to their needs. What do you think we could do to help our patients feel like we were more responsive to their needs?" Now team members would perceive that they need to figure out how to help patients feel like their needs are being met. The need to work on behavior would seem more meaningful, connecting with the "why" of work—the larger purpose that caregivers are seeking to accomplish in their careers.

What we need, then, aren't more metrics-focused initiatives. We need specific strategies that individual caregivers can use that bring them closer to purpose. In this chapter, I present a few such strategies—simple, easy techniques that caregivers can try in their daily work. These strategies aren't the *only* techniques that will work, but they will help caregivers do more of what we know makes a difference to the people for whom we care and to our colleagues. If caregivers deploy these strategies, patient loyalty, caregiver engagement, and healthcare outcomes will all improve. Caring for patients will become more of what it should be: a fulfilling and enriching pursuit, not just for patients but for everyone.

56 Seconds

When I managed other nurses, some younger team members would remark that making a connection with patients was important but that they simply didn't have time. With so much else to do, they couldn't afford to spend 10 or 15 minutes chatting with a patient. If they did, their other work wouldn't get done.

Sound familiar? Well, maybe there's a way to handle this very legitimate concern.

When I became Press Ganey's CNO, I began speaking about patient and caregiver experience before groups of nurses, administrators, and board members. I got the idea of including a bit of audience role-play. I would ask a volunteer from the audience—a total stranger—to sit or stand near me for a brief conversation. I would ask another audience member to time our interaction. Sitting down with the volunteer, I would say, "Hi, Ms. Atkinson, I'm Christy, and I'm going to be your nurse today. What would you like me to call you?"

"Call me Sandy," she might have said.

"Sandy? Great. Sandy, is this a good time for you?"

She might have nodded her head.

"Great," I would say. "You know, we talked in bedside shift report this morning about the procedure you'll have this afternoon and the changes in your medication. But I've never taken care of you before. So, when you're not here, what do you like to do?"

Sandy, or any other audience member I called up, might have talked about her family, her job, her hobbies, her pets, and so on. No matter how she responded, I would always be able to find a way to connect with her. If she were to tell me she had three kids, I could ask how old they were, whether they were boys or girls, where they went to school, or what sports they played. At some point, I would decide to wrap up the conversation because I controlled it. When I was ready to wrap it up, I would say something like, "I hope I can meet your kids when they come to visit. I'll look for them and make sure they get to the right room. In the meantime, I need to do an assessment. I'm going to ask you lots of questions, and you ask me any questions that come to mind, OK? We're in this together!"

I have performed this exercise thousands of times in many kinds of venues. Guess what? These interactions have never taken longer than two minutes! In fact, they take an average of *56 seconds*.

Consider how powerful even a conversation this short can be. From now on, every time you walk into Sandy's room to hang another IV, administer medications, change her dressing, or get her to the bathroom, you can exchange a few words about her children, what they like to do, and how proud she is of them. You and Sandy will have a lot to talk about, and none of it will have anything to do with the reason for her hospital visit. That's the point! Sandy will now know that you know her not as the mastectomy in 902, but as a person—as Sandy who has three children who all play sports, and the baby is a girl who loves to dance. As a result of that personal connection, Sandy will feel safer, knowing that you're looking out for her. And to enhance that feeling, you can introduce Sandy to her other caregivers so that she feels safe with them, too. Because Sandy feels safe, she'll be more likely to reveal information that might affect her care. She'll be more likely to comply with her care plan and to participate actively in her care—because she trusts her caregivers. A mere 56 seconds will have completely changed her experience. Fifty-six seconds!

If you're a caregiver, or if you're managing a team of caregivers, you'll want to go back and practice this 56-second-long conversation. Just start doing it with colleagues, and eventually you will do it with patients. You might fear that these conversations will take longer than two minutes—that you'll be trapped in a room with a patient who won't stop talking. This might happen at first, but with a bit of practice, you'll become more adept at controlling the conversation.

I recommend that managers and caregivers set aside time at least once every quarter to practice the "56 seconds" exercise. You can't just perform this exercise a single time and assume you've nailed it. Have caregivers pair up with one another, with one playing the role of the patient and the other of the caregiver. To make the role-playing more realistic, have the "patient" drink a liter or two of water first, leave the call light on the floor, leave the door open, and have the "caregiver" leave the room. The "patient" will have to go to the bathroom, but he or she will lack a way of getting anyone's attention. When the "caregiver" comes in, have another team member film the interaction (you can do this on a smartphone, no need for expensive video equipment). As I find, team members who see themselves on film in a role-play scenario often experience epiphanies about themselves and their behavior. Managers and coworkers can also use these videos to provide coaching and feedback, asking questions like, "When you saw the patient's facial expression just then, what do you think she was feeling?" or "Is there something you could have said or done that would have made the patient feel safer and more at ease?" Have team members switch roles, and repeat the role-play exercise until every team member has had a chance to play both the patient and the caregiver. If you perform this exercise regularly, you'll find that you and your colleagues will improve your ability to convey empathy, thus improving patient experience.

Now, you might object that not every patient is as amenable to a friendly conversation as Sandy was. What about all those patients who are belligerent or angry? In this situation, you have to take some steps to calm or soothe the patient. One young nurse I know, Julie, had a patient with congestive heart failure who had made frequent trips to the hospital. She went into this patient's room and very cheerily said, "Hi, Frank! How's it going today?" The patient became visibly upset, ordering the nurse out of the room and bellowing for her to "get the head nurse in here now!" Julie was confused and very upset. She had no idea what she'd done wrong. She had gone in and tried to connect with her patient, but clearly she had failed miserably.

The nurse manager asked her to tell her what happened. Julie recounted the story and her bewilderment at the patient's response. The nurse manager then went into the patient's room and sat down. "Mr. Patterson," she said, "I understand that you had a problem with Julie this morning. She asked me to come to see you. Could you tell me what happened?"

"That little chippie came in here and called me Frank!" the patient responded. "She doesn't know me, and she didn't ask permission or bother to inquire what I wanted to be called. I am 'the Judge.' Everyone calls me that. I worked hard for that title. Why, even my wife calls me Judge!"

The nurse manager apologized for the misunderstanding and said that Julie would be happy to call him "the Judge" going forward. She assured the Judge that Julie was a very good nurse and would take great care of him. She asked the Judge to allow Julie to demonstrate her skills and to call if there were any further issues. The Judge replied that he would. He thanked the nurse manager for listening and addressing the issue.

Julie went in and apologized for addressing the Judge informally. She told him she was very happy to care for him, and then she asked him, "Would you tell me how you got the title the Judge?" The patient explained that he had been a judge in juvenile court for 25 years. He was proud of it—his career and his title were a big part of his identity.

Julie understood what was happening here. Her patient had lost control over his life, was frightened, and felt at the mercy of his caregivers. Recognition of his identity was now exceptionally important to him.

In some cases, we can forestall anger by asking a couple of easy questions up front. How does a patient like to be addressed? Does he or she have a professional title? If the patient is elderly, does he or she hear us when we're speaking, or do we need to speak a little louder? It doesn't take long to ask questions like these and document them on the chart. And sometimes, having an initial 56-second conversation can prevent patients from becoming frustrated later on in their care. Their educations, jobs, families, hobbies—these are important to them, and it means more than we might think for us to ask about them. The trust we build can help us avoid misunderstandings, and the extra context can allow *us* to empathize more and prevent us from becoming frustrated ourselves.

In conducting these conversations, we should always remember what's likely the real culprit behind patients' anger: fear. Our patients are afraid of what will happen to their bodies, how long it will take, what it will do to their lives and the lives of their family, and how much it will cost. Sometimes when people feel frightened, they mask that fear with anger. As psychologist and clinician Leon Seltzer has explained, anger is "almost never a primary emotion. For underlying it . . . are such core hurts as feeling *disregarded, unimportant, accused, guilty, untrustworthy, devalued, rejected, powerless,* and *unlovable.* And these feelings are capable of engendering considerable emotional pain. It's therefore understandable that so many of us might go to great lengths to find ways of *distancing* ourselves from them."[2] Anger serves to help us keep our sense of vulnerability in check, and it does that so effectively that we tend not to know the function that anger is serving. The good news is that we can take action to mitigate our patients' feelings of vulnerability and hence their expressions of anger. By allowing patients to make more decisions and by helping them to feel safe, we can prevent anger from erupting.

Remember, patients might also harbor concerns that don't bear directly on their disease or treatment. They might worry about who will watch their children while they receive treatment, who will take care of their pets during their rehab stay, or how they will tell their boss that they will be out of the office every week for chemo. Burdened with such concerns, they might well not want to talk to you and make a connection. By asking open-ended questions during those 56-second conversations, you can elicit their concerns and possibly find ways to help them address them. As we saw in Chapter 4, a patient who has a headache might be stressed out over a nasty divorce. Offering the patient Tylenol and asking questions about the symptoms don't address the real issue, nor do they meet the patient's needs. Delving just a bit deeper with patients might help. At the very least, it will increase your chances of forming a positive connection. By acknowledging suffering, you can ease or prevent anger.

I am hardly suggesting that we can deescalate or please every patient all the time. Still, the vast majority of the time, we can either forestall anger or calm frustrated patients. It's tempting to think that most patients are angry and that only angry patients fill out surveys. The truth is otherwise. Most patients who complete surveys rate the organization or provider as "good" or "very good." Far fewer than 10 percent typically rate the organization or provider as "poor" or "very poor."[3] Let's find ways to help all patients, including those 10 percent.

Offer Choices

As caregivers, we can and should *offer patients as many choices as possible* to help minimize the sense they might have of losing control. We might ask patients: "Would you prefer to take your bath in the morning or in the evening?" or "Would you like ice in your water or no ice?" These choices don't materially impact the care we offer, nor do they place an additional time burden on us. But these questions present opportunities for patients to exert control over the seemingly uncontrollable experience of being a patient.

You might think that the ability to make decisions big and small doesn't matter much to patients, but that's not what the research says. In one study, researchers asked 274 patients to identify which changes they would most like to see implemented in their relationship with their physicians. The top answer: more information, autonomy, and shared decision making. [4] Significantly, patients don't just want caregivers to provide them with options. They want *information* about their care, which in turn allows them to participate more fully. Information, autonomy, and shared decision making topped "easier access to more sophisticated medical services," "shorter queue[s] for tests," and "continuity of care" on the list of patient desires—that's how important they were.[5]

Talk with Patients About Their Pain

Physical pain is an abiding reality in healthcare.[6] In recent years, responding to the epidemic of opioid addiction, the Joint

Commission has changed the way that healthcare organizations should care for patients in pain. When prescribing pain medication, caregivers must identify "psychosocial risk factors that may affect self-reporting of pain; involve patients to develop their treatment plan and set realistic expectations and measurable goals; focus reassessment on how pain impairs physical function (e.g., ability to turn over in bed after surgery); monitor opioid prescribing patterns; and promote access to nonpharmacologic pain treatment modalities."[7] Let's be clear: the existence of an opioid epidemic doesn't mean that many patients don't continue to suffer excruciating pain. They most certainly do. To avoid either overprescribing opioid medications or treating all patients as "drug seekers," we must strive to understand our patients better and get at the underlying issues relating to their perception of pain. That means having more conversations about pain that will help us determine appropriate levels of medication.

As a consultant, I once followed a nurse into the room of a woman on her first postoperative day after a total knee replacement. The nurse did a great job in connecting with this woman as she went about her duties. However, when I looked at the whiteboard, I was shocked. It said "Pain Goal: 0." A goal of zero pain on the first day after a total knee replacement? That's impossible! You simply cannot get to zero pain after that surgery. This nurse set herself up to fail when she wrote that on the whiteboard, and worse, she set her patient up to fail. She thought she was allowing the patient to participate in her care and make decisions. But she neglected to set *realistic* expectations with her.

Chances are, a whole team of caregivers failed. A patient having an elective knee replacement might have received counseling about the pain she would experience at many points along the way: at the provider practice when she first sought treatment for her knee; when surgery was scheduled; at the preoperative call or appointment prior to the day of surgery; on the day of surgery when the surgeon, anesthesiologist, and perioperative nurses interviewed and spoke with her; when she arrived in her inpatient bed; and at every encounter in between.

Caregivers could have told her something like this: "Mrs. Smith, you are going to have a total knee replacement. After surgery, you are going to experience some pain, and we are going to do everything we can to help you manage that pain. We aren't going to be able to get to zero pain. So, when you are at home and you have a headache or your knee hurts, what's a reasonable amount of pain for you before you need something? Does your pain rank as a three out of ten? Or maybe a five out of ten? That's what we'll manage to, knowing that we just can't get to zero right after surgery. But rest assured, we will do everything we can to help you manage your pain."

With counseling such as this, Mrs. Smith would know to expect at least some pain. Instead of feeling surprised, upset, or fearful when she first experienced pain, she would know that the pain is normal and that caregivers will help her manage it. Caregivers would have made her feel safe.

Small as they may seem, these kinds of conversations about pain make a big difference. We asked patients if they had received pain medication and if the doctors and nurses did everything they could to help them manage their pain. Some patients said yes to both questions. Others said that they had not received pain medication, but that doctors and nurses had done everything they could to help them manage pain. As Figure 5.1 shows, the group that did not receive pain medication rated the ED more highly and indicated that they would recommend the hospital more. In other words, it's not about the drug. It's about the connection, communication, and information.

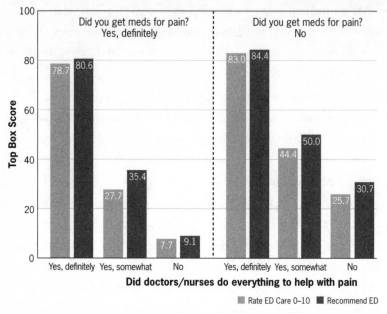

Figure 5.1   How conversations about pain affect patients' willingness to recommend

Round Like You Own It

I have yet to meet a nurse who is not in a patient's room at least hourly. We've always done that. But is hourly rounding a good idea? The clear answer is yes. And just as important as rounding hourly is rounding *purposefully*. Caregivers must be in the room frequently to accomplish tasks required for patient care, whether they are in the hospital, the provider's office, a rehab facility, or an outpatient clinic. Purposeful rounding allows staff to be proactive and anticipate patient needs. When nurses feel that they can be proactive and watch out for patients, the incidence of falls and pressure injuries declines. And our research has demonstrated that patients who experience hourly rounds during their stay evaluate their care more highly in all areas across both Press Ganey and HCAHPS survey measures. Items on the Press Ganey survey most impacted by hourly rounds are "Response to concerns and complaints made during your stay" and "Promptness in responding to the call button." The more consistently hourly rounds occur, the more positively patients evaluate their care experiences and the more likely they are to recommend the hospital. [8]

If rounding is essential, how should individual caregivers best perform their rounds? Here we have no shortage of good advice. One 2006 article in the *American Journal of Nursing* suggested guidelines that caregivers should follow in every patient round, such as inquiring about pain, asking about toileting assistance, assessing positioning, and assuring that personal items were within reach. After the authors consistently deployed these strategies, they found that patients used their call lights less frequently and that their overall experience improved.[9]

To drive consistency, the authors used scripting and checklists. While these approaches help drive consistency, they also come with an unwanted side effect: they make caregiver interactions seem less genuine. When Aaron was in the rehab hospital, the staff did amazing work with patients with head and spinal cord injuries. Miracles happened there every day, thanks to their good work. And yet every time new caregivers entered the room to introduce themselves, they said exactly the same thing—not kind of the same thing, but *exactly* the same thing. Obviously, their communications had been scripted. While these team members delivered great care, their demeanor came across to us as somewhat less authentic than if they had simply talked to us in their own, idiosyncratic ways. Scripting is a fine tool when used over the short term to help team members begin to understand how to communicate. But it can only help after they understand the deeper purpose behind it. And we should quickly look past the script so as to sustain the authenticity that helps us to connect with others. We should script the *sentiment* we are trying to convey, not the words themselves.

As caregivers, we can become too checklist oriented, task driven, and, in this case, script reliant. So what can we do about it? An important strategy is to take more time practicing how to connect. Ask for help during orientation sessions, and if you're having trouble connecting with patients, ask for follow-up coaching. Focus on specific behaviors, like how to let patients know that you're listening to them. If certain colleagues of yours seem to excel at making connections, try to observe them, learn their "secrets," and incorporate those secrets into your own work with patients. Small investments of time like these can reap huge returns, enhancing the experience not only of patients but of your fellow caregivers, too.

While we individual caregivers should work on improving our own rounding practices, managers should round as well. Unfortunately, many managers struggle to understand how to help their staff round better, and they also struggle to model desired behaviors. Once while touring a hospital, I asked a CNO what she had done to improve how individual caregivers perform their rounds. She recounted that they had tried many techniques and initiatives that hadn't worked (this organization had been at the forefront of lean methodology in healthcare and had applied that thinking to rounding). Ultimately, this CNO related, the hospital's leadership had decided that it "couldn't really hold people accountable for rounding unless we knew that they were competent to round." The committee developed a checklist that described components of good rounding by nursing staff. It then trained staff around the checklist, including ample discussion of purpose. Each manager then had to observe each staff member on three separate occasions to assure that the staff member was rounding correctly and to coach him or her when need be. After three "good" rounds, the staff member was "checked off" as competent. "We can now hold them accountable," this CNO said. "We know they are competent."

But this organization's efforts didn't stop there. Managers performed unannounced observational audits to assure that employees were still rounding correctly. These audits took place on an ongoing basis indefinitely. As a result of this effort, team members were now so well practiced in rounding that they "owned" it. They did it effortlessly and automatically, as part of the standard way they cared for patients. They still used a rounding tool to log the rounds, but the observational audits and coaching made the real difference, driving consistency and sustainability.

As vital as it is, accountability is not enough to make caregiver rounding successful. Individual caregivers have to *own* rounding. We shouldn't just treat rounding as one more thing we have to do during our workdays. Rather, we should partake of it as a way to demonstrate the empathy, compassion, and desire to serve that prompted us to enter healthcare in the first place. Working as a caregiver isn't just a job, but a calling. When we reduce this calling to a series of tasks, the work itself loses meaning. Whether you're a nurse, physician, or tech rounding on patients or a leader doing so on staff, the act of rounding affords a chance to forge connections with the very people who have put their trust in us. It is simply the way we do what we do.

Practice Both Consistency *and* Critical Thinking

I wish I had a nickel for every time I heard, "Yeah, we tried that, but it hasn't worked so far." When I hear people at an organization saying this, I will often ask to walk around and observe as a "secret shopper." I will have attended leadership meetings by then, having heard all the right things. I will also see purposeful rounding logs in rooms that, amazingly, show that rounds are happening exactly at the same time in every room. Imagine that!

Of course, rounding isn't happening uniformly at these hospitals. And that points to a broader issue. We talk about the patient experience and patient safety, but all too often we flounder by failing to practice the required behaviors *consistently*. As Figure 5.2 demonstrates, we don't achieve reliability by focus, evidence, patient centeredness, or financial motivation alone. These are all important, but it's consistent focus over time that leads to highly reliable, zero-harm clinical excellence, patient experience, and efficiency—all of which, in turn, lead to better reimbursement.

Consistency is so important, of course, because it helps us reduce variability, which often lurks as the enemy of quality. During the late 1980s and early 1990s, when clinical pathways began to gain popularity, several physicians said to me, "Don't tell me how to take care of my patients! This is cookbook medicine!" Clinical pathways were developed to standardize care for high-risk and problem-prone conditions. As research has documented, total joint replacement patients who followed a clinical pathway that standardized and organized care experienced reduced lengths of

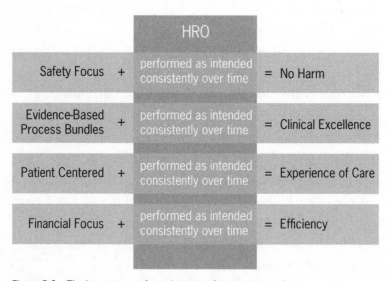

Figure 5.2　The importance of consistent performance over time

stay and fewer postoperative complications like deep vein thrombosis (DVT), pulmonary embolism, and infections.[10] Consistency drove quality improvement. So my response to those physicians was usually, "You're right! It is cookbook medicine. Why do you use a cookbook? To get the best result *every time!*" Consistency is important in everything we do as caregivers, from the way we care clinically for patients to the way we round and interact with our patients and colleagues.

By emphasizing consistency so strongly, I am by no means suggesting that caregivers should think and behave like robots. Absolutely not! To consistency, they must add another vital competency: critical thinking.

As caregivers, we talk a lot about critical thinking. It's part of virtually every curriculum in healthcare education. In a 2013 brief, the Council for Aid to Education observed that "while there are many desirable outcomes of college education, there is widespread agreement that critical thinking skills are among the most important." In particular, the council noted, critical thinking skills "are seen as essential for accessing and analyzing the information needed to address the complex, non-routine challenges facing workers in the 21st century."[11] Likewise, in their book, *Critical Thinking Tactics for Nurses*, M. Gaie Rubenfeld and Barbara Scheffer describe their efforts to identify a common definition for critical thinking in nursing. They arrived at 17 dimensions: 10 "habits of mind" ("confidence, contextual perspective, creativity, flexibility, inquisitiveness, intellectual integrity, intuition, open-mindedness, perseverance, and reflection") and seven cognitive skills ("analyzing, applying standards, discriminating, information seeking, logical reasoning, predicting, [and] transforming knowledge").[12] Considering each of these elements, we can readily understand how they help caregivers achieve the Institute for Healthcare Improvement Triple Aim of better experience of care, healthy populations, and lower cost. We can also see how they help us achieve the IOM (Institute of Medicine) charge of achieving the following five competencies:[13]

- **Provide patient-centered care**—identify, respect, and care about patients' differences, values, preferences, and expressed needs; relieve pain and suffering; coordinate continuous care; listen to, clearly inform, communicate with, and educate patients; share decision making and management; and continuously advocate disease prevention, wellness, and promotion of healthy lifestyles, including a focus on population health.

- **Work in interdisciplinary teams**—cooperate, collaborate, communicate, and integrate care in teams to ensure that care is continuous and reliable.

- **Employ evidence-based practice**—integrate best research with clinical expertise and patient values for optimum care, and participate in learning and research activities to the extent feasible.

- **Apply quality improvement**—identify errors and hazards in care; understand and implement basic safety design principles, such as standardization and simplification; continually understand and measure quality of care in terms of structure, process, and outcomes in relation to patient and community needs; design and test interventions to change processes and systems of care, with the objective of improving quality.

- **Utilize informatics**—communicate, manage knowledge, mitigate error, and support decision making using information technology.

Clearly, it's critical for caregivers to *think critically*. And yet for all the talk, we in healthcare don't employ critical thinking enough. As individual caregivers, we must dedicate ourselves to it, tempering our decision making by constantly questioning, searching for evidence, analyzing data, and synthesizing data. We must challenge ourselves to avoid behaving in certain ways simply because "that's the way we've always done it." To drive the patient experience and safety in healthcare, we must sustain situational awareness, attention to detail, 360-degree communication, clarification of information, appropriate use of protocol, and reasoned decision making. We must validate information, asking ourselves if a given contention makes sense and verifying what we think we know with evidence from independent, qualified sources. When peers think critically and watch out for one another, providing situational awareness and immediate feedback, the number of errors decreases.

At the extreme, as we become increasingly proficient at critical thinking, seeking feedback and becoming more self-aware, we can achieve what Maslow, in his Four Stages of Learning theory, called "unconscious competence" (see Figure 5.3). Maslow conceived of four stages that span a continuum, starting with unconscious incompetence (an inability to perform a task well, coupled with a lack of awareness of the deficit) and going all the way up to unconscious competence (an individual's ability, grounded in intensive practice, to perform a task not only well, but effortlessly and unconsciously).[14]

In the case of nursing, caregivers who achieve unconscious competence have not only applied their critical faculties to improve. They've mastered skills to such an extent that, as Patricia Benner and her colleagues noted, they "do not rely on rules and logical thought processes in problem-solving and decisionmaking. Instead, they use abstract principles, can see the situation as a complex whole, perceive situations comprehensively, and can be fully involved in the situation."[15] These nurses and other caregivers "can perform high-level care without conscious awareness of the

Unconscious Incompetence	**Conscious Incompetence**
The individual does not understand or know how to do something and does not necessarily recognize the deficit.	Though the individual does not understand or know how to do something, he or she does recognize the deficit.
Conscious Competence	**Unconscious Competence**
The individual understands or knows how to do something. However, demonstrating the skill or knowledge requires concentration.	The individual has had so much practice with a skill that it has become second nature and can be performed easily. He or she may be able to teach it to others, depending upon how and when it was learned.

Figure 5.3   Maslow's Four Stages of Learning

knowledge they are using, and they are able to provide that care with flexibility and speed."[16] Ultimately, then, caregivers require critical thinking to excel, and they arrive at such a state of mastery that the task becomes second nature, and consistency ensues.

All of us, not only nurses, must adopt critical thinking skills in order to provide the best care possible to the patients we serve. In Chapter 7, when we discuss how organizations become more compassionate and connected, we'll delve into critical thinking from a systemic perspective, not merely an individual perspective. In their book *Critical Thinking Tactics for Nurses,* Rubenfeld and Scheffer represented this thinking for both organizations and individuals as a medallion representing the IOM competency of applying quality improvement (see Figure 5.4).[17] Using Donabedian's triad of structure, processes, and outcomes, Figure 5.4 captures the behaviors, attitudes, and abilities we in healthcare require to achieve quality of care and continuous improvement, both as individuals and as interdisciplinary teams.

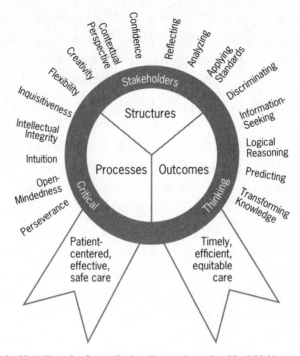

Figure 5.4   Medallion of safe, quality healthcare through critical thinking

Cultivate Your Resilience

Although few caregivers would dispute that the behaviors described in this book would reduce the suffering of patients and colleagues, we often see a disconnect between what we caregivers want to do and what our "compassion tank"—our internal storehouse of compassion—allows. That's where the quality of resilience comes in. We can define resilience as "that ineffable quality that allows some people to be knocked down by life and come back stronger than ever. Rather than letting failure overcome them and drain their resolve, they find a way to rise from the ashes."[18] In effect, resilience is a shield that allows us to repel some of the inherent and avoidable suffering prevalent in healthcare today. It is both the opposite of and the antidote to burnout, allowing us to withstand suffering in all its guises and to deliver Compassionate Connected Care to our patients.

So what fuels resilience? The rewards and benefits attached to healthcare do. If the pain for caregivers exceeds the reward or benefit, we become disengaged and burned out. But if we perceive the reward as greater than the pain, we bounce back and continue to reengage. Significantly, that reward need not be monetary or even tangible. Intangible rewards like recognition, praise, and intrinsic motivation often suffice to keep us on track and engaged on the job.

Individual caregivers also can take steps to build up their resilience. For instance, we can embrace a mindfulness practice. In today's fast-paced world, it's hard to be mindful. Smartphones by our side, we are constantly bombarded by stimuli, both at work and at home. I once asked my daughter, a teacher, why educators paid so much attention to bullying these days. Hasn't it always been a problem? "Mom," she told me, "it used to be that kids would be bullied at school, but then they could come home and be safe and get away from the bullying. But now, with cell phones, Facebook, and other social media, kids cannot ever get away from it. It's always there and they can't turn it off. There is no safe place anymore." That's true for all of us.

To become more mindful, try turning off your phone for a few minutes. Allow yourself to be in the moment. If you're eating, sense what's on your tongue. If you're touching something, sense the feeling on your fingers. If you're sitting comfortably, sense what every part of your body feels like. As simple as these practices are, they're also immensely powerful. According to psychologists Daphne Davis and Jeffrey Hayes, "Mindfulness meditation promotes metacognitive awareness, decreases rumination via disengagement from perseverative cognitive activities and enhances attentional capacities through gains in working memory. These cognitive gains, in turn, contribute to effective emotion-regulation strategies."[19] Davis and Hayes go on to enumerate further benefits, like stress alleviation, working memory enhancement, increased focus, reduced emotional reactivity, increased cognitive flexibility, more relationship satisfaction, greater self-insight, a more acute moral sense, greater intuition, a better ability to control fear, increased immune functioning, and improvement in well-being.[20] Most remarkable, perhaps, research has shown that mindfulness and positive thinking actually had a beneficial effect on the DNA of breast cancer patients (i.e., the lengthening of telomeres), suggesting that the effects of mindfulness meditation on the body may be far more extensive than we had ever imagined.[21] In all these ways, consistently practicing mindfulness reinforces your resilience shield, fueling your "compassion tank" so that you can deliver more Compassionate Connected Care.

Not only must caregivers practice mindfulness; to become more resilient, they must also avoid certain missteps, like personalizing negative situations that are not their fault, or assuming that an obstacle in one area will apply to *all* areas, or believing that a particular emotion (for instance, joy or sadness) will last forever.[22] Caregivers can also enhance resilience by adopting a gratitude practice. Try taking five minutes each day to write down three things that went well. Or try writing a letter of appreciation to someone explaining something the person did, how it made you feel, and the benefits you received.[23] Or try taking a few minutes to admire and feel inspired by a beautiful sunset. Or try writing about challenges or negative experiences and the positive benefits gleaned from them. When people think about good things that come out of bad experiences, they report less distress, fewer disruptive thoughts, less negativity, and more meaning in their lives.[24]

You must also remember to care for your body and mind. Being physically and mentally fit isn't just about looking great. It's about feeling great and having enough energy for yourself and the people for whom you care. You can't give of yourself to others unless and until you give of yourself to *you* first. The American Nurses Association "defines a healthy nurse as one who actively focuses on creating and maintaining a balance and synergy of physical, intellectual, emotional, social, spiritual, personal and professional wellbeing. A healthy nurse lives life to the fullest capacity, across the wellness/illness continuum, as they become stronger role models, advocates, and educators, personally, for their families, their communities and work environments, and ultimately for their patients."[25] It's a lofty ideal, and one to which we all should strive—for ourselves and for the sake of reducing or preventing suffering in our patients.

Does all of this sound "fluffy" to you? It did to me, until I began to practice mindfulness during my breast cancer treatment and then later with Aaron's shooting and rehabilitation. It was amazing what just 10 minutes a day of being mindful and reducing the clutter and noise in my head could do. I was able to think more clearly, accomplish more in my work, and be more present for my family, colleagues, and clients.

In one class on mindfulness I attended, the leader gave us raisins and had us just look at them, noticing the color and the shape. Then we spent time smelling the raisins. Then we were asked to really feel the raisins, their grooves and squishiness. Then he had us put our raisins on our tongues and notice how they felt in our mouths. Then he had us savor their sweetness and the sensation of biting into them. While each of us was eating our raisins, we couldn't think about anything else because our minds and our senses were totally devoted to this extended act. I found this exercise astounding—and I don't even like raisins. As one study has shown, mindful eaters experience "lower body weights, a greater sense of well-being, and fewer symptoms of eating disorders."[26]

After the raisin class, I attended a mindful writing class. During this session, the leader asked a simple question, something like, "Tell me about your best day." The participants were asked to start writing on a blank sheet of paper. We were told to be specific and to really think about what made that day great. How did it feel physically, emotionally, and spiritually? Then we shared what we wrote. Several of my classmates cried while recounting why they had chosen to write about a particular day. The experience was profound.

I challenge you to try the resilience-building exercises I've described, whether it's a gratitude practice, mindful eating, or something else. As with other strategies discussed in this book, you can't just "do resilience" once and check it off your list. You must practice it daily so that it becomes something that you habitually do and thus becomes a part of you. Make yourself unconsciously competent.

The Impact of a Compassionate Connected Caregiver

Some caregivers might have an easier time taking tangible steps to make Compassionate Connected Care a reality. Over the course of their careers, they might have seen the impact of the behaviors I've described on patients and families and felt inspired to integrate these behaviors into their everyday practice. Or as patients themselves, they might have experienced firsthand the wonderful difference that caregivers make when they deliver care compassionately and in a connected way.

My colleague Julie, a nurse for 35 years, recently found herself in pain so horrific that it sent her to the emergency room for the first time as a patient. Julie quickly underwent lab and imaging tests. Her husband had overheard imaging personnel talking with the surgeon on call, Dr. Lee Zho. "I don't know what you're going to do with this one!" they said. "Good luck." As you can imagine, Julie and her husband were terrified.

Julie met Dr. Zho for the first time in the emergency room after her tests were completed. After introducing himself, he immediately put Julie at ease. He leaned in, looked her in the eye, took her hand, and said: "I'm *so* glad you came in when you did." As Julie remembers it, the expression on his face conveyed deep concern but also comfort. In just a few short seconds, he let her know that he truly cared about her as a person and a patient.

Dr. Zho proceeded to inform Julie of his plan to perform immediate, emergency surgery resulting in an ostomy. Because of her nursing experience, Julie knew full well what an ostomy was. She had cared for many a patient with one, and yet she still reacted with shock and disbelief. Dr. Zho paused to watch for Julie's reaction and understanding of what he'd just stated. As Julie recounts, she found his gentle tone of voice and the look of genuine caring in his eyes deeply reassuring. "I'll never forget that interaction," Julie says. "It made me feel completely safe, cared about, informed, and as prepared as I could be. I felt at ease for the first time in over a week."

Julie was fortunate to have other caregivers who lived the Compassionate Connected Care model. Her nurse Lisa was fully present at every interaction, reading every nonverbal cue Julie threw her way in order not to miss an unstated need or concern. And as Julie later learned, Lisa remained focused even though she had two small children and a terminally ill husband. Lisa maintained appropriate professional boundaries, and yet she and Julie connected. "Watching Lisa," Julie says, "I learned a lot about how to be mindful in the moment, even in the face of major life and work distractions. And I also learned about how much a caring, healing environment affects both patients and the caregiver's own health and resilience." Tears come to Julie's eyes as she tells me that she will forever feel grateful for Lisa's care and that Lisa's family will always be in her prayers.

What a life-changing connection in a matter of days! Imagine the connections that you could make with your patients and colleagues, each and every day, as you put the Compassionate Connected Care model to work.

CHAPTER

6

Compassionate
Connected Teams

During the early 1990s, I had an unusual opportunity to observe and study up close the functioning of teams in healthcare. I was working as a nurse in the PACU of Wickerland Health Center (not its real name), a large, level 1 trauma center in the Midwest. At the time, healthcare organizations across the country were moving toward universal, "managed care" as part of Hillary Rodham Clinton's reform efforts. Buying up physician practices, organizations hoped to integrate care and render it more efficient. Under this new model, primary care physicians would serve as "gatekeepers" for patients, helping them navigate the many specialties and subspecialties now located under one organizational roof. Organizations were worried that healthcare reform might lead to lower reimbursement, so they were working preemptively to reduce the cost of healthcare and improve access to care.[1] At Wickerland, administrators had brought in consultants to redesign the hospital's surgical services so as to reduce waste and cut costs. Administrators needed someone to serve as the liaison between the consulting firm and the hospital, and they asked me if I'd like the job. I wasn't quite sure what I was getting myself into, but I liked the challenge, so I agreed to take it.

Wickerland had 26 operating rooms at two locations inside the hospital. We performed scheduling tasks the old-fashioned way, using a paper scheduling log to keep track of both surgical cases and staff schedules. Since we only had a few operating rooms dedicated to specialties, such as heart/vascular or lithotripsy, we tended to allocate space on a first-come, first-served basis. In a given operating room, we might have booked a tonsillectomy, then a hernia repair, and then a total joint replacement, moving staff between rooms to assure that we assigned them cases in which they had the requisite experience and expertise. The system was chaotic and fraught with delays, leading to problems with staffing and overtime. Staff never knew where they would be working or with whom, so they became stressed and frustrated. Surgeons were forced to wait around between cases, but they couldn't leave the hospital because they didn't know if a room would open up and they'd have to go to work. Patients had to wait for long periods, and they often had their surgeries canceled or moved. The hospital was making money, but it certainly wasn't maximizing its margins.

To push ahead our reform efforts, we established cross-disciplinary task forces to handle each of the primary projects: staffing, materials management, OR scheduling, and information technology. A steering committee oversaw the work, setting rules for the task forces to follow based on requirements dictated by hospital leadership. Operating within these rules, the task forces conducted research and came up with specific recommendations for reform. Only when the steering committee had approved these recommendations and leadership had signed off would the hospital implement them. The real power lay with the task forces. The steering committee had agreed to support task force recommendations, provided that they stayed within established guidelines and that hospital administrators served on the steering committee. So as our task forces got to work rethinking how we would organize the OR, we felt confident that we would be able to effect real change.

After some initial difficulties that I'll describe a bit later, we did manage to transform the OR. Over a six-year period, we implemented a number of recommendations that our task forces had generated, including block scheduling of the OR, the reduction of instruments in our surgical instrument sets, and strategic reductions in staff hours. We held weekly team meetings to review data and make adjustments in our strategy, monitoring a number of metrics, including block time utilization, on-time starts, scheduling, and staffing relative to expertise and aptitude. We started self-scheduling and convened teams that reviewed elements such as surgeon preference lists and room stock. At all times, we worked collaboratively and communicated transparently, taking care to include representatives from the OR staff.

The results exceeded our expectations. Surgical cases increased by over 5 percent, while the number of operating rooms necessary for surgical cases on weekday afternoons and evenings declined by 45 percent. Thanks to the increased efficiency, we boosted revenues to the general/trauma surgeon group by more than 6 percent. Because we also enabled the nursing floors to predict their evening and night-shift staffing requirements more accurately, we reduced overtime by 2 percent. Caregiver suffering declined, as evidenced by improvements in "staff morale and retention." Our improvements were so dramatic that industry experts cited us as models for scheduling, team-based care, on-time starts, and overall flow.[2] We took an average OR and put it on the map!

The experience of redesigning the OR at Wickerland taught me a great deal about teamwork and its relationship with suffering. Poor organization of our surgical teams had been causing considerable suffering for our caregivers and our patients. Staff often couldn't work in the specialties they wanted and in which they were most skilled. Surgeons had to deal with expensive gaps in their schedules, as well as incomplete instrument sets. Patients and families underwent long waits. But by coming together across disciplinary boundaries as cohesive teams, we had been able to redesign our operations so that our operating teams could work better. Within each redesign team, colleagues shared information and discussed our current practices, best practices at other organizations, our goals for the future, and what it would take to realize them. Our final recommendations improved scheduling accuracy and on-time starts, reduced case duration and turnover time between cases, and improved staff and physician engagement. Patients waited less and received higher-quality care. Staff and physicians enjoyed their jobs more. All of us suffered less.

To reduce suffering under the Compassionate Connected Care model, it's not enough for individual caregivers to embrace the right kinds of behaviors. We also must support Compassionate Connected Care through teamwork, on two distinct levels. First, we must improve the way teams operate in general. Disorganized teams fragment the provision of healthcare, leading to a host of issues for patient and caregiver experience. We can have the world's most compassionate and connected caregivers, but we'll never reduce suffering in meaningful ways unless teams at healthcare organizations also operate at optimum levels. On top of this, patient-facing teams in particular can take specific steps when interacting with patients to make connections and improve their experience. By focusing on both levels at once, we can support the good work that individual caregivers do to reduce suffering, solidifying our gains in the patient and caregiver experience.

The Value of a Good Team

Before examining how to reduce suffering by improving team performance generally, let's first review the kinds of teams that commonly exist in healthcare settings and the impact these teams have on patient experience. In a 2012 discussion paper, the Institute of Medicine defined team-based healthcare as "the provision of health services to individuals, families, and/or their communities by at least two health providers who work collaboratively with patients and their caregivers—to the extent preferred by each patient—to accomplish shared goals within and across settings to achieve coordinated, high-quality care."[3] The authors go on to report that "in order to benefit from the detailed information and specific knowledge needed for his or her healthcare, the typical Medicare beneficiary visits two primary care clinicians and five specialists per year, as well as providers of diagnostic, pharmacy, and other services."[4] But groups dedicated to caring for patients aren't the only kind of interprofessional or cross-disciplinary teams that exist in healthcare. Organizations also bring caregivers and staff together as "project teams" to address operational issues, as we did at Wickerland. If organizations are to improve experience and reduce suffering, it's critical that both kinds of teams function well, with fluid coordination, collaboration, and communication taking place among all team members.[5]

Our research shows that patients intuitively perceive a connection between teamwork and the suffering they experience. As we saw in Chapter 3, strong teamwork helps patients feel safe, loyal, and cared for. In particular, patients' perceptions of the coordination of care within hospitals, measured by the survey item "How well staff worked together to care for you," strongly influence whether patients recommend the hospital across service lines, including both inpatient and ambulatory care. Patients who ranked staff the highest for their ability to collaborate were far more likely to recommend a hospital than patients who gave staff lower marks for working together (see Figure 6.1). Caregivers also recognize teamwork's relevance for reducing their own suffering. As I recounted in Chapter 4, I asked a group of 500 clinicians to

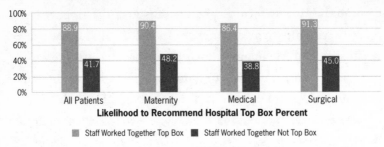

Figure 6.1   Impact of staff teamwork on HCAHPS "likelihood to recommend"

rank the six themes of Compassionate Connected Care for the Caregiver. They ranked teamwork the highest by double-digit percentages.

Such patient and caregiver impressions are not hard to understand. In sports, a lack of communication, accountability, and preparation by teams causes them to lose games. In healthcare, the consequences of poor teamwork are potentially much more severe. When teams function poorly, care becomes fragmented, leading to at least some amount of suffering in the form of duplication of care, patient confusion, and so on. As quality deteriorates, patients and their families suffer even more due to potential medical errors, adverse events, complications, and readmissions. Even when a world-class care team delivers high-quality care, patients and families will never rate the care they received as excellent if the patient is harmed in the process. A growing body of research has uncovered meaningful links between clinical safety, the effectiveness of healthcare, and patient experience.[6]

Unfortunately, teamwork often breaks down in healthcare organizations today. More than one-fifth of U.S. hospital patients reported system problems, including the provision of conflicting information by staff and the inability of staff to tell them which physician was taking charge of their care.[7] When poor teamwork impinges on the patient experience, caregivers often don't realize it. Some analyses find vast disparities between physician and

Table 6.1 Patient and Physician Rankings of Teamwork at a Healthcare Facility

	Patient	Employee Leader	Employee Nonleader	Physician
Facility 1	94.8	68.3	74.0	86.0
Facility 2	67.9	91.2	67.1	97.5
Facility 3	77.7	64.4	69.2	97.2
Facility 4	86.6	79.8	77.2	87.3
Facility 5	62.9	88.9	91.4	83.6
Facility 6	81.2	96.4	62.4	84.0

patient perceptions of teamwork. At one facility, patients ranked teamwork at the 67.9th percentile, while physicians at the same facility ranked it at the 97.5th percentile (see Table 6.1).[8] That's a huge difference! Clearly, we must do better at educating all caregivers (not merely physicians) about how to function well on teams, and also about the specific components of teamwork that matter most to patients. But how exactly should we do this? If our goal is to reduce suffering, how might we best focus to attack the difficult problem of improving teamwork?

Optimizing Teams

According to organizational behaviorists Anna Mayo and Anita Williams Woolley, strong teams "can aggregate, modify, combine, and apply a greater amount and variety of knowledge" in the service of decision making, problem solving, idea generation, and task execution better than any one individual could do alone.[9] But as these scholars also attest, putting a bunch of smart people together and calling them a team does not make them one. Press Ganey chief medical officer Tom Lee agrees, distinguishing between pickup teams that form casually on playground basketball courts and professional teams. Pit a pickup basketball team against the Cleveland Cavaliers, and even if the individual members of the pickup team are as talented as those on the Cavaliers, the pickup team will lose every time. Why? Because the pickup team isn't truly a team. It's just a group of people who share a common interest in playing basketball. The Cavs, and every other NBA team for that matter, are made up of highly experienced experts who constantly train and study their craft together and who are motivated to excel as a group rather than just as individual players. Each Cavs player not only commits to the group but is accountable to it for his own play and preparation. The team "owns" the game. Team members win or lose together, which is why losing is never an outcome they readily accept.

When it comes to reducing suffering, the question thus becomes, how might we best transform groups of healthcare providers into genuine teams capable of delivering on patient experience? For starters, we should focus on improving *leadership*. All teams in healthcare, both patient care and project teams, need strong leaders—visionaries who can define a common purpose, inspire confidence, promote skill building, recruit team members with the right skills, remove issues that might prevent the group from performing, and work side-by-side with staff.[10] All too often, such leadership doesn't exist, if only because organizations form teams haphazardly. When a hospital convenes a group of people who have the same interests and says, "Your goal is patient care," it's a pickup team. When we hire based on the strengths that we need for the team, provide a vision that the team can not only buy into but truly own, and help team members navigate through conflicts when they first begin working together, then we have real teams that can accomplish great things in patient experience, safety, clinical quality, and staff engagement.

Certain areas of leadership seem ripe for improvement on healthcare teams. Leaders in any context must promote psychological well-being, creating safe climates that facilitate learning. Team members will more likely take risks when leaders give each of them an equal voice and when they trust that leaders will support them even if they fail. When leaders themselves push change by monitoring their environment, identifying processes or behaviors that require change, and coordinating change efforts, team members feel even more comfortable proposing new ideas.[11] In too many cases, leaders don't invite team members to participate, and they don't proffer support. Rather than seeking change, they seem to resist it. As a result, teams go adrift and fail to take steps that would reduce suffering and improve the patient experience. Organizations embark on ambitious patient experience initiatives, but come away with little to show for them.

The Wickerland perioperative steering committee I mentioned earlier was a case in point. After our task forces delivered their recommendations and the steering committee approved them, hospital leadership was supposed to implement them in due course. That's not what happened. The task force on OR staffing recommended that the hospital cut back on surgical staff. But it also recommended that the hospital provide more patient care assistants or environmental services personnel for room cleaning, turnover between cases, and transport. Another task force examined the number of instruments contained in each instrument set and gained consensus from surgeons on what was critical to maintain in these sets (no small accomplishment). This task force recommended that the hospital could place fewer instruments in the instrument sets, but only if the hospital made more instruments available as "separates" on an individual basis. The OR scheduling task force recommended that the hospital streamline operating rooms by scheduling time in blocks. But it also recommended that the hospital leave 25 percent of staffed surgical time "open" or unblocked to accommodate unscheduled or add-on cases.

All these recommendations passed the steering committee. However, when it came time for hospital administrators to implement the recommendations, they did so selectively, breaking with the procedural rules that they themselves had set. Administrators agreed to fewer staff in the OR, but they refused to commit to providing additional patient care assistants. If at some later date the data demonstrated that we needed more of these assistants, the hospital leaders said they would provide them then. Administrators likewise agreed to fewer instruments in the instrument sets, but they declined to provide more single instrument separates. They would provide those "if needed." Finally, administrators agreed to the block scheduling, but they refused to allow for open time in the schedule.

Keep in mind, the task forces had collaborated closely for months. They had performed time and motion studies, examined endless amounts of data, and surveyed the people who did the work, including surgeons, surgical technologists, circulating nurses, and other personnel. They had evaluated the data together and deliberated as a group to arrive at their recommendations. Hospital administration didn't take any of this into account. They violated the rules of our redesign process, leaving the staff to do the same work with fewer employees in each room, fewer instruments in the sets, and no flexibility in the schedule. The last of these led to more "add-on" cases that went late into the night.

Staff members were frustrated, and they soon decided that they weren't going to take it anymore. Months after working in these frustrating conditions, every single member of the operating room staff walked out. Administrators rushed to bring in replacement staff from the organization's sister hospitals, but that wasn't enough to prevent surgical cancellations. The walkout lasted three days, ending when leaders agreed to a series of demands, including more staff input into decisions and a review of policies and procedures. Three administrators lost their jobs, including the CEO. My job wasn't at risk, but I thought about leaving anyway. I suspected that staff and physicians would lump me in with leadership, blaming me for the way that their recommendations had been undermined. Happily, my fears were misplaced. The staff sent me flowers, saying they knew it wasn't my fault. They asked me to stay, and I did.

When leaders at Wickerland didn't fully accept the recommendations even after the work hewed to the requirements that leadership itself had set, any semblance of psychological safety evaporated. Nobody felt comfortable addressing issues openly. Although the people in management had invited collaboration, their actions suggested that it had all been a sham—they were calling the shots, and full participation by other stakeholders wasn't welcome. No wonder staff members abandoned the process and walked out. To address suffering, leaders should create conditions for psychological safety and refrain from taking actions that compromise it. First and foremost, they should set clear guidelines for inclusive participation and stick with the rules, even if the results aren't entirely to their liking. Let our experience at Wickerland stand as a cautionary tale.

Another important leadership area to address in order to improve teamwork in general is recruiting. When the National Football League holds its annual draft, teams arrive with specific needs, and they attempt to draft players who will best fit those needs. Teams in healthcare must do the same. In particular, they must do a better job of making sure that they contain representatives of all the disciplines that care for patients. Research has repeatedly shown the benefits of teams that integrate direct caregivers into the mix and that are comprehensive (for instance, including pharmacists, not just prescribing physicians, in the management of medication). Such teams help forge alliances among providers, patients, and families,[12] serve patients' needs better,[13] and leave them feeling supported,[14] with better quality care. As a result, suffering decreases.

After the consultants left Wickerland and the staff ended its walkout, we developed a robust Perioperative Services Guidance

Committee. This committee reviewed all the prior recommendations from our task force teams, evaluating whether and how to implement each one and promulgating policies to implement approved recommendations. We recruited for this committee thoughtfully, including leaders in each surgical specialty, the chair of anesthesia, the nurse managers of each of the areas of perioperative services (OR, PACU, preop, ambulatory surgery), the manager of materials management, and the VP responsible for perioperative services. The committee was cochaired by the director of perioperative services and the OR's medical director, and it was small enough to make decisions quickly (as research shows, small groups tend to perform better than larger ones).[15] The group had a "checkwriter," a person authorized to make decisions so that we didn't have to obtain additional approvals at every turn. The group also included leaders who embraced change and continuous improvement. Their energy and enthusiasm allowed us to make rapid progress, correct for errors along the way, and achieve our goals.

Leaders can also improve teamwork—and help reduce suffering—by improving how they manage teams day to day. So often leaders don't empower team members to take ownership over their results. They dictate solutions, trying to solve problems themselves, without drawing on the team's talents. To work together more effectively, we must push authority—and responsibility—downward to team members themselves. This isn't easy, but with determination and focus, it can be done.

When I became the director of perioperative services, one especially vocal trauma surgeon on our team never hesitated to let me know when a case didn't run smoothly. He was almost always right, but his domineering style undercut his message. I counseled him about this, and we finally agreed to "Christy's rule," a stepwise process for addressing problems and changing our processes. Christy's rule was the following:

1. If you brought a problem to management (me), I would do what I could to address it.

2. If I couldn't address it and the problem persisted, the person who brought the problem to management would join a committee to address the problem. If a committee did not yet exist, that person would cochair a new committee with me.

3. If the person who brought the problem didn't want to help resolve the problem, he or she could no longer raise the issue.

This "rule" gave team members more ownership over work processes in our operating rooms. If issues arose, they were no longer "someone else's problem." We *all* owned what happened in the OR for our patients and staff. When staff members grew concerned about how we scheduled holidays, we laid down clear guidelines (for instance, we specified that staff members couldn't have the same holidays off every year, that all cases must be staffed, and so on) and then convened a staff team to come up with a policy. Team members arrived at a great policy, and they owned it. Similarly, when surgeons approached me and said they needed us to assign them staff members who always knew their routines so that cases would go smoothly, a team of staff and surgeons convened to determine what a "team" looked like for each specialty. This work reduced the time required to complete cases, increasing staff satisfaction and engagement and reducing suffering for patients (as our data show, higher staff engagement translates directly into better patient experience).

One reason the Perioperative Services Guidance Committee succeeded was that it also gave strong ownership to team members. The committee approved of and often developed policies related to the operations of perioperative services. For example, it developed a detailed on-time start policy for the OR. The data were collected and shared weekly with the committee, and penalties were established for surgeons who started their blocks late more than 10 percent of the time. The committee agreed that surgeons who violated this policy would not be able to start before 9 a.m. (7:30 a.m. was the first case start time) and that their blocks could not extend longer because of a late start. This policy was a big deal, and it helped improve our on-time start rate from only 30 percent to 90 percent, reducing overtime pay, delays, and cancellations. The policy succeeded because it was developed by the committee, enforced by the committee, and continuously evaluated by the committee. The committee was a team, and each member of the team had an equal vote, regardless of his or her role or title. Each member brought unique insight and experience to the committee, and the committee relied on these strengths during its deliberations. Although the committee had its growing pains, it gelled during its first six months together and went on to perform exceptionally well. Patients and caregivers suffered less as a result.

Besides empowering team members, leaders can help their teams run more smoothly and get vastly more done by improving how they run meetings. In my work with organizations across the country, I have heard many physicians lament that they no longer participate in meetings "because nothing ever happens." Meetings are an investment in time and effort, and when they fail to produce results, people become disengaged. In many cases, the culprit is "analysis paralysis." We in healthcare have more data than ever before, and many teams just don't know what to do with all this information. So we study it. And study it. And study it. We talk about the data and the issues, but we fail to take action.

For teams to function properly, meetings must be efficient and purposeful and be scheduled appropriately. When forming our Perioperative Services Guidance Committee, we knew the committee wouldn't function properly if it held monthly meetings. So we held weekly meetings, and to assure maximum attendance, we scheduled these meetings at 6:30 in the morning to fit the needs of surgeons and anesthesiologists. In many cases, the team met for 30 minutes and sometimes an hour. Participation in the meetings was mandatory, but rarely did anyone want to miss a meeting because we made decisions at every meeting. We shared data so that we could evaluate how well the policies we had adopted were functioning, but we didn't overanalyze the data. We stuck to a clear agenda, which called for taking action and making progress. At the end of each meeting, we specified actions that team members would take, as well as deadlines for achievement. At the following team meeting, we reviewed progress since the previous meeting, holding team members accountable for their results.

Properly organized meetings can yield amazing results that significantly reduce suffering, and they can do it quickly and efficiently even when teams are quite large. I witnessed a good example of this firsthand when I observed the real-time demand capacity team at a large academic medical center.[16] Committed to streamlining the patient discharge process, the team held daily meetings at 10 a.m., gathering representatives from every area of the organization into a large meeting room. This group included people from the OR, ED, inpatient units, EVS, imaging, patient access, facilities, food service, administration, transport, and others. Their goal was to increase the number of patients discharged by 2 p.m. The more patients the hospital discharged, the fewer delays other patients would experience as they were admitted from the emergency department, the operating room, the intensive care unit, or the hospital clinics. By fixing the discharge process, the hospital could significantly reduce suffering due to wait times that patients might have regarded as interminable—and that could, in fact, compromise their care.

The real-time demand capacity team met daily—appropriate scheduling given the team's desire to increase discharges rapidly. The team kicked off each meeting with a review of its success the day before. How accurate was the team in predicting which patients would be discharged by 2 p.m.? Team members discussed why some of their predictions had not panned out and what they would need to do to overcome barriers going forward. Then the representatives of the individual units discussed what was occurring within their units, how many available beds they had, and how many people they thought would be discharged and could leave by 2 p.m. More important, each unit identified the obstacles team members were encountering.

For example, one manager alerted radiology that a certain patient was simply waiting for a chest x-ray before he or she could leave. Noting that information, the radiology representative made this patient a priority in order to get the patient discharged without an excessive wait for a follow-up test. In another instance, a manager stated that a room of hers was out of service because of a broken call light. The facilities representative made sure it was fixed immediately. In this way, daily interprofessional team meetings assured that the people who could make things happen were all in the same place to address the issues immediately, without multiple phone calls or approvals. The improved communication streamlined the discharge process, making it more predictable and less chaotic for caregivers and patients alike. Patients could better arrange for rides home, and they could prepare emotionally to leave the hospital. Better discharge processes, in turn, improved the admissions process, as staff could predict better when beds would come open for other patients. Improved communications also enhanced staff members' collegiality. When they convened each day, they could solve problems as they occurred, rather than allowing them to fester. They could devise meaningful solutions, not merely a series of disconnected work-arounds.

Optimizing Patient-Centered Teams

In addition to improving teamwork generally, organizations can reduce suffering by taking more specific steps to enhance how patient-facing teams operate. These steps include:

Improving Team Huddles

In his book *Mastering the Rockefeller Habits* (2002),[17] Verne Harnish advised companies to hold daily, short meetings in which the team stands or "huddles" together to address questions and issues. The point of such meetings was to keep goals well aligned and to allow teams an opportunity to address issues quickly and hold team members more closely accountable. In healthcare, many patient-centered teams have come to implement huddles to discuss relevant issues, make a plan, and follow up on whatever happened at the previous day's huddle. The problem is that patient-centered teams often don't perform these huddles consistently or well. As a result, teams don't function as well as they might, with caregivers and patients paying the price.

Once, while visiting a healthcare organization, I had a chance to follow a nurse manager who led a unit that was achieving mediocre results. I asked her if she held huddles, and she said that she did so "sometimes." When I inquired about how staff received information, she said that she sent out a monthly newsletter. On other occasions, managers have told me that they communicate via e-mail, Twitter, and text messaging in lieu of huddling. All of these are wonderful forms of communication, but they lack something critically important that huddling provides: a chance for real-time *dialogue*. To achieve sustainable results, you have to talk through challenges, discuss the data, and arrive at consensual solutions. Simply pushing out information does not assure that people understand and act upon the information to improve patient care.

In healthcare, huddles frequently work better than conventional meetings that last longer and are held less frequently. In 2013, Advocate Healthcare did away with its usual team meetings, replacing them with frequent 15-minute team huddles. Good thing: the number of safety issues uncovered by teams jumped 40 percent. By meeting daily for short periods, nurses could review safety and quality issues that arose the day before or that they could anticipate arising in the day to come.[18] Think of the suffering the team was able to avert! In inpatient settings as well as provider practices, teams that begin the day without checking in might find that they experience delays, bottlenecks, and challenges throughout the day that bleed over into patient delays, dissatisfaction, and rescheduling. By starting off the day with a huddle, everyone can understand what issues to expect. They can strategize on how to address them, and they can agree on a plan before patients arrive.

What makes for effective huddling? I've found that following a number of commonsense tactics makes huddles more effective. Hold huddles at the same time every day or shift. Start huddles promptly. Stick to a clear agenda. Require that team members participate. Keep huddles short, no more than 15 minutes. Begin and end huddles in a positive way. Focus on solutions, not just the exposure of problems. I once followed a nurse manager at Henry Ford Health System who ran one of the system's "star" units. It was immediately apparent why this unit was so successful. Maria was engaged and enthusiastic. She couldn't wait to show me her unit, introduce me to the team, and talk to me about what team members were doing. She invited me to one of her huddles. It was short, to the point, and engaging. She talked about the team's progress on its quality metrics and asked staff members to address challenges they were experiencing. Instead of bringing up problems, as so many people do in team settings, staff members brought up solutions. The team left feeling empowered and eager to take on the day's work.

Implementing Interdisciplinary Rounding

In Chapter 5, we discussed how purposeful hourly rounds and leader rounds benefitted both patients and caregivers. Interdisciplinary or interprofessional rounds are a bit different and, as you might expect, trickier to execute. Such rounds take the team approach to the bedside, incorporating the patient as part of the team. In an interprofessional round, representatives from each discipline caring for the patient huddle together at bedside, sharing information about the plan of care, the patient's progress, and next steps. Although brief, these rounds should allow time for the patient to ask and answer questions about his or her care.

Organizations that have implemented interprofessional rounds have seen better patient experience scores, lower lengths of stay, better employee engagement, reduced mortality, and fewer adverse events.[19] Nevertheless, some providers fear such huddling for the same reason they fear connecting one-on-one with patients: they envision being trapped in a room by patients or family members barraging them with "too many questions." There's no doubt that interprofessional rounds are not easy. They require a great deal of coordination, teamwork, and leadership. Still, caregivers can minimize the chances by keeping the rounds well organized.

The team should come together prior to initiating rounding and agree on a template to follow. The mere act of doing so serves as a good team-building exercise, and the existence of a template can help keep conversations on track. The team should also define a leader for these rounds, someone (not necessarily a physician) who can keep the conversation moving and end it at the appropriate time. Choose a team member who knows the patient well, who has demonstrated good facilitation skills, and who can assure that the team (including the patient and family) stays focused and initiates therapies discussed during the huddle. Finally, team members should *practice* interdisciplinary rounding. Just as we must teach caregivers how to connect with a patient, we must also teach caregivers how to perform rounds, exploring who is involved, how each member should participate, and how to end rounds efficiently and respectfully.[20]

Improving Bedside Shift Reports

After nursing school, I worked in a neuro unit, spending alternating weeks in the ICU and the step-down unit. During my shifts in the latter, we recorded our patient reports on cassette tape (yes, it was a long time ago). Team members in the incoming shift listened to the report and asked any questions they might have before we left for the day. The process wasn't ideal. Because we didn't engage in a dialogue and because we didn't include patients and their families, we frequently experienced communication gaps that compromised the care we delivered.

Our care would have improved dramatically had we conducted bedside shift reports. These reports bring information right to the patient at bedside. Not in the hallway outside the patient's room. Not in the room but on the other side of the curtain. In the patient's room at bedside, preferably using the whiteboard in the room and involving the patient in the discussion. Bedside shift reports are an important way of helping patients feel like they are part of the care team. They build trust, accountability, and a sense of camaraderie. The ability to participate and to learn about their care gives patients at least some sense of control, which reduces suffering.

To build trust with patients, introduce yourself and your colleague when commencing these reports. Walk together into the room and greet Mrs. Riley, letting her know that you trust this colleague of yours who is coming on shift and who will be caring for her. Say something like, "Mrs. Riley, this is Gail. She's going to be your nurse tonight. I've worked with her for about five years now, and she's my go-to person when I have a question. She's a fantastic nurse." This helps Mrs. Riley to feel safe in Gail's care. If you think Gail is a good nurse, and if Mrs. Riley thinks you're a good nurse because you've met her needs and reduced her suffering, then Mrs. Riley will likely think Gail is a good nurse, too.

Here the 56-second conversations described in Chapter 5 come into play. Because you've connected with Mrs. Riley during your shift, and you've learned something about her that has nothing to do with the reason she is in the hospital, you can reference that information when introducing the oncoming nurse. This provides the oncoming nurse with a conversation starter to build her own connection with Mrs. Riley. Then you and the oncoming nurse can talk together about Mrs. Riley's progress toward her goals, her upcoming procedures or lab work, her discharge needs, and so on, all along making sure to involve Mrs. Riley in the conversation.

Some caregivers worry that by conducting bedside shift reports in semiprivate rooms, they'll compromise patient privacy. They claim that in these situations, bedside shift reports simply aren't feasible. On the contrary, caregivers should still perform bedside shift reports, albeit with a twist. Instead of conducting the report at the foot of the bed, caregivers should join patients at the head of the bed and speak quietly with the curtain pulled between the beds. This way, caregivers can maintain patient privacy and still invite patients to participate in the conversation.

Minding the Whiteboard

In conducting bedside reports, caregivers should make ample use of the whiteboards that are virtually omnipresent in patient rooms.

Whiteboards in healthcare settings come in various sizes and shapes and contain varying levels of information. But no matter what form they take, caregivers must recognize that *the information belongs to the patient.* If it belonged only to the care team, we would have no need to locate whiteboards in patient rooms. In keeping with this philosophy, caregivers conducting these reports should keep the whiteboard where the patient can see it and populate it with information that the patient needs to know, including caregivers' names and roles, some information about the plan of care and goals for the day, instructions about diet or exercise, and, ideally, the anticipated date and time of discharge. Patients will wish to know this basic information, and they'll ask about it repeatedly if caregivers don't provide it. Merely possessing this information provides autonomy for a vulnerable person who otherwise feels out of control. By providing the information and keeping it updated, you help patients feel safe, and thereby you reduce suffering.

It's not enough to provide this information as part of bedside shift reports. You also have to confer with patients about it. I have often asked patients what the numbers on the whiteboard in their room mean. "Oh, I don't know," they say. "It's something for the nurse." When I ask the nurse, she says, "Oh, that's the phone number for the family to call when they're ready to talk with the doctor!" We need to discuss the information on the whiteboard with patients. How will the family members know the plan of care and actively participate in it if they don't understand how to contact the physician? Simply writing it on the whiteboard isn't enough. Have the conversation and make it very clear to the patient and family. It's a seemingly small detail, but it improves the patient experience and reduces suffering.

Often staff members don't update the whiteboards, or they leave the information recorded there incomplete. Patients in treatment rooms, exam rooms, or inpatient rooms don't have much to look at besides a TV, a window, the ceiling, or the whiteboard. So they look at that whiteboard all day long. When the information is wrong or incomplete, patients have a hard time scoring caregivers "always" on anything. If the team members couldn't keep the whiteboard updated, what else did they miss? An incomplete whiteboard gives patients the impression that you weren't always there to care for them. In their minds, gaps in information suggest that there must have been gaps in care as well.

Getting Discharges Right

When I worked as a staff nurse, I often found it maddening to receive a physician order that read, "Discharge to nursing home today." That order came with no notice that the patient was going to a nursing home. The patient didn't know about it, the family had not chosen a nursing home, no arrangements had been made, and now everyone had to scramble. Sound familiar? Many healthcare organizations take a bit more care than this in discharging patients, but they still don't do enough to prevent emotional and physical pain.

It's so important to discharge our patients carefully and thoughtfully, with thorough and repeated provision of information. If patients don't understand how to take care of themselves, or if their families don't know how to care for them, patients and families both feel anxious. Even worse, they stand a greater chance of making mistakes in providing follow-up care, with potentially disastrous results, including the need for rehospitalization. In a study published in the *Journal of the American Medical Association* (2016),[21] researchers found that in over a quarter of readmitted patients, the readmission was considered potentially preventable. In over half of these patients, the readmission might have been prevented if caregivers had taken the right steps during the first admission. Researchers discovered that many of these readmissions owed to factors like failing to schedule follow-up appointments, a lack of awareness on the patient's part about whom to contact after discharge, or excessively early discharge of patients.

Effective discharge preparation might mitigate many of these common causes of readmission. In some cases, for instance, patients don't understand how to take their medication, and they ask questions only after experiencing an adverse reaction. Mistakes such as these are potentially quite serious. In a study involving patient cohorts from Brigham and Women's and Vanderbilt Hospitals, researchers revealed that nearly a quarter of heart disease patients endured "medication errors" within a month after their discharge from the hospital, despite receiving instructions and follow-up. Of these errors, 23 percent were serious medication errors, and 2 percent were life-threatening. The problems identified by researchers included unclear written instructions, poor communication between primary caregivers and hospitals, and physicians' failure to check on their patients' recovery often enough. The researchers recommended including the patient and family in discussions about their medications and encouraging patients to play active roles in their care.[22]

We caregivers have no excuse for failing to discharge patients properly. We know that they will eventually leave the hospital, finish treatments, or move to other levels of care. Our job is to set them up for success when they do. That means we must provide information throughout their care that will help them to succeed. We can't do that 20 minutes before the patients go home from the hospital, 5 minutes before they leave the emergency department, or 30 seconds before they leave the doctor's office. Providing information throughout their encounter and in multiple ways helps to assure their success.

To understand how an effective discharge might work, consider a fictional scenario. Let's suppose that Mr. Jones has been admitted for a right total knee replacement. When he saw his surgeon the week before, he learned that he would likely spend about three days in the hospital. His surgeon told him that he would need a ride to come for him around midday on his day of discharge, but that the nurses on the unit would keep him posted on progress leading up to that. The surgeon also told Mr. Jones about the medications he would probably be taking and the physical therapy he would need. He gave Mr. Jones numbers for physical therapists, along with information about the procedure's risks, benefits, and alternatives, handing Mr. Jones an information packet and going over it with him. Mr. Jones then went to an appointment for preadmission testing, where he also received information about his procedure and what he would need both in the hospital and after his discharge.

When Mr. Jones arrives at the hospital on the morning of his surgery, his preop nurse verifies all this information with Mr. Jones and his family. Then she asks that they repeat back the information about physical therapy, medications, and discharge plan along with asking if they have any questions about the process. The anesthesiologist then sees Mr. Jones, reinforcing the importance of follow-up physical therapy and taking medications exactly as prescribed. She also confirms that Mr. Jones will need someone to give him a ride home after discharge. When Mr. Jones arrives in his room after the surgery and PACU stay, his nurse assesses him, speaks with his family, and writes on his whiteboard:

Mr. Jones is a retired professor of math at the university.

He is a grandfather of three and has two dogs named Macie and Moose.

Provider: Dr. Jon Allen

Nurse: Sally

Patient Care Assistant: Matthew

Diet: Clear liquids

Exercise goal: Up in chair tonight

Anticipated date and time of discharge: Thursday, 11 a.m.

The next morning, someone in the physical therapy department helps Mr. Jones to ambulate and tells him how the physical therapists would work with him after discharge. His nurse enters and talks to him about issues he might have with walking, asking about throw rugs and stairs at his house. She further inquires about who might take Mr. Jones to physical therapy and talks to him about the medications he would take at home. She asks him to repeat the medication instructions back to her to make sure that he will be safe when he is discharged. She also talks with his family members about what they can expect and what side effects, infection, and complications to look out for. That evening, the next nurse on duty talks to him about the same items and gives him a packet that lists all the information they had discussed. On the final day of Mr. Jones's hospitalization, the provider comes in and tells him that he can go home. Mr. Jones had already arranged for his daughter to pick him up at 11, and she is there waiting for him. Together, they review the same instructions he has been given by the surgeon in the office, the preop nurse, the anesthesiologist, all of the nurses who cared for him on the orthopedic unit, and the physical therapists.

In this scenario, Mr. Jones is much more likely to succeed after discharge than if he had been discharged with a minimum of notice or information. His caregivers have repeated their instructions not because they're disorganized. It's the opposite: they're working well together as a team, coordinating their messages because they know patients and their families often require repetition in order to process information about their follow-up care. Mr. Jones and his family feel empowered because they *are* empowered. They know what to do to assist his recovery and to minimize his suffering.

Putting It All Together

As we've seen in this chapter, we cannot prevent suffering under the Compassionate Connected Care model without addressing care on the level of the team. By improving the way project teams function, we can improve operations across our organizations, reducing wait times, waste, miscommunication, serious safety events, and many other sources of patient and caregiver suffering. By improving the way patient-facing teams function, we can directly enhance the ability of caregivers and patients to connect with one another. Patients feel safer and better cared for, while staff engagement soars. Healthcare becomes more of what it is supposed to be: a healing and enriching experience for all involved.

At the extreme, healthcare organizations should endeavor to provide seamless, team-based care for patients suffering from specific conditions. Some organizations are already doing this. MD Anderson's Head and Neck Cancer Program has been lauded as a model not only for cancer care but also for team-based care. In the early 1990s, Dr. David Hohn recognized that "seventy percent of cancer patients required treatment by more than one specialty" and that seeking such care was difficult. Processes typically were organized around clinical specialties (surgical, medical, or radiation technology) that required patients to navigate an unwieldy and bewildering system. To remedy this situation, MD Anderson created its Head and Neck Cancer Center, a collaboration among multiple specialties serving cancer patients. The center locates most specialties in one building. Patients have initial contact through the Patient Access Services Staff, and within 24 hours a surgeon decides whether the patient would benefit from services at the center. If the answer is yes, then the center obtains all the relevant patient data and diagnostics. Patients receive a diagnostic plan and undergo testing before even meeting with clinicians for the first time. After just a day or two on-site, most patients have received a diagnosis and a treatment plan and have completed all their specialty consultations.[23] By deploying teamwork to meet patient needs for speed and safety, MD Anderson's team-based approach has reduced the avoidable suffering and mitigated the inherent suffering that cancer patients experience.

Virginia Mason Medical in Seattle has built a similar system for patients with lower back pain. Traditionally, patients who suffer from such pain have usually seen multiple physicians and therapists and tried multiple medication solutions, to no effect. But at Virginia Mason, patients call one number and are typically seen the same day by a team consisting of a physical therapist and a board-certified physiatrist. For most patients without a malignancy or infection, treatment such as physical therapy also begins on the same day. According to one account, Virginia Mason "eliminated the chaos by creating a new system in which caregivers work together in an integrated way. . . . Compared with regional averages, patients at Virginia Mason's Spine Clinic miss fewer days of work (4.3 vs. 9 per episode) and need fewer physical therapy visits (4.4 vs. 8.8)."[24] Since Virginia Mason founded the clinic in 2005, MRI scans decreased by almost a quarter. Despite having the same infrastructure and staffing, the new clinic sees approximately 2,300 new patients annually—that's nearly 900 more patients than it administered under the old framework.[25]

As both these examples teach us, reducing suffering requires not simply that we colocate caregivers but that we organize care around the patient, providing the full continuum of services around the patient's needs. In our interdisciplinary teams, we must acknowledge and capitalize on each team member's experience and expertise. Only by working together in comprehensive and efficient ways can we achieve breakthrough results, reducing suffering far below traditional levels.

In all healthcare organizations, even those with more traditional care models, we must never stop pursuing excellence in teamwork. At one point during a Perioperative Services Guidance Council meeting at Wickerland, we shared positive data trends relating to block utilization, on-time starts, and cost controls. The chair of the anesthesia department nodded at me, saying "We're doing so well. Can't we take a break from performance improvement initiatives for a little while?"

"No," I responded. "We can *never* stop because other organizations are not stopping. More important, the journey will never be over."

I continue to believe that. We will always find ways to improve the experience of patients and caregivers, and that makes working well together all the more important. By creating a vision that reflected our goals of world-class, efficient, and effective surgical care by world-class providers and staff, the new administration at Wickerland was able to optimize the strengths of all the stakeholders on the council. That, in turn, positioned us to make ever greater gains going forward—gains that improved the experience of patients and caregivers alike.

Our challenge, and the challenge of all high-functioning teams, was to sustain and deepen this healthy and vibrant collaboration over time. In all organizations, the Compassionate Connected Care model cannot succeed unless the organization itself proffers strong support for both caregivers and teams. It is to this topic we now turn.

The Compassionate Connected Organization

THE YEAR WAS 2009, and Amy Cowperthwait, a veteran nurse and coordinator of the Skills and Simulation Lab at the University of Delaware's School of Nursing, realized that her program needed to change. Like many other institutions, the university had trained young nurses by relying on electronic mannequins. Yet these mannequins weren't preparing students very well for what they would encounter in their future work with live human patients. "It was impossible," Cowperthwait recalls, "to cultivate simulations that focused on essential communication skills for healthcare providers"—skills like developing rapport, empathy, and therapeutic communication. The mannequins didn't behave like human patients did.[1] They were "unable to follow commands or express emotions in a way that was believable." Although the mannequins could verbalize pain as well as emotions like sadness or anger, they couldn't wince or make other facial gestures that evoke emotion.

On one occasion, Cowperthwait was running a code blue simulation that included postmortem care for the patient. After having nursing students identify that the "patient" had coded, Cowperthwait had them deliver several rounds of CPR, code drugs, and shock treatment. Addressing the students over a loudspeaker, Cowperthwait called the code and the time of death. What she saw next startled her. The nursing student who had been performing the final round of CPR "picked up her hands and slammed them down on the chest of the patient. 'You're dead,' she shouted." Then the student slapped her hands together to indicate that her work there was done. Cowperthwait was mortified. As she says, "I remember thinking that this patient would be someone's father, someone's brother, and that abusing a corpse is a federal offense!" At that moment, Cowperthwait realized that her students "weren't equating the manikin with a human life. The manikins had no ability to provide the needed reference to humanity. If I'm being honest, it scared me a bit."

Cowperthwait realized that she needed to inject more real human contact into the simulation program. But how? She got an idea: drama students. Collaborating with the university's theater department, she helped create a program called "Healthcare Theatre" in which nursing students engaged in simulations on theater students who had been trained to behave like sick patients and family members. Immediately after the simulations, faculty members from the theater department directed the theater students and helped them develop feedback for the nursing students in the room.

Debuting in 2009, Healthcare Theatre was a rousing success. Over several years, it grew to become two fully approved university courses that were cross-listed in the theater and nursing departments. Students were incorporated into all nursing simulations run by the simulation lab, as well as into skill labs that did not include invasive procedures. According to Cowperthwait, nursing students benefited from "over 650 hours of quality simulation and patient-centered feedback each semester." They learned to attend to the human dimensions of caring for patients, gaining experience that would help them to minimize suffering during their future work as nurses. The program was so successful that the School of Nursing featured Healthcare Theatre to help recruit top academic candidates. A number of university administrators likewise referenced Healthcare Theatre when highlighting the university's interprofessional work. Healthcare Theatre has expanded to include physical therapy, medical anthropology, behavioral health, and nutrition programs at the University of Delaware. The course has also attracted undergraduate students from many other majors including psychology, engineering, communications, marketing, premed, biology, criminal justice, political science, exercise science, and medical laboratory sciences.

As the example of Healthcare Theatre suggests, the ability of healthcare organizations to deliver Compassionate Connected Care hinges on more than just the efforts of individual caregivers and localized teams. It requires that *organizations* engage to provide support, encouragement, and resources. Health systems, hospitals, ambulatory practices, long-term care facilities, and other organizations must educate present and future caregivers so that they truly understand how to meet the needs of patients and their families. But their obligations extend far beyond education. These organizations must create nurturing *cultures* that at once reduce suffering for caregivers and energize them to provide the best possible patient experiences. Without strong organizational support, caregivers and teams will feel hamstrung and ultimately defeated in their attempts to provide compassionate and connected care. The best care today—that which combines patient safety, clinical excellence, *and* excellence in the healthcare experience— occurs within organizations large and small that have dedicated themselves wholeheartedly to the mission of reducing suffering for everyone.

The Power of Culture

You might wonder: Do organizations really impact the amount of suffering patients and caregivers experience? Don't individual caregivers and teams—the people who actually interact with patients and one another—have the most influence over experience in healthcare settings? Yes, individuals and teams are critical, but the evidence shows that organizational support—in particular, a strong organizational *culture*—matters a great deal. When the culture of an organization supports the processes of care provided by teams, caregivers feel more satisfied with their jobs, and the quality of patient care improves. Outcomes improve, even in facilities with complex and intense care requirements.[2] The suffering of both patients and caregivers decreases.[3] As the authors of one study have noted, organizational support impacts individual and team effectiveness, as they rely on "leadership, shared understanding of goals and individual roles, effective and frequent communication, . . . shared governance, and [empowerment] by the organization."[4] All these elements, of course, contribute to and help constitute organizational culture.

Conversely, organizations that don't support teams with strong cultures of excellence see lower caregiver engagement and care quality, which correspond with increased suffering. When a general sense of diminished expectations pervades an organization, teams tend to communicate and collaborate poorly. Team members *expect* poor information, which as researchers have noted, "leads to errors because even conscientious professionals tend to ignore potential red flags and clinical discrepancies. They view these warning signals as indicators of routine repetitions of poor communication rather than unusual, worrisome indicators."[5]

Unfortunately, many healthcare organizations lack dynamic cultures that promote and reward excellence in quality, safety, and patient experience. One culprit is industry consolidation.

As hospitals and provider practices have acquired one another and merged, the resulting cultures have often suffered, becoming uneven and incoherent. CEOs at larger systems often make excuses for their cultures, claiming that "they're different" from the industry-leading organizations because their patients are sicker or because they serve economically challenged areas that create staffing challenges. Although such challenges might exist, the fact is that efforts to integrate an array of smaller organizations, each with its own culture, policies, staff, and patient care practices, often fail. In addition, the very economic pressures that prompt healthcare organizations to consolidate have led to cost cutting and staff layoffs. In the best of circumstances, layoffs hit employee morale hard, but when organizations fail to communicate properly, employees become disengaged and disillusioned. The culture of the organization feels inadequate and unhelpful, if not outright hostile. Suffering increases.

The Importance of Leadership

If caregivers' ability to reduce or mitigate suffering hinges on organizational culture, how might organizations build their cultures so as to implement the Compassionate Connected Care model most effectively? As with teams, *leadership* makes all the difference. No organization of any kind can build or sustain a high-performance culture, and realize the business results that accrue to such a culture, without leadership's full support and attention. That holds especially true in healthcare. Researchers have investigated the organizational factors that exist in high-performing academic medical centers. As they've found, the leaders at these medical centers tended to work harder than most on personally affirming cultural standards of excellence. They focused on quality and safety during meetings, used leadership rounds to identify and address performance issues, perceived "excellence in service, quality, and safety as a source of strategic advantage," and enlisted practitioners to improve areas like "timeliness, customer service, facility cleanliness, and safety."[6] In addition, CEOs at top-performing institutions were "passionate about improvement in quality, safety and service and had an authentic, hands on style."[7] They made their desire to serve patients clear to employees, including lower-level staff. In sum, these leaders shaped the cultures of their organizations by engaging *everyone* around treating patients well.

At lower-performing organizations, employees weren't as clear about the organization's dedication to patient care, teaching, and research. Leaders at these sites typically seemed satisfied with their organizations' current quality and safety performance, despite data demonstrating quality and safety issues. Some of these leaders touted their organization's scientific accomplishments as evidence of clinical quality, discounting data that showed subpar performance in quality or other areas. In general, leaders of lower-performing organizations didn't make service excellence a high priority, viewing quality and safety as moral imperatives but not strategic business concerns. As a result, these organizations had lower HCAHPS scores, which as we've seen, translate into higher levels of patient and caregiver suffering. At these organizations, we may extrapolate that more patients felt unsafe, and more caregivers felt unappreciated.

This study and other research point to a number of specific areas on which leaders can focus to align organizational culture better with the Compassionate Connected Care model. Leaders must translate the organization's core mission, vision, and values into tangible and tactical practices and processes for the people who care for patients every day. They must also focus on areas like transparency and safety. Let's briefly review each of these areas in turn.

Articulate the Organization's Mission, Vision, and Values

What exactly does an organization seek to accomplish? Why does it exist? Employees of any organization can't work toward common objectives without understanding their organization's common purpose or *mission*, and they certainly can't do it passionately or energetically. A similar situation exists in healthcare organizations, and it relates directly to caregiver and patient suffering. If leaders don't define a strong mission, caregivers become disengaged. As we've seen, this disengagement leads to corresponding declines in the quality of care, safety, and patient experience. Further, if leaders don't define a patient-centered mission, the organization isn't helping caregivers to focus on practices that will improve the patient experience. Patients again suffer, experiencing greater wait times, poorer communication, less frequent emotional connections with caregivers, and so on.

Research has confirmed a link between well-articulated organizational missions and employee engagement. In any organization, an important component of employee engagement is meaning. Employees must see their work as having an impact or serving a significant purpose. They must feel that they are contributing in their own limited sphere to the organization and its goals. Northwestern University graduate student Carrie Gibson studied individuals representing a variety of different industries, organizational departments, and lengths of employment to understand employee engagement. Her study, like those undertaken at Press Ganey, found a "strong positive correlation between organizational missions and the meaning of employee existence."[8] When organizations utilize missions, they provide employees with a strong sense of purpose, which in turn enhances "the meaningfulness condition of employee engagement." People feel that they are worthwhile, valuable, and useful. They feel more energized to do their best. In healthcare settings, higher engagement again leads to better patient experience and reduced suffering.

If a mission constitutes an organization's purpose, *vision* is, by one definition, "a mental image of a possible and desirable future state of the organization."[9] It's where the organization is headed. Research performed with small professional services firms has found positive correlations between leaders who communicate visions well and financial performance, productivity, and retention.[10] Other research has suggested that having a vision motivates employees to perform better, which in turn leads to performance results.[11] In healthcare, as we've seen, when caregivers feel motivated and committed, engagement rises, leading to higher HCAHPS scores—resulting in less suffering for patients and caregivers. Communication of vision by leadership helps caregivers feel a stronger sense of belonging and shared purpose. Leaders who start every meeting by reminding team members how the meeting, policy, practice, or process flows from both the mission and the vision help caregivers connect their work with the organization's shared purpose. Team members come to "own" the organization's success or failure in a way they wouldn't otherwise.

Leaders must take care to translate the vision into specific performance goals. As the management thinker Peter Drucker observed, service organizations (like those in healthcare) can't improve performance and achieve desired results unless leaders execute their primary responsibilities, which include setting goals as well as defining the business, prioritizing, measuring performance, using the metrics for feedback, and auditing objectives and results.[12] If an organization doesn't clearly articulate its larger goals, it can't reward people for helping to attain them or dock them if they don't contribute. People don't understand how to manage and improve their performance or contribute to the organization's success. I've related how when I began my career as a staff nurse, my hospital had a plaque on the wall by the elevator that articulated its mission, vision, and values. However, it was only a plaque. I had no idea that the words it contained related to my work or to the hospital's success. My manager and other leaders had to make that connection for my colleagues and me. They had to discuss specific goals in huddles and meetings, explaining how each line item in the budget, performance improvement project, capital budget expenditure, and hiring decisions tied back to the vision. To reduce suffering, we leaders need to specify clear goals and connect them to the guiding principle of bettering the patient and caregiver experience.

Beyond defining a clear sense of an organization's mission and direction, leaders can help build a supportive culture for caregivers by defining and affirming the shared values that inform *how* work gets done. The values and the shared beliefs they reflect help underpin an organization's "deep culture." Research has shown "that clear organizational values improve employee morale," in part because these values implicitly hold each person "to the same, value oriented obligations."[13] Employees also thrive on the feeling that the organization's values mirror their own[14]—a finding that Press Ganey has confirmed specifically in connection with healthcare organizations. Employees feel more committed to their organizations and like their jobs better. They also feel more loyalty to their organizations and seem to experience less stress.[15]

To build a culture consistent with and supportive of Compassionate Connected Care, leaders must align the organization's values with its mission and vision, and they must also assure that these values truly center on the patient. Of these two tasks, alignment might prove the trickiest. Even if physicians, nurses, administrators, and others agree to certain values, we all tend to look at those values differently. When I worked with the outspoken trauma surgeon mentioned in Chapter 6, he and I realized that we didn't approach patient care in exactly the same way. As a physician who was responsible for his own group of patients, he advocated primarily on their behalf. I, however, bore responsibility for the care of all the unit's patients and employees, as I was the unit manager. Further, when I was promoted to VP and administrator for large areas of the healthcare system, I bore responsibility for larger groups of patients and employees across the entire continuum of care. From my perspective, a singular focus on any one group of patients over others could prove detrimental—it was the bigger picture that counted. As a result, this surgeon and I diverged in how we *interpreted* and *actualized* our organization's vision.

For instance, this surgeon might have respected the work of a given nurse on the unit and requested that she care for his patients whenever possible. As a manager, however, I might have known that this nurse would not always be able to care for his patients. Further, I might have known that having her attempt to care for his patients might interfere with her workflow. As a manager, I had to assure that we met the needs of all patients and staff, not just those of one surgeon. Neither this surgeon nor I was "right" or "wrong" in trying to live by our organization's values. Our focus was just different.

This surgeon tended to focus on the short term because he was trying to meet his patients' immediate needs. Most physicians and caregivers probably do this. Leaders of healthcare organizations, in contrast, should focus on positioning the entire organization for the future, serving the greater community, and assuring that the organization allocates limited resources effectively so that it can achieve its broader goals.[16] Understanding these different perspectives helps foster empathy between leaders and caregivers, and allowing each colleague to articulate his or her perspective helps leaders and caregivers to arrive at better decisions. Once this surgeon and I understood the differences in how we perceived organizational values around patient care, we could tackle the problem in ways that spoke to each of our concerns. The result, in this case, was better scheduling practices for staff and patients—and ultimately, a better experience for all.

The implication here is that leaders should regard the articulation of values as an ongoing process of negotiation. As the leadership expert James Burns noted, guiding people in such a process is actually a defining quality of "transformational" leadership. "The essence of leadership in any polity," he wrote, "is the recognition of real need, the uncovering and exploiting of contradictions among values and between values and practice, [and] the realigning of values. . . ." Leaders needed to help people to become more alert to their perspectives—"to feel their true needs so strongly, to define their values so meaningfully, that they can be moved to purposeful action."[17] Just as compassionate caregiving is about understanding and serving patients' human needs, so we might describe compassionate and connected leadership as "clarifying human values and aligning them with the needs of the organization."[18] Put differently, there are many ways to "focus on the patient." By ensuring that those perspectives all come to the surface, and by helping negotiate what "focus on the patient" ultimately means in each situation, leaders can help establish a strong and meaningful culture that galvanizes caregivers to reduce suffering.

Prioritize Safety

By attending to mission, vision, and values, leaders can align their organizational cultures behind the Compassionate Connected Care model. Yet they can take other actions as well to render their cultures more compassionate and connected. First, they can prioritize improving safety, quality, and patient experience and become a high-reliability organization (HRO).

According to the Agency for Healthcare Research and Quality, "high reliability organizations are organizations that operate in complex, high-hazard domains for extended periods without serious accidents or catastrophic failures."[19] Healthcare organizations have only recently begun to embed the notion of high reliability into their cultures, but this notion has long defined organizations in industries like aviation and nuclear power, where mistakes can cause catastrophic outcomes.

In healthcare, HROs embrace the culture of safety as their operating system and, as a result, experience higher staff engagement and better patient experience. Indeed, cross-domain analyses of the Press Ganey patient experience, engagement, and NDNQI databases suggest that the elements of safety, quality, experience of care, and caregiver engagement are all intimately interwoven with one another. Further, we've found that improving these three elements also leads organizations to improve their financial outcomes. Focusing on improving patient experience and lowering suffering can also yield safety gains. In our research, systems in the top quartile for HCAHPS patient experience metrics (those assessing interactions with nurses and physicians, as well as those evaluating cleanliness, likelihood to recommend, and the overall hospital rating) see lower rates of hospital-acquired conditions (see Figures 7.1 and 7.2). They also chart shorter lengths of stay and fewer readmissions than systems that perform in the bottom quartile for patient experience. Increasing safety and reducing suffering go hand in hand.

Leaders can take a number of steps to build more concern for safety into the culture. As a 2017 Press Ganey white paper has recommended, leaders should identify safety as a top organizational priority. They should also create an environment that encourages individuals at all levels to report errors or close calls without fearing repercussions. As vulnerabilities become apparent, they should promote collaboration across ranks and departments to develop

Median HAI Scores by Patient Experience Quartile

HCAHPS Domain	CLABSI	CAUTI	MRSA	C. Diff
Nurse	0.59 ◆—● 0.95	0.71 ◆—● 0.87	0.81 ◆—● 0.94	0.84 ◆●—● 0.97
Physician	0.89 ● 0.90	0.67◆—● 0.87	0.92◆● 0.94	0.73 ◆—● 0.97
Cleanliness	0.74 ◆—● 0.97	0.67◆—● 0.89	0.77◆—● 0.97	0.83◆—● 0.98
Likelihood to Recommend	0.74 ◆●● 0.93	0.77 ◆◆ 0.87	0.76◆—● 0.98	0.89 ◆●◆ 0.93
Overall	0.71 ◆●—● 0.94	0.81◆● 0.83	0.70◆—● 1.00	0.91◆● 0.93

Scale axes: 0 — 1.0 — 2.0 | 0.5 — 1.0 — 1.5 | 0.5 — 1.0 — 1.5 | 0.5 — 1.0 — 1.5

HCAHPS Domain Quartile: ● Bottom Quartile ◆ Top Quartile

CLABSI (Central Line-Associated Blood Stream Infection); CAUTI (Catheter-Associated Urinary Tract Infection); MRSA (Methicillin-Resistant Staphylococcus Aureus); C. diff (Clostridium difficile colitis)
[1] Hospital Compare, 2015
Production: Press Ganey Data Science, March 10, 2017

Figure 7.1 Clinical safety/quality versus patient experience, median HAI score by patient experience quartile

Median Clinical Quality Scores by Patient Experience Quartile

HCAHPS Domain	PSI 90	30-Day Readmission	LOS	HAC Score
Nurse	0.87 ◆●—● 0.89	15.4 ◆—● 15.7	3.1 ◆—————● 4.4	4.1 ◆———————● 5.9
Physician	0.88◆●—● 0.89	15.4 ◆—● 15.8	3.2 ◆—————● 4.4	3.9 ◆———————● 5.8
Cleanliness	0.86 ◆—● 0.9	15.4 ◆——● 15.7	3.2◆————● 4.5	4.1 ◆————————● 6.0
Likelihood to Recommend	0.86 ◆●—● 0.88	15.3 ◆—● 15.7	3.5 ◆—● 4.1	5.1 ◆●● 5.3
Overall	0.86 ◆—● 0.89	15.3◆—● 15.8	3.3 ◆———● 4.3	4.9◆—● 5.6

Scale axes: 0.8 — 0.9 — 1.0 | 15.0 — 16.0 | 3.0 — 4.0 — 5.0 | 3.0 — 4.0 — 5.0 — 6.0

HCAHPS Domain Quartile: ● Bottom Quartile ◆ Top Quartile

[1] Hospital Compare, 2015
Production: Press Ganey Data Science, March 10, 2017

Figure 7.2 Clinical safety/quality versus patient experience, median clinical quality scores by patient experience quartile

solutions. Finally, they should allocate sufficient resources to address safety concerns.[20]

Organizations that move aggressively to prioritize safety can make rapid progress. In 2012, Tennessee-based Community Health Systems (CHS) began a safety journey across all its 150 hospitals. CHS obtained certification as a patient safety organization (PSO) from the Agency for Healthcare Research and Quality. Subsequently, CHS formed another organization, CHS PSO, LLC, a component PSO of CHS that would be able to provide a secure and confidential environment for collecting and analyzing safety data from CHS's hospitals. The objective: to identify and reduce or eliminate the risks and hazards associated with patient care. Meanwhile CHS took action to construct a high-reliability culture, drawing on the expertise of HPI/Press Ganey and deploying evidence-based tools. As we wrote in our white paper, "By consistently practicing proven safety behaviors and measuring serious safety events in a highly reliable way, determining their causes, and changing procedures to prevent their recurrence, the health system has reduced its serious safety event rate by nearly 80 percent."[21]

Pursuing an HRO designation doesn't just have to be about improving safety. Healthcare organizations moving to become HROs often seek to improve metrics in a number of areas, including quality, experience of care, caregiver engagement, and efficiency. In fact, some organizations are using the HRO concept to improve in all these areas at once. Whichever areas an organization wishes to enhance, it can use the HRO concept as a means of supporting the Compassionate Connected Care model. Clearly, improving safety will prompt an organization to break down silos and forge better connections between disciplines and between caregivers and patients. Likewise, HROs require compassion in order to function well. After all, improving safety means deferring to the expertise of colleagues throughout an organization. That, in turn, implies the prevalence of mutual respect—a cultural trait inculcated via humanistic and relationship-oriented leadership styles. Just as caregivers deploy relationship skills to treat patients compassionately, so leaders can to help entire organizations become more compassionate—and safer. Suffering will lessen in turn.

Improve Communication

As we've seen, poor communication among caregivers increases suffering. While teams and individuals can address that problem, leaders also can address it by embedding strong communication into the organization's culture. Hospitals routinely encourage physicians and nurses to raise concerns whenever appropriate, but individuals lower down in the hierarchy often fear doing so.[22] Their concerns go unexpressed, preventing organizations from identifying and remedying safety and patient experience issues and perpetuating those issues by causing individuals to become disengaged and disenchanted in their jobs. Leaders should implement comprehensive policies and strategies for listening to the concerns of employees, stakeholders, and community members. As the Society for Human Resource Management (SHRM) has noted, "Listening to employee issues and concerns builds loyalty and improved productivity. Organizational leaders can learn through listening about issues or concerns *before* they become formal grievances or lawsuits. They can also discover potential employee relations issues and learn about attitudes toward terms and conditions of employment." To improve communication, SHRM advises that organizations link communication to their strategic plans—and specifically to their mission, vision, and values. They also suggest that organizations communicate consistently, seek input from all constituencies, and take steps to assure the organization's credibility.[23]

As regards this last piece of advice, it's especially important that healthcare organizations communicate *transparently* with stakeholders, especially patients. Consumers of healthcare have more information than ever before. They can visit websites like https://data.medicare.gov to compare hospitals on clinical quality, patient experience, and outcomes, and they can also go online to post their perceptions in far less scientific ways. Indeed, a study published in the *Journal of the American Medical Association* discovered that "59% of American adults find online ratings to be an important consideration when choosing a physician. Over one-third of those who used online reviews chose their doctor based on positive reviews, and 37% reported avoiding physicians with negative reviews."[24]

Despite concerns about the reliability of online reviews, organizations have much to gain by promoting greater internal and external transparency about their data. Leading-edge organizations are already publishing their physicians' quantitative and qualitative patient experience data on their own websites. They post every rating and comment, whether positive or not, attributing each one to the physician who delivered care. As a result, these organizations gain more control over the scientific validity of the data that appear online, and they ensure that patients get the most accurate picture possible of the quality of care these organizations have provided. Physicians gain more confidence in the data and tend to become more engaged in the organization's improvement efforts.

Transparent communication through online reviews mitigates avoidable patient suffering by empowering patients to make the best choices they can for their care. Selecting a physician can prove challenging even for a healthy patient. For patients seeking care for illness or injury, it can cause a great deal of anxiety. Treating patient experience data in a transparent manner honors the right of patients to make informed decisions about care. For organizations, transparency is a proactive strategy for connecting with patients and treating them with compassion and empathy before they even make their first appointment.

To move toward greater transparency, organizations should expand the volume of data they collect about physician performance outcomes. It's hard to be transparent if you don't know how your caregivers are performing. Moreover, all patients deserve a voice in rating the care they have received. By surveying entire patient populations rather than just a random sample, organizations can tell a story about the care they provide that truly reflects the patient experience. They can further use the survey data to identify areas for improvement and to unleash an epidemic of empathy among providers. Physicians will embrace valid and reliable data that help them better understand how they are performing and where they might improve. Transparent communication of data also reduces patient suffering by engaging and enabling patients to collaborate actively in their own care.[25]

Enhance the Work Environment

Yet another way leaders can build organizational cultures that support Compassionate Connected Care is by enhancing the work environment. Some nurse leaders perceive staffing as the greatest challenge that prevents us from optimizing patient and caregiver experience, but that's not exactly true. The work environment often plays a greater role. As a bedside nurse, I knew how good I felt when my manager voiced appreciation for my work, when my colleagues and I helped one another and agreed that we provided great care, and when I felt that I was paid a fair wage. I also know that I was more inclined to work an extra shift, take an extra patient, and cover for my colleagues' breaks. My work environment helped enable me not only to provide compassionate and connected care for my patients but to maximize my own potential as a nurse and as an employee. The work environment enabled me to do what it took to reduce suffering for patients and my fellow caregivers.

The data bear out my experience. Although higher staffing levels are associated with more positive nurse perception, more positive patient experience, and fewer negative patient outcomes, cross-domain analytics demonstrate that the perceived status of nursing in the organization—a direct product and characteristic of the work environment—exercises a greater influence over caregiver experience.[26] When nurses perceive that the organization has valued them sufficiently to provide them with enough supplies and staff training, to hire qualified and skilled nurses, and to take other steps to ensure nurse engagement and job satisfaction, their experience improves, and their degree of suffering declines—as does patient suffering. Further, organizations that empower nurses to enact professional nursing standards or best practices tend to see rises in the overall quality of performance and patient care.[27] As the 2015 Press Ganey "Nursing Special Report" noted, "An organization's own caregivers are uniquely qualified to comment on the quality of care delivered by the organization. The strong relationship between nurses' assessment of quality and work environment creates further imperative for focusing on this foundational aspect of leadership."[28]

Research shows that supportive work environments foster safety and quality of patient care by boosting how *engaged* nurses are with their jobs. Engaged nurses feel a sense of ownership and loyalty on the job. They dedicate themselves to creating a safe environment for patients and an effective and efficient working environment for their colleagues.[29] The safety and quality of care rises in due course.[30] Conversely, defects or dysfunction in the nursing work environment can lead to both minor disruptions and major systemic consequences, both of which lower engagement and, in turn, influence the quality, safety, cost, and patient experience of care. If you don't get the work environment right, everyone suffers, including patients. In an era of high nurse turnover and vacancy, you also render the organization vulnerable to severe staffing shortages, which further increase patient and caregiver suffering.

Organizations that perform well on patient experience, caregiver engagement, and nurse-sensitive clinical quality will work hard to assure that caregivers feel safe in their practice and can care for patients in proactive ways. To improve in this area, leaders can pursue a number of strategies including safe patient handling and mobility (SPHM) based on the American Nurses Association's safe patient handling and mobility standards.[31] These standards provide a comprehensive framework for ensuring the safety of both patients and nurses. They include measures such as creating a culture of safety, establishing a sustainable SPHM program, implementing ergonomic design, installing proper SPHM equipment, and establishing a system for training to maintain competency. Other strategies include providing for adequate breaks during work shifts, avoiding extended work shifts, hiring more highly trained RNs (those with a bachelor's degree or specialty certifications), and assigning nurses to patients in equitable ways.[32]

Since the same factors that help nurses feel safe and proactive in their caregiving are frequently those that help them to feel more engaged, leaders should build a culture of nursing excellence that supports all these objectives. Just as we try to provide compassionate and connected care to patients, so leaders should try to meet caregivers' needs by acknowledging the complexity and importance of their work, providing the resources they need to do their jobs, promoting teamwork as a vital component for success, and removing barriers to a positive work-life balance.

Support Caregiver Education

To build cultures that support Compassionate Connected Care, there's one more area in which leaders can and should focus: caregiver education. Given how unprepared many young caregivers are today and how potentially jaded some seasoned caregivers are, leaders must emphasize ongoing professional education and training if they are to have any hope of optimizing patient and caregiver experience. Innovative programs such as Amy Cowperthwait's Healthcare Theatre, described at the beginning of this chapter, have an important role to play in training caregivers how to connect emotionally with patients. These programs do cost money: Healthcare Theatre's projected budget for 2015 was about $110,000. Still, any investments that organizations might make in such programs yield important returns. When comparing costs and potential benefits, leaders should remember that direct caregivers constitute the largest line item on any healthcare organization's operational budget. As such, they have the greatest impact on patient experience and the organization's ability to achieve high safety and quality metrics. With a considerable portion of reimbursement pegged to patient and caregiver experience and safety, organizations stand to lose hundreds of thousands of dollars if caregivers *don't* perform well in these areas. A small investment in teaching the art of connecting makes clear financial sense.

Healthcare Theatre is hardly the only innovative way to help caregivers understand the patient experience. Northwell in New York has created simulation labs that take caregivers through an exercise of both "being a patient" and acting as a caregiver. Renown Health in Reno, Nevada, has implemented a fairly unique orientation exercise in its emergency department to help foster empathy and compassion for patients. On their first day on the job, all new employees, no matter who they are or what their roles are in the emergency department, are asked to place all their belongings in a locker. They are then taken, without explanation, to the waiting room and left there for four hours, with no communication during this period. Then they are brought to a treatment room and the curtain is drawn. The new employees can hear all the ambient noise, and they can also hear other staff members talking about them. Again, no explanation is provided until the end of the day. At that time, the preceptor pulls aside the curtain and says, "This is what your patients go through every day. Don't forget it."

As I know firsthand, the experience of being a patient or a family member of a patient changes a caregiver's perspective. Renown Health engineered a way for caregivers to begin to experience this shift in perspective without actually being a patient. How might your organization help caregivers better understand and connect with patients' points of view? As the example of Renown Health suggests, a little imagination in this area goes a long way.

Mobilizing the Organization—and the Industry

During her time in Healthcare Theatre, a junior nursing student at the University of Delaware named Annie Gardner had a chance to portray a number of patients, including a diabetic teenager, a patient with cerebral palsy, an adult woman from the Appalachian Mountains with hypertension, and a depressed college student. As Gardner reflected, "Playing all of these different patients [opened] my eyes to different thought processes people have, why they say the things they do, and where people come from."[33] But the chance to interact with nurses during the role-play sessions also opened her up to the different ways that caregivers can treat patients. "After several interactions, it became clear who the 'good' nurses were; not because they did all the techniques right or they knew all the side effects to the medication I was prescribed, but because they made me feel like a person and not a patient."

We desperately need more "good" nurses. But as we've seen in this chapter, caregivers and teams can't make real progress in reducing suffering unless healthcare organizations themselves take this goal as their guiding principle. Leaders must believe passionately in the need to reduce suffering, and they must dedicate themselves to building cultures that are compassionate and connected. They can do this by articulating a clear mission and vision for the organization as well as clear values. But that is only the beginning. Leaders must also attend to a number of other factors that bear on culture, including safety, communication, workplace experience, and education. Combine these elements together, and you arrive at a culture and an organization that is fully mobilized around enhancing patient and caregiver experience. Impressive reductions in suffering will follow.

The Compassionate Connected Care framework transports us to the intersection of clinical excellence, operational efficiency, caring behaviors, and culture. Organizational leadership and structure must influence and drive these components. But is the healthcare industry itself ready to optimize care for patients and caregivers? In the next chapter, we examine the history of healthcare reform and what we must do as an industry to make compassionate and connected care the norm, rather than the exception it largely is today.

CHAPTER	A Compassionate
8	Connected Healthcare Industry

EARLY IN THIS book, I described my own experiences as a patient and as a family member of patients. In this final chapter, I'd like to tell you a bit about my mother-in-law, Norma. She is 85 years old, but sadly, not a "young" 85. A retired nurse, she smoked and struggled with her weight for decades, eating a diet rich in high-calorie, fried foods. Such a diet was the norm where she lived, part of the culture. My husband recalls that when we were first dating and my mother invited him over for dinner, she served alfalfa sprouts. "I had never seen them before," he says. "I thought it was grass. I grew up eating fried pork chops, fried potatoes—everything fried. That's what we ate."

By her late forties, my mother-in-law had developed type 2 diabetes. She did stop smoking in her late fifties, but her health woes worsened nonetheless. Years of walking around with excess weight took a toll on her joints, leading her to undergo two knee replacement surgeries. By her early seventies, she was going blind from the diabetes and developed kidney problems, among other ailments. As of this writing, she is completely blind, in kidney failure, and dependent on others for her basic needs. She relies on a walker to get around and has to be accompanied to meals at her assisted-living center because she tends to fall if left on her own. Suffering pervades her daily life. As she says, "I'm tired. I can't even see the faces of my grandchildren. I can't walk without falling down. Honestly, I don't want to do this anymore."

Is the suffering my mother-in-law experiences inherent, simply a part of growing older? Not exactly. Although genetics obviously affects how we age, lifestyle choices play an important role. Had my mother-in-law stopped smoking or never started, and had she kept her weight under control with exercise and a healthy diet, she likely would not be where she is today. My own mother, also a former nurse, offers a helpful counterpoint. She, too, smoked as a young woman and quit in her forties. Otherwise, though, she has largely cultivated healthy habits. She has eaten a healthy diet throughout her life (lots of alfalfa sprouts), and today she is a vegetarian. She exercises daily and hikes a portion of the Appalachian Trail every fall. She takes a multitude of vitamins and a statin to lower her cholesterol. She is the healthiest person I know and endures none of the chronic conditions that makes my mother-in-law's life so difficult.

In recent years, the healthcare industry has come to recognize the importance not just of offering excellent care for sick people but of preventing people from getting sick in the first place. Medical science knows a great deal about how to keep people out of the hospital and enjoying life longer through nutrition, exercise, mindfulness, and preventive measures. What better way to prevent suffering—and reduce the burden on our healthcare system—than that? And yet the healthcare industry hasn't gotten behind wellness as much as it might. We've improved at caring for patients at home after they've been in the hospital, but we don't reimburse healthcare organizations enough for keeping people well, nor do we give patients enough financial incentives to keep themselves well. As a result, Americans suffer more from chronic illness than residents of other developed countries. As a 2015 report by the Commonwealth Fund found, the United States had "poor health outcomes, including shorter life expectancy and greater prevalence of chronic conditions" than 12 other high-income countries, even though we spend more on healthcare than these countries.[1]

Wellness is just one area in which the healthcare industry as a whole might mobilize to reduce or alleviate suffering. By engaging on the level of policy around safety, waste, provider diversity, population health management, and a number of other issues, we can not only cut costs and improve outcomes but improve the patient and caregiver experiences and reduce suffering. As we've seen, action at the individual, team, and organizational levels is essential to bring the Compassionate Connected Care model to life. Still, we'll never achieve deep, sustainable changes unless the larger *system* of healthcare delivery changes. All of us—individuals, teams, and organizations—need support from systemwide policies and mandates that put the experience of patients and caregivers first.

The History of Healthcare Reform

Supporting compassionate and connected care at the industry level isn't just a matter of adopting policies that enable frontline caregivers to put people and their needs first. In the broadest sense, we cannot provide state-of-the-art, patient-centered care unless we simultaneously address another basic factor: cost. The economics of healthcare *matter*—they are an inescapable reality. Our healthcare system can expend endless effort trying to reduce suffering, but if it doesn't also contain costs while also assuring high quality, our efforts on behalf of patient and caregiver experience won't be sustainable. Healthcare must be safe, effective, patient centered, *and* efficient.

To understand the link between patient experience and cost, consider for a moment why an aspirin costs $10 in the hospital even though you can buy a whole bottle of aspirin at retail for less than half that amount. Have you ever thought about this? Your local drugstore's price contains a markup that reflects the drugstore's own costs, including compensation for clerks and other team members as well as the money the drugstore must pay to distributors to buy the aspirin. The price also reflects a profit margin for the drugstore.

Hospitals have an entirely different—and more formidable—cost structure. Yes, hospitals must buy the aspirin from a distributor, which costs money. But after the hospital receives the aspirin, it goes to a pharmacy, which must be staffed. The pharmacists and technicians cannot dispense the medication without an order from a provider (more costs there). Meanwhile, in order to receive the aspirin, patients must be admitted, which means that the hospital must pay costs associated with their room and nursing care. Oh, and that electronic medical record the physician uses to enter the order for aspirin? That entails a *huge* capital outlay to buy, implement, and maintain. In short, each step in the provision of aspirin to a patient in a hospital setting costs money. And each step also holds the potential for suffering, in the form of waiting, error, duplication, and adverse outcomes. What if the provider misses a potential drug interaction when prescribing aspirin? What if the nurse provides the aspirin as ordered without waiting for the pharmacist or the alerts in the electronic medical record? What if such errors lead to significant bleeding for the patient? And what if the whole process takes so long that a patient suffering from a headache has to wait three hours or more for pain relief?

These questions aren't hypothetical. They arise every day in healthcare organizations. And they don't just apply to aspirin but to everything in healthcare—every drug, every procedure, every test. Out-of-control costs and out-of-control suffering are facts of life, and the welfare of patients and healthcare organizations themselves hangs in the balance. Hospitals aren't like banks, whose profit margins exceed 20 percent.[2] As I've noted, many hospitals limp by on margins of 3 percent. If the hospital doesn't offset its cost of ordering, supplying, stocking, distributing, and providing medications, it will operate at a loss and eventually close its doors.

The bottom line is this: we must keep patients at the center of our business models, treating them with compassion and connection. But if we can't afford to keep the doors open, we can't treat patients in the way that we should. That begets the question: How might we structure the provision of care to increase access, reduce costs, maintain quality, *and* improve the experience of patients and caregivers? For much of the past century, government policymakers and healthcare leaders had sought answers, with varying degrees of success. Before we examine policy areas that the healthcare industry should address in order to reduce suffering, let's pause for a moment to glance back at previous reform efforts.

During the 1940s, in the wake of the New Deal, healthcare consumed a greater portion of our gross domestic product, and Americans were increasingly unable to pay for care, especially when they were aged or indigent. To solve this problem, President Harry Truman pursued universal healthcare coverage. The American Medical Association (AMA) fought this idea, and legislation promoting universal coverage died in Congress. Truman's efforts did ultimately lead to the Hospital Survey and Construction Act (1946), which provided federal grants and loans to support the growth and modernization of hospitals.

A subsequent push to increase access to healthcare for all Americans took place during the Kennedy administration. In particular, President John Kennedy supported legislation that would provide health insurance coverage as part of Social Security to Americans aged 65 or older. Once again, interest groups including the AMA defeated the bill. Lyndon Johnson finally signed a version of the legislation in 1965, creating the Medicare and Medicaid programs. These laws provided coverage for healthcare at hospitals and other facilities to Americans 65 years of age and older, as well as to poor, blind, and disabled individuals.

During the 1970s, President Jimmy Carter took up the fight for universal healthcare coverage, but he didn't accomplish much, despite weak support from the American Hospital Association and the AMA. His successor, President, Ronald Reagan, was concerned primarily about reducing healthcare costs, and during his presidency, several laws were passed to reduce federal spending and to improve efficiency. The legislation accomplished these goals by changing Medicare's reimbursement methods, and specifically, by reducing reimbursement to hospitals and physicians and boosting antifraud measures. These efforts to curb costs continued under President George H. W. Bush, who signed into law the Stark I legislation that prohibited physicians from referring patients to the physicians' own clinical lab services.

The Clinton administration tried anew to make healthcare accessible to all, this time via "managed competition." Championed by First Lady Hillary Rodham Clinton, this approach called for private insurance companies to vie for patients in, as one historian called it, "a highly regulated market, overseen and coordinated by regional health alliances to be established in each state. All health plans would be required to provide a minimum level of benefits. Employers would be required to provide insurance coverage for their employees and pay 80 percent of the premium."[3] Although this legislation died after failing to receive broad support in the healthcare and insurance agencies, the Clinton years did see passage of "The Health Insurance Portability and Accountability Act, a significant expansion of the Stark physician self-referral law (Stark II), and the State Children's Health Insurance Program." Another significant expansion of coverage occurred under

President George W. Bush, with passage of a law—the Medicare Drug Improvement and Modernization Act of 2003—that provided prescription drug coverage under Medicare Part D.[4]

The most notable piece of healthcare reform legislation passed in recent decades was, of course, the Patient Protection and Affordable Care Act (PPACA), also known as the Affordable Care Act, signed into law by President Barack Obama. The legislation restructured the healthcare system in a bid to lower costs, improve coverage, and improve quality of care. The PPACA mandated that employers of a certain size buy health coverage for employees, that almost all private citizens have some sort of health coverage, that insurers provide minimum levels of benefits, and that they no longer deny coverage based on preexisting conditions. The law also provided federal payments to the states to help cover more low-income patients.[5]

From its inception, the PPACA was highly controversial, and it remains so to this day. Following the election of President Donald Trump, the House of Representatives passed healthcare reform legislation that would modify the PPACA (as of this writing the Senate was considering its own version of this legislation). According to the Congressional Budget Office, the American Healthcare Act passed by the House in 2017 would cause 23 million people to lose insurance by 2026 and decrease the deficit by $119 billion. The Senate bill was similar to its counterpart in the House, though it also allocated funds to stabilize health insurance exchanges created under the Affordable Care Act. Notably, the Senate's bill did not penalize people for lacking coverage, as the Affordable Care Act did.[6]

The challenge of providing for access, quality, and cost has been a formidable one, and today the overall direction of reform remains uncertain. The good news is that by taking steps at the industry level to address suffering, we can simultaneously move toward other critically important goals that efforts at healthcare reform have sought to address. Let's now consider five areas that policymakers should address in order to support the drive for more compassionate and connected care.

Policy Focus #1: Promote Safety

In Chapter 7, I argued that organizations need to prioritize safety and become high-reliability organizations (HROs) in order to reduce patient and caregiver suffering. We need to take action on safety industrywide, mandating that *all* organizations become HROs. Healthcare in the United States is not nearly as safe as it should be. Each year, poor care delivery causes as many as 440,000 patient deaths. Just think of the untold human suffering that this represents.

We can turn to industries outside healthcare in order to drive our own, industry-level action. Craig Clapper, a colleague at Press Ganey, worked for a decade as a nuclear engineer and engineering leader at two power companies, Arizona Public Service Company and Public Service Electric and Gas. He later applied these methods as a consultant in power, transportation, manufacturing, and, most recently, healthcare. While working in nuclear power, Craig personally observed work at 64 of the 103 operating nuclear reactor sites in the United States. All these sites deployed high-reliability organizations or another methodology known as safety science, in part through the Institute of Nuclear Power Operations (INPO), an industry group dedicated to promoting the highest safety standards. As a result of these efforts, the number of significant safety events per reactor site fell from a high of 0.90 events per reactor site in 1989 (that is, nearly one event at every one of those 100 reactor sites every year) to 0.01 events per reactor site in 2014 (that is, only one event for *all 100 of the reactor sites* in one year). This amounts to a reduction of 98.9 percent over a 25-year period. Moreover, those significant safety events were only "precursor" events. No actual damage to the reactor cores at these facilities occurred during those years.[7]

Imagine if the entire healthcare industry could achieve comparable results. We might, by focusing—as nuclear power facilities did—on cultural transformation. In truth, nuclear power facilities approached the challenge of increasing reliability in two ways. First, they streamlined and standardized processes and fixed equipment. But second, they used people and culture to enhance the ability of workforces to anticipate and adjust to complex situations as they arose. This latter approach mobilized specific tools and universal skills—called "safety behaviors" or "error prevention techniques"—that leaders use every day. Together the tools and the skills formed the foundation of a *safety culture* at these facilities. INPO eventually standardized the elements of nuclear safety culture in its publication "Traits of a Healthy Nuclear Safety Culture." The publication included elements such as personal accountability, the avoidance of complacency, effective communication, a respectful work environment, and continuous learning.[8]

As we saw in Chapter 7, the HRO methodology helps organizations improve not only safety but quality, experience of care, engagement of caregivers, and efficiency. Used industrywide, the methodology would lead to substantial reductions in patient and caregiver suffering across our healthcare system. Significantly, the HRO and safety science approaches don't add more cost or work to our already-strained healthcare system. That's because HRO is not another thing we need to do. Rather, it's about changing *how we do what we already do.*

In effect, every outcome in healthcare today has its own subculture, and as a result, our processes for delivering care are woefully suboptimized. We improve one outcome to the detriment of other outcomes. What kind of progress is that? We need *real* system improvement that results in better outcomes (and indirectly, lower patient and caregiver suffering) without adding more control, cost, or work. In the nuclear power industry, a focus on safety provided better outcomes while actually *lowering* costs. According to the Nuclear Energy Institute, the number of significant safety events in the nuclear power industry fell by 70.6 percent between 1995 and 2005. During those same years, quality of production (what is called the unit capability factor, or the amount of electricity produced) rose by 13.3 percent. Power plants became more efficient, cutting the cost of operations, maintenance, and fuel by 28.7 percent.[9]

Think about the connection between safety and cost as applied to healthcare. How much would you pay for safer healthcare? Would you pay 100 percent more? Probably not. How about 50 percent more? Again, probably not. Most people would probably not pay in excess of 25 percent more for improved safety. But what if you *cut* costs by 28 percent and still received care that was much safer? That's the promise that safety science and HRO hold for healthcare. We all should be using safety science and HRO to improve care delivery to sharply reduce harm, significantly increase quality, connect care, and—above all—inject more compassion back into care. Our industry should mandate it.

Policy Focus #2: Reduce Waste

When I served as director of perioperative services, I realized pretty quickly that waste was endemic, not only in perioperative care but in healthcare overall. Over the years, as I did research and worked with lean, six sigma, PDSA, and other performance improvement tools, I came to understand that if we were ever to optimize reimbursement, reduce cost, and improve patient and caregiver experience, we had to get rid of the waste. Make no mistake: waste is absolutely a precursor for suffering. When patients wait, when they receive too much treatment, and when they experience errors and adverse events, we find both waste and suffering.

Researchers have documented the proliferation of waste in healthcare. In a 2012 article in the *Journal of the American Medical Association*, former CMS administrator Donald Berwick and Andrew Hackbarth, an assistant policy analyst at the RAND Corporation, identified six categories of waste in healthcare: "overtreatment, failures of care coordination, failures in execution of care processes, administrative complexity, pricing failures, and fraud and abuse." As they observed, these categories account for, at a minimum, "20% of total healthcare expenditures." The industry could save much more if it cut back on waste than if it cut back on the care it provided to patients.[10] The Institute of Medicine (IOM) has evoked the magnitude of waste by comparing healthcare to other industries. Imagine waiting days for an ATM transaction instead of seconds. Imagine if tradespeople all worked from different blueprints when performing renovations on your house. Imagine if individual airline pilots could check their plane's safety in their own way, or not perform a safety check. That's what would happen, the IOM observed, if banking, construction, and the airline industry embraced healthcare's inefficient and wasteful ways.[11]

One especially obvious form of waste in healthcare is the duplication of services. Many providers lack information about diagnostic tests performed on patients, whether due to poor communication, a lack of available information, fragmentation of services, or human error. Rather than waiting to learn if a test has been performed or not, providers simply order one, often duplicating the testing. Patients suffer more in turn from the stress of waiting and the inconvenience and pain of having to submit to unnecessary tests—not to mention the additional costs.

To reduce the risk of duplication, the IOM has advocated more shared decision making on the part of hospital staff. By making decisions collaboratively, caregivers can "encourage open communication among patients and ensure the development of an evidence-based care plan free of duplication and waste. Once properly informed about their care options, patients often reveal preferences for lower-cost and less-intensive treatments, which can reduce costs associated with overuse."[12]

It's not enough to focus on reducing duplication or other forms of waste at the organizational level. We must do so across the healthcare industry. As data about patient experience, caregiver engagement, and clinical quality show, waste translates into waiting for patients, families, and caregivers. When patients call providers to schedule an appointment, how many people must they speak with? Do they even have an opportunity to speak with a live person? When patients appear at provider practices, how long do they languish in the waiting room before a staff member shows them to an exam room? Once in the exam room, how long does it take for providers to arrive and see patients for 10 minutes? If diagnostic testing occurs, how long does it take to schedule and perform those tests or to get the results back? When patients come to the ED, how long must they wait in a waiting room, scared and in pain and looking for answers? How long must they wait for admission to hospital beds? Will caregivers even place them in beds, or will they place them on gurneys in hallways? How long will they have to wait to go to the OR?

Quantified hourly, all this waiting amounts to *tens of billions of dollars of waste* in our healthcare delivery system every year. A study published in 2015 in the *American Journal of Managed Care* calculated the opportunity costs that patients accrued while waiting in ambulatory care alone. Researchers found that patients spent, on average, 121 minutes per visit. This included 84 minutes spent in the clinic itself and 37 minutes spent traveling. "The average opportunity cost per visit was $43 which exceeds the average patient's out-of-pocket payment." In 2010, physician visits in the United States exacted $52 billion in total opportunity costs, a heavy burden indeed. "For every dollar spent in visit reimbursement," concluded the study, "an additional 15 cents were spent in opportunity costs."[13] Significantly, these data date from 2010. Despite the Affordable Care Act, not much has changed. As journalist Mattie Quinn observes, "The average wait time at a hospital in 2014—the first year that Americans were required to have health insurance—was 24 minutes, down only four minutes from 2012."[14]

Wait times matter, and while they are difficult to address, we must do so. More broadly, we must mobilize our professional associations to demand a wholesale reduction of waste across our healthcare system. And we must mandate the universal use of tools like lean and six sigma and guidelines proffered by organizations like the IOM to reduce waste inside organizations. We have the technology and knowledge to significantly reduce waste. But do we have the will?

Policy Focus #3: Foster Transparency

In Chapter 7, I argued that organizations should pursue more transparent communication with stakeholders, given patients' preference today to engage as consumers. One organization that has benefited from transparent communications in an especially impressive way is Geisinger Health System in Pennsylvania.[15] Nearly a decade ago, Geisinger took pay-for-performance medicine to a new level with its ProvenCare evidence-based approach for ensuring care quality. Geisinger charged a flat fee for standardized, best practice care processes associated with certain high-volume diagnosis-related groups, essentially attaching a service warranty to these procedures. For coronary artery bypass surgery, for example, clinical work groups established a bundle of 40 evidence-based practices and designed improved workflow processes. Information technology staff hardwired each element of the bundle into the electronic health record through templates, order sets, and reminders. If the patient suffered a complication, infection, or some other abnormality, Geisinger, not the patient's health insurance, would bear responsibility for the cost of that care, regardless of how much it exceeded the flat rate. More recently, Geisinger Health System has extended its ProvenCare model for ensuring care safety and quality into the patient experience domain with its innovative ProvenExperience program, which offers a money-back guarantee for care experiences that don't meet patients' expectations. Online physician ratings, family participation in morbidity and mortality conferences, patient presentations to executives, patient access to physician notes, and leadership and board rounding provide patients and providers unprecedented access to information and to one another.

ProvenExperience was radical, but as Geisinger's chief patient experience officer, Dr. Greg Burke, explains, it was the right thing to do. "If you have a bad cup of coffee at Starbucks," he said, "they give you your money back or a new cup of coffee. Healthcare is a profession bound by an oath. We have to be even more accountable."[16] As Burke has recounted, Geisinger first unrolled ProvenExperience for patients undergoing back and bariatric surgery. The organization asked patients who weren't happy with their care to explain why and state (via an app) how much of a refund they believed they should receive. "Geisinger is riding the risk for this," Burke allowed. "There is the possibility that people might try to take advantage of us, but our experience to date is that most people don't. A lot of the requests have been small copays. What this comes down to is trust. We include a comment in the app: 'You put your trust in us, so we should put our trust in you.'"[17]

On the strength of this program and other initiatives, Geisinger joined the Employee Centers of Excellence Network (ECEN), an organization that, according to a *Harvard Business Review* profile, "helps employers identify quality providers and negotiate bundled payments."[18] Participating firms pay for all employee travel and medical costs accrued at specific healthcare organizations, with employees of these companies paying nothing out of pocket. ECEN's rigorous selection process assures that companies secure quality care for their employees, at a considerable cost savings due to the fixed rates negotiated for bundled care. Meanwhile, healthcare organizations like Geisinger that provide the care gain access to a lucrative market, while also maintaining and improving care delivery. Everyone wins—and it all hinges on transparency in the communication of outcomes, as well as on measuring the specialty-specific patient-reported outcome measures. Instead of contenting itself with standard metrics like length of stay, infection rate, or return to surgery, Geisinger transparently reports metrics that patient care about: Can they walk after total joint surgery? Can they breathe after their coronary artery bypass graft? Were *their* goals and life needs met?[19]

We need the entire industry to follow the lead of organizations like Geisinger and move toward innovative, patient-centered, bundled care. More fundamentally, we need the entire industry to measure what matters to patients, to report it transparently, and to take real responsibility for meeting patients' needs efficiently and effectively.

Policy Focus #4: Population Health Management

As my mother-in-law's story suggests, the healthcare industry must take care of people *before* they get sick. Only then will we be able to reduce suffering while cutting cost and improving value. At present, however, it isn't lucrative in medicine to keep people healthy and out of the hospital. It *is* lucrative to perform procedures, keep people in hospital beds, and provide prescriptions for people who are not healthy.

So how do we move from sick care to healthcare? One solution is to care for entire populations of people, reimbursing organizations based on the number of people for whom they care and whom they keep healthy rather than for the number of procedures, tests, or office visits they provide. Caring for populations in this way incentivizes organizations to prevent people from getting sick in the first place—through more prevention, screening, rapid diagnostic testing and treatment, and innovation so that organizations and insurers can offer the right treatment in the right location by the right provider. In short, population health management is *proactive* care, delivered on an individualized basis. By emphasizing prevention and customization, it minimizes suffering while lowering cost and improving value.

Population health management is a key feature of the Affordable Care Act. Under this legislation, providers across the healthcare continuum could form accountable care organizations (ACOs), taking responsibility for a patient population, including the costs and quality of its care. As Melinda K. Abrams and her colleagues at the Commonwealth Fund explain, "Beginning in 2012, the ACA established the Medicare Shared Savings Program to encourage the development of ACOs. If participating ACOs meet quality benchmarks and keep spending for their attributed patients below budget, they receive half the savings that result, with the rest going to the Centers for Medicare and Medicaid Services (CMS), which administers the program."[20] In order to retain an even larger share of savings (up to 60 percent), ACOs could employ a "two-sided risk" model, repaying "a share of losses if healthcare spending for attributed patients exceeded the budget target."[21]

Policymakers hoped that this kind of "bundled payment" would encourage continuity and coordination of care, prompting organizations to focus more on disease prevention and health, which would in turn drive costs down. According to the *Harvard Business Review*, "By definition, a bundled payment holds the entire provider *team* accountable for achieving outcomes that matter to patients . . ."[22] The risk adjustment of bundled payments incentivized providers to care for even difficult cases. If organizations didn't provide care efficiently or if they provided it inappropriately, the government penalized them. Policymakers hoped that if they held providers accountable for outcomes that encompassed the entire continuum of care, organizations would add new services, interventions, or diagnostic tests that improved outcomes or lowered the cost of care. Michael Porter and Robert Kaplan suggested that costs could potentially decrease by up to 20 or 30 percent, without compromises in quality.[23]

So far, some ACOs have delivered promising results. Health policy experts Jessica Schubel and Judith Solomon, for example, document their effectiveness in Minnesota. "Building upon its existing managed care program," they write, "Minnesota implemented an innovative model to lower Medicaid spending and improve beneficiary health outcomes. The state allows its Medicaid health plans to partner with different types of organizations to deliver integrated medical, behavioral, and social services." One such ACO, Hennepin Health, reduced ER use by over 9 percent between 2012 and 2013 and saw a 50 percent reduction in hospitalizations.[24] When patients are not waiting in emergency department waiting rooms or admitted to the hospital for care, their suffering declines. When providers are not overwhelmed by the sheer number and complexity of patients, their suffering also declines. When the healthcare industry lowers costs by keeping people healthy, the industry, and indeed the country, suffers less. Why would we not want to keep people healthy?

Caring for populations is indeed the wave of the future. As of 2017, there were 744 ACOs that covered a total of 23.5 million lives.[25] The number of organizations and covered lives had grown more than tenfold since 2011. In January 2015, the Department of Health and Human Services stated that by the end of 2018, it would shift half of all Medicare payments to "alternative payment models."[26] Meanwhile, the largest payer in the United States,

United Healthcare, took population health management to a new level. In February 2015, the organization stated that its "total payments to physicians and hospitals" that were "tied to value-based arrangements" had nearly tripled over a three-year period.[27]

In the course of shifting to population-based compensation, the industry can migrate healthcare encounters to lower-cost options while also maintaining and improving quality care delivery by embracing telehealth. According to HealthIT.gov, "The Health Resources and Services Administration of the U.S. Department of Health and Human Services defines telehealth as the use of electronic information and telecommunications technologies to support and promote long-distance clinical healthcare, patient and professional health-related education, public health and health administration. Technologies include videoconferencing, the internet, store-and-forward imaging, streaming media, and terrestrial and wireless communications."[28] In the future, as healthcare services continue to consolidate, patients increasingly will not see specialty providers in the traditional doctor's office setting, but in their homes or primary care physicians' offices via electronic means. This will render access to care easier and timelier, reducing suffering.

Telehealth does not come without its challenges. Healthcare organizations will have to operate seamlessly together. Reimbursement and licensure may prove tricky to navigate for providers practicing in multistate organizations, while data integrity and safety will remain important concerns. However, the movement toward delivering value (as defined by outcomes divided by cost) makes telehealth a logical alternative, one that patients will increasingly demand because of its convenience, quality, and lower cost.

In moving to telehealth, the healthcare industry must work to preserve the patient experience in its totality. Suffering remains a concern in the digital world. In Chapter 2 we discussed the unintended isolation that technology often brings about, leading to fear, anxiety, and a lack of trust. In providing telecare, the healthcare industry must assure that it involves patients in its care, encouraging them to ask questions and share in decision making. Just as making the connection with a patient in a "live" environment takes practice, so, too, does connecting in a virtual environment. But compassion, empathy, and the reduction of suffering remain paramount, regardless of the mode of care.

Policy Focus #5: Provider Diversity

Regardless of where it is delivered, healthcare today depends at least in part on people to provide it. However, workforce experts agree that a widening gap exists between the supply of and demand for primary care physicians. In 2015, the workforce added some 8,000 primary care physicians. A decade earlier, that number was 7,500. Doesn't sound like much of a shortage, does it? It is, though, when you consider that "the number of primary care physicians who retire each year is projected to reach 8,500 in 2020." The number of primary care physicians retiring exceeds the number entering practice, even as the aging U.S. population is requiring both more care and more expensive care.[29]

So what do we do about this problem? In a 2013 article, Thomas Bodenheimer and Mark Smith suggested that we plug the supply-demand gap by turning to a combination of clinicians, licensed practitioners, nonlicensed practitioners, technology, and patients themselves.[30] If each professional on the care team works to the top of his or her license or training, the healthcare industry can spare the highest-skilled and highest-trained providers from performing tasks that don't require their level of skill and training. With the burden on caregivers reduced, they'll suffer and burn out less on the job. At present, if physicians can't document the care they provide in the medical record due to issues with computer placement, lack of easy access, or poor setup and deployment of the information system, they might have to document that care during break times or during precious time at home, leading to stress and burnout. Some organizations solve this problem by utilizing scribes to document the care while the physicians interact with patients. Physicians can devote their full attention to the patient, while the scribes assure that the documentation is complete and accurate.

Nonclinicians can provide a great deal of standardized preventive care based on the U.S. Preventive Services Task Force guidelines, including "immunizations; screening for cervical, breast, and colorectal cancer; or cardiovascular risk reduction (smoking cessation, healthy eating, and physical activity)."[31] Quality remains intact when nonclinicians provide these services, and more patients gain access. "In some practices," health experts Bodenheimer and Smith note, "registered nurses or pharmacists have standing orders to take total care of patients with diabetes, only rarely involving the clinician."[32]

Based on the projected numbers, it seems possible that relying on a diversity of providers can help us bridge the gap between supply and demand. The number of nurse practitioners, physician assistants, pharmacists, physical therapists, and others has already begun to rise. Some 3.1 million RNs practice in the United States, and between 2012 and 2025, that number will grow by an astonishing 33 percent. The Bureau of Labor Statistics anticipates that the number of PAs will rise by 30 percent through 2024, and that the number of nurse practitioners, certified nurse midwives, and certified registered nurse anesthetists will rise by almost a third.[33] These nonphysician medical providers "diagnose conditions and counsel and treat many patients in many settings, including primary care and acute care settings, and the results are usually comparable to physicians, and include high rates of patient satisfaction."[34]

According to Bodenheimer and Smith, we aren't yet using licensed practitioners such as nurses, pharmacists, psychologists, licensed clinical social workers, and others to their full capacity, nor are we using nonlicensed personnel like medical assistants, front desk staff, and health coaches.[35] Still, some sectors of the healthcare industry are moving to rely more on diverse caregivers. "High-performing practices," they write, "empower medical assistants to provide algorithm-based, periodic chronic and preventive care services. Other practices utilize registered nurses, pharmacists, or medical assistants as health coaches, assisting patients with chronic conditions to engage in behavior change and improve medication adherence."[36] The Veterans Administration proposed an expansion of practice authority that would allow a range of advanced practice nurses to assess, diagnose, and prescribe medications and interpret diagnostic tests to the full extent of their education and abilities without a physician's clinical supervision.[37]

As much as utilizing diverse clinicians can help to optimize the total value of care, significant barriers remain. Physicians harbor concerns about clinical quality, while state health departments remain concerned about reimbursement and regulatory issues. However, if the healthcare industry ensured a consistency of professional standards for all healthcare providers, and if it strengthened accountability, it would "facilitate interprofessional collaboration, foster innovative practice, and enhance the accessibility of high-quality primary care."[38]

The Perfect Healthcare System

I began this chapter by describing my mother-in-law's considerable health woes. Her chronic conditions, shared by so many in our society, derived in part from her behaviors. But they were also enabled by a healthcare industry that has traditionally emphasized sick care over healthcare, and that has been marked by enduring inefficiency, subpar quality, and poor patient and caregiver experience. It's a system that has also, alas, been rife with suffering.

When I sit with my mother-in-law, or hear my husband talk about how she is faring, I find myself imagining what a perfect healthcare system might look like. Invariably, it contains many of the features described in this chapter. I think of a child born today whose mother would have had excellent prenatal care and whose parents would have been healthy. This child would have immunizations and wellness visits to his provider throughout his life, with screenings for various cancers and diseases at the appropriate times. As the child grows, his provider would would encourage him to wear helmets and seatbelts and to eat a healthy diet. When the teen's behavior slipped, his provider would check in with his parents to understand if the teenager needed any kind of referral for care.

This teenager, as I imagine it, would grow to adulthood, and wellness visits would continue with appropriate immunizations and interventions. The government would pay for all this care because policymakers would understand that keeping people healthy costs much less than taking care of them when they become sick. The providers in this scenario would not all be physicians, but also advanced practice nurses, physician assistants, and pharmacists. All these providers working at the top of their licenses would provide excellent medical care for people when they get sick and perform procedures where medically indicated.

But my imaginary scenario goes on. Providers and healthcare employees would be skilled communicators, building connections, fostering trust, and spending just 56 seconds assuring that they truly know the patients who are trusting them with their health. Hospitals would be reserved for the truly sick and would become de facto ICUs equipped with the best technology. Care would be primarily ambulatory because the goal would be to keep people healthy. Patients would have a vested interest in keeping themselves healthy, with financial incentives encouraging them to eat right, exercise, give up smoking, and so on. Only sick visits would have a copay. Wellness visits would cost nothing out of pocket, and patients could accumulate points for each visit that would offset their copay if they happened to fall ill. This perfect system would also incentivize providers to keep people healthy, perhaps paying the providers a "bonus" for each cohort of patients that achieves wellness thresholds.

In this system, we would reduce waste, minimizing waiting times, duplication of services, overutilization and underutilization of services, and care in inappropriate places. The federal government, working with provider organizations, would assure that organizations maintain quality and continuously work to improve it, penalizing poor performance and rewarding optimal performance. Providers and healthcare organizations would communicate transparently, and so would patients, sharing their concerns, issues, and healthcare challenges. We would all be held accountable for the care we provide in totality—clinically, operationally, culturally, and behaviorally.

As I imagine it, that healthy baby would live to be a centenarian on account of his healthy habits. When he does finally die, as we all do, his will be a death with dignity, as free from pain and suffering as we in the healthcare industry can make it. All of this is a wonderful dream, and right now, it is only that. It's up to the individuals, teams, and organizations to make this dream a reality. Try as we might as individuals, team members, and organizations, we cannot do so without real, substantive, and difficult reform in the industry itself. Let's roll up our sleeves and get started. Together, we can accomplish so much.

Why We Do
What We Do

ON SEPTEMBER 16, 2016, a 34-year-old editorial production manager named Laura Levis suffered a severe asthma attack that stopped her breathing. Although paramedics managed to restart her heart, she never regained consciousness and died days later. In the wake of her death, her husband, Peter, posted an open letter of gratitude on Facebook, addressing it to the staff members in the intensive care unit who took care of his wife. The letter was so poignant that it caught the eye of the *New York Times*, which republished it.[1]

"Every single one of you," Peter wrote, "treated Laura with such professionalism, and kindness, and dignity as she lay unconscious. When she needed shots, you apologized that it was going to hurt a little, whether or not she could hear. When you listened to her heart and lungs through your stethoscopes, and her gown began to slip, you pulled it up to respectfully cover her. You spread a blanket, not only when her body temperature needed regulating, but also when the room was just a little cold, and you thought she'd sleep more comfortably that way."[2]

Peter went on to recount the many small acts of kindness the staff rendered to Laura's parents, including their willingness to answer questions and involve them in her care. He described how the staff cared for him, checking on how he was doing, consoling him, and assisting him with small tasks as he attended to his wife. The staff bent the rules in a show of compassion, allowing him to bring in the couple's cat to say goodbye. On his wife's final day, caregivers allowed Peter to be alone with her for an hour one last time in the ICU. "I will remember that last hour together for the rest of my life," he wrote. "It was a gift beyond gifts . . ."[3]

In presenting my ideas about Compassionate Connected Care to audiences around the country and the world, I tell my own story as a patient and that of my son-in-law Aaron. But at the end of my presentation, I often tell people about Laura, Peter, and the letter that he wrote. Peter's letter doesn't talk about the clinical care that his wife received, although he implied that the care was excellent. Rather, it talks about how the staff, up to and including the people who cleaned the room, made Laura's loved ones *feel*. It talks about how the staff cared, how they understood the vulnerability of Laura's loved ones, their pain, their suffering. As Peter recounts, the caregivers treated him like a *person*, and that simple fact made such an impact that he, in turn, remembered their names.

Real caring transcends the medical diagnosis or the clinical care we provide. It's about providing that care, but doing so much more: feeling empathy, showing compassion, and easing suffering. Isn't that why we in healthcare have spent so many years pursuing our degrees and receiving our professional training? Isn't that why we put up with the hardships inherent in caring for others, and also the hardships that, as we've seen, are avoidable?

When I take audience members through my presentation slides, most of them seem to pay attention, and many nod their heads. But when I describe this letter, most people start to cry, including myself. This is the way we want *all* our patients and their families to feel after being in our care. And we want caregivers to feel grateful, too, for having been treated respectfully and compassionately.

All too often in healthcare today, people don't experience compassion, and they don't forge connections with others around them. Although healthcare providers haven't traditionally used the word "suffering" to describe patient and caregiver experience, it's pretty clear to most clinicians, nonclinicians, leaders, and staff with whom I speak that suffering is real. It's also pretty clear that all of us—individuals, teams, organizations, and the industry as a whole—need to offer Compassionate Connected Care. I can honestly say that no audience has ever argued with Compassionate Connected Care. The concept and the model resonate with people in a way that the usual talk about tactics and strategy does not. That's because Compassionate Connected Care brings us back to why we are in healthcare and why we must always strive to do better.

In this book, I've told the stories of a number of people, in most cases, masking their identity. Before I leave you, let me fill you in on how they have fared. The man who shot my son-in-law, Aaron Pearson, was found guilty on all counts and given life in prison plus 115 years. That's small consolation to Aaron and our family, but it is something. Much bigger consolation is the progress that Aaron himself has made in his recovery. During the late summer of 2015, he threw out the first pitch at our local minor league stadium. The following year, he did the same at a major league game between the Kansas City Royals and the St. Louis Cardinals. This is a young man who doctors said would never speak again or use the right side of his body for much of anything. Today, Aaron can play with his kids and enjoy conversation with his wife. In December 2016, he achieved a milestone: he obtained his driver's license and can now drive a car! Aaron has significant and irreversible challenges with language and cognition, and he'll likely never be able to work again, but he is a walking miracle, thanks to God and all the people who cared for him. I will forever feel grateful for their compassionate and connected care.

My daughter Amanda has shown a kind of strength that I hope most people will never have to muster. All along, she has been there for her husband and for her children, helping them to persevere through any number of frightening and painful times. Before Aaron was shot, she was a kindergarten and certified special education teacher. I'm happy to report that in the fall of 2017, she returned to teaching. Jackson, my grandson, started kindergarten at the same time, and Jovie, my granddaughter, turned three. The entire family has made it through this horrific ordeal stronger and more passionate about both law enforcement and healthcare.

Kylie, Aaron's nurse, no longer works as a nurse. My heart is heavy about that, but perhaps one day she will come back. Right now, though, she is a full-time, stay-at-home mom to a baby boy, Miller. Although I've repeatedly conveyed to her what an impact she had on our lives, she'll never really know the extent of it. I will always remember her and the little things she did to make Aaron's tragedy bearable. So many people at Mercy of Springfield, Missouri, and at the Shepherd Center in Atlanta showed us empathy and compassion, truly connecting with us. We will always remember and feel grateful.

Brandy and her family are optimistic about her cancer treatment, and she continues to receive care both at home and at MD Anderson. Amy Cowperthwaite continues her work in Healthcare Theatre. I applaud her innovation and passion and look forward to her continued success in teaching future nurses and healthcare providers the importance of connecting, empathy, and compassion. Julie has returned to work and is healthy and whole again. We continue to wait for answers for Olivia's pain but have, thankfully, ruled out the really bad things. They are doing well.

I am cancer-free. In September 2018, I will mark my five-year survival. I look forward to continued health and appreciate all the people who cared for me.

Although this book has pointed to the many ways that we in healthcare need to change, there is also a lot of good happening in our industry. Slowly but surely, the safety and quality of care in the United States is improving, as is the experience of healthcare. Over the past five years, the percentage of patients giving their hospital top box scores for "Overall Rating" has increased. Between 2015 and 2016, healthcare providers improved on nearly every HCAHPS measure, although the improvement was uneven. According to a report released by the U.S. Department of Health and Human Services, hospital-acquired conditions (HACs) dropped 21 percent between 2010 and 2015, representing 3.1 million fewer adverse events over that period compared with what we would have seen if rates had held steady at 2010 levels.[4] Nearly 125,000 fewer patients died in the hospital from HACs, and our country saved some $28 billion in healthcare costs.

Patients' perception of their care is also improving. Between 2013 and the first quarter of 2017, the percentage of patients giving their hospital top box "Overall Rating" on the HCAHPS increased by about 0.6 percentage points per year. That might not sound like much, but it's significant, representing an increase in the industry's baseline standards. If a hospital scored at the fiftieth percentile in 2013 and its scores had remained steady, it would have scored at only the thirty-fifth percentile today.[5]

Results like these are promising, and they stem from the collective efforts of individuals, teams, organizations, and the healthcare industry. But they are not nearly enough. Suffering remains an urgent problem, for patients and for caregivers. And as long as we haven't addressed suffering as well as we might, we also haven't addressed fully other aspects of care that matter to us all, including quality, efficiency, safety, and cost. Let's all rededicate ourselves, our teams, our organizations, and our industry to doing right by the patients and families we're serving, and to doing right by one another. Let's all focus on connecting with one another empathically, as fellow human beings. Let's all rediscover our deepest purpose, the impulse that drew us into healthcare to begin with: easing people's pain and helping them to heal.

Notes

Chapter 1

1. *Merriam-Webster*, s.v. "patient," accessed July 7, 2017, https://www.merriam-webster.com/dictionary/patient?utm_campaign=sd&utm_medium=serp&utm_source=jsonld.

2. Because of its unfortunate etymology and association with passivity (e.g., waiting around *patiently* for doctors or nurses), some medical professionals seek to retire the term "patient" (Ann Robinson, "Some Doctors Want to Scrap the Term 'Patients'. As a GP, I Have a Better Idea," *Guardian*, May 11, 2017, https://www.theguardian.com/commentisfree/2017/may/11/healthcare-patients-radical-idea-gp-people).

3. Thomas H. Lee, "The Word That Shall Not Be Spoken," *New England Journal of Medicine* 369 (November 2013): 1,178, doi:10.1056/NEJMp1309660.

4. W. F. Bynum and Roy Porter, eds., *Companion Encyclopedia of the History of Medicine* (Routledge, 1993).

5. Bevin Cohen et al., "Frequency of Patient Contact with Health Care Personnel and Visitors: Implications for Infection Prevention," *Joint Commission Journal on Quality and Patient Safety* 38 (December 2012), https://www.ncbi.nlm.nih.gov/pmc/articles/PMC3531228/.

6. Amy Witkoski Stimpfel, Douglas M. Sloane, and Linda H. Aiken, "The Longer the Shifts for Hospital Nurses, the Higher the Levels of Burnout and Patient Dissatisfaction," *Health Affairs* 31 (November 2012), doi:10.1377/hlthaff.2011.1377.

7. Heather Punke, "Infographic: What's the Cost of Nurse Turnover?" *Becker's Hospital Review*, March 21, 2016,

http://www.beckershospitalreview.com/human-capital-and-risk/
infographic-what-s-the-cost-of-nurse-turnover.html.

8. Christina Dempsey and Barbara A. Reilly, "Nurse Engagement: What Are the Contributing Factors for Success?" *Online Journal of Issues in Nursing* 21 (January 2016), doi:10.3912/OJIN.Vol21No01Man02. The discussion, including the two graphs, is significantly adapted from this article.

Chapter 2

1. The Institute of Medicine (IOM) (2003) defines patient-centered care as the ability to "identify, respect, and care about patients' differences, values, preferences, and expressed needs; relieve pain and suffering; coordinate continuous care; listen to, clearly inform, communicate with, and educate patients; share decision making and management; and continuously advocate disease prevention, wellness, and promotion of healthy lifestyles, including a focus on population health" (M. Gaie Rubenfeld and Barbara K. Scheffer, *Critical Thinking Tactics for Nurses: Achieving the IOM Competencies*, 2nd ed. [Massachusetts: Jones and Bartlett Publishers, 2010], p. 71).

2. In *Best Care at Lower Cost*, the Committee on the Learning Health Care System in America found that "a growing body of evidence highlights the potential benefits of patient-centered care for clinical outcomes, health, satisfaction among health care workers, and providers' financial performance. For example, several hospitals that encourage patient-centered care by paying greater attention to patient needs and preferences, as well as care coordination, have found that adverse events decrease, employee retention increases, operating costs decrease, malpractice claims decline, lengths of stay are shorter, and the hospital's costs per case decrease (Mark Smith et al., eds., *Best Care at Lower Cost: The Path to Continuously Learning Health Care in America* [Washington, DC: Institute of Medicine, 2013], p. 194).

3. Michael Porter and Elizabeth Olmsted Teisberg, *Redefining Health Care* (Massachusetts: Harvard University Press, 2006), p. 4.

4. Steven D. Pearson and Lisa H. Raeke, "Patients' Trust in Physicians: Many Theories, Few Measures, and Little Data," *Journal of General Internal Medicine* 15 (July 2000), doi:10.1046/j.1525-1497.2000.11002.x.

5. Thomas H. Lee, *An Epidemic of Empathy in Healthcare: How to Deliver Compassionate, Connected Patient Care That Creates a Competitive Advantage* (New York: McGraw-Hill Education, 2016), p. 77.

6. Ibid.

7. Walter Kiechel, "The New New Capital Thing," *Harvard Business Review*, July–August 2000, https://hbr.org/2000/07/the-new-new-capital-thing.

8. Ethan Kross et al., "Facebook Use Predicts Declines in Subjective Well-Being in Young Adults," *PLOS One* 8 (August 2013), doi:https://doi.org/10.1371/journal.pone.0069841.

9. Akanksha Jayanthi, "The New Look of Diversity in Healthcare: Where We Are and Where We're Headed," *Hospital Review*, March 8, 2016, http://www.beckershospitalreview.com/hospital-management-administration/the-new-look-of-diversity-in-healthcare-where-we-are-and-where-we-re-headed.html.

10. According to the Agency for Healthcare Research and Quality's (AHRQ) Healthcare Cost and Utilization Project, older age groups average more frequent and lengthy hospital stays (Audrey J. Weiss and Anne Elixhauser, "Overview of Hospital Stays in the United States," *AHQR*, Statistical Brief #180, October 2014, https://www.hcup-us.ahrq.gov/reports/statbriefs/sb180-Hospitalizations-United-States-2012.pdf).

11. Rose M. Leavitt, "Generational Differences in Work Motivation of Healthcare Workers" (PhD dissertation, University of Nebraska, 2014), p. 27 passim.

12. Ibid., pp. 28–29.

13. "Nursing Shortage," American Nursing Association, http://www.nursingworld.org/MainMenuCategories/ThePracticeofProfessionalNursing/workforce/NursingShortage.

14. Rebecca Grant, "The U.S. Is Running Out of Nurses," *Atlantic*, February 3, 2016, https://www.theatlantic.com/health/archive/2016/02/nursing-shortage/459741/.

15. The Health Resources and Services Administration's (HRSA) Health Workforce Simulation Model examined trends and projections in the supply and demand for registered nurses in 2014 using data from 2012. Their findings projected a 33 percent increase in RN supply nationally by 2025 given the current pace of training and attrition. However, while not considered in the study, the HRSA suggested that the emerging care delivery models with a focus on management of health and populations would further increase the demand for nurses ("The Future of the Nursing Workforce: National- and State-Level Projections, 2012–2025," U.S. Department of Health and Human Services, Health Resources and Services Administration, National Center for Health Workforce Analysis, 2014, https://bhw.hrsa.gov/sites/default/files/bhw/nchwa/projections/nursingprojections.pdf).

16. "New Research Confirms Looming Physician Shortage," Association of American Medical Colleges, April 5, 2016, https://www.aamc.org/newsroom/newsreleases/458074/2016_workforce_projections_04052016.html.

17. Ann E. Rogers et al., "The Working Hours of Hospital Staff Nurses and Patient Safety," *Health Affairs* 23 (July 2004): 205, doi:10.1377/

hlthaff.23.4.202. The study further said: "Fourteen percent of the respondents reported working sixteen or more consecutive hours at least once during the four-week period. The longest shift worked was twenty-three hours, forty minutes . . . analysis showed that work duration, overtime, and number of hours worked per week had significant effects on errors. The likelihood of making an error increased with longer work hours and was three times higher when nurses worked shifts lasting of 12.5 hours or more (odds ratio = 3.29, p = .001). Working overtime increased the odds of making at least one error, regardless of how long the shift was originally scheduled (OR = 2.06, p = .0005). Our data also suggest that there is a trend for increasing risks when nurses work overtime after longer shifts (OR = 1.34, 1.53, and 3.26 for scheduled eight-hour, eight-to-twelve-hour, and twelve-hour shifts, respectively), with the risks being significantly elevated for overtime following a twelve-hour shift (p = .005)" (Rogers et al., pp. 205–207).

18. Amy Witkoski Stimpfel, Douglas M. Sloane, and Linda H. Aiken, "The Longer the Shifts for Hospital Nurses, the Higher the Levels of Burnout and Patient Dissatisfaction," *Health Affairs* 31 (November 2012), doi:10.1377/hlthaff.2011.1377.

Chapter 3

1. "Building a High-Performing Workforce," Press Ganey.
2. Kelly M. Pyrek, "Perception of Care, Contact Precautions Entwined in Patients' Minds, Studies Find," *Infection Control Today*, December 17, 2013, http://www.infectioncontroltoday.com/articles/2013/12/perception-of-care-contact-precautions-entwined-in-patients-minds-studies-find.aspx.
3. "The HCAHPS Survey—Frequently Asked Questions," cms.gov, https://www.cms.gov/medicare/quality-initiatives-patient-assessment-instruments/hospitalqualityinits/downloads/hospitalhcahpsfactsheet201007.pdf.
4. "Building a High-Performing Workforce," Press Ganey.
5. Arlie Russell Hochschild, *The Managed Hearth: Commercialization of Human Feeling* (Berkeley: University of California Press, 2012), p. 7. Author's original italics removed.
6. Please see "Building a High-Performing Workforce," Press Ganey.
7. This story draws on Diana Mahoney, "Quality Health Care Is a Team Effort," *Industry Edge,* January 2017, http://www.pressganey.com/resources/articles/quality-health-care-is-a-team-effort.

Chapter 4

1. "Empathy: The Human Connection to Patient Care," Cleveland Clinic, YouTube video, 4:23, published February 27, 2013, https://www.youtube.com/watch?v=cDDWvj_q-o8.

2. *English Oxford Living Dictionary*, s.v. "sympathy," accessed July 6, 2017, https://en.oxforddictionaries.com/definition/sympathy.

3. *Merriam-Webster Dictionary* defines "empathy" as "the action of understanding, being aware of, being sensitive to, and vicariously experiencing the feelings, thoughts, and experience of another of either the past or present without having the feelings, thoughts, and experience fully communicated in an objectively explicit manner (*Merriam-Webster*, s.v. "empathy," accessed July 6, 2017, https://www.merriam-webster.com/dictionary/empathy). Many people believe that empathy is an emotion, but in fact it's an ability to understand conceptually what someone else is experiencing. As scholars have written, "Literature supports a simulation theory of empathy, which proposes that we understand the thoughts and feelings of others by using our own mind as a model. In contrast, theory of mind research suggests that medial prefrontal regions are critical for understanding the minds of others" (Lian T. Rameson and Matthew D. Lieberman, "Empathy: A Social Cognitive Neuroscience Approach," *Social and Personality Psychology Compass* 3, no. 1 [2009]: 94).

4. *Cambridge Dictionary*, s.v. "compassion," accessed July 6, 2017, http://dictionary.cambridge.org/us/dictionary/english/compassion?q=compassion.

5. Marlaine C. Smith and Marilyn E. Parker, eds., *Nursing Theories and Nursing Practice*, 4th ed. (Philadelphia: F. A. Davis Company, 2015).

6. Mary Tonges and Joel Ray, "Translating Caring Theory into Practice: The Carolina Care Model," *Journal of Nursing Administration* 41, no. 9 (2011).

7. The list is directly adapted from Christina Dempsey et al., "Reducing Patient Suffering Through Compassionate Connected Care," *Journal of Nursing Administration* 44 (October 2014): 520–521, doi:10.1097/NNA.0000000000000110.

8. K. J. Swayden et al., "Effect of Sitting vs. Standing on Perception of Provider Time at Bedside: A Pilot Study," *Patient Education and Counseling* 86, no. 2 (2012), doi:10.1016/j.pec.2011.05.024.

9. Gerald B. Hickson et al., "Patient Complaints and Malpractice Risk," *Journal of the American Medical Association* 287, no. 22 (2002), doi:10.1001/jama.287.22.2951.

10. Howard B. Beckman et al., "The Doctor-Patient Relationship and Malpractice: Lessons from Plaintiff Depositions," *Archives of Internal Medicine* 154 (June 1994): 1365, 1367.

11. Paul Kalinithi, *When Breath Becomes Air* (New York: Random House, 2016), p. 166.

12. "2016 Nursing Special Report: The Role of Workplace Safety and Surveillance Capacity in Driving Nurse and Patient Outcomes," Press Ganey.

13. Maryann Abendroth, "Overview and Summary: Compassion Fatigue: Caregivers at Risk," *Online Journal of Issues in Nursing* 16 (January 2011), doi:10.3912/OJIN.Vol16No01OS01.

14. Henry D. Mason and Juan A. Nel, "Compassion Fatigue, Burnout and Compassion Satisfaction: Prevalence Among Nursing Students," *Journal of Psychology in Africa* 22, no. 3 (2012): 451.

15. Julie Apker, Kathleen M. Propp, and Wendy S. Zabava Ford, "Investigating the Effect of Nurse-Team Communication on Nurse Turnover: Relationships Among Communication Processes, Identification, and Intent to Leave," *Health Communication* 24 (2009): 107, doi:10.1080/10410230802676508.

16. Michelle O'Daniel and Alan H. Rosenstein, "Professional Communication and Team Collaboration," in *Patient Safety and Quality: An Evidence-Based Handbook for Nurses*, R. G. Hughes, ed. (Maryland: Agency for Healthcare Research and Quality, 2008), pp. 2–3.

Chapter 5

1. In his well-known "Golden Circle" model, leadership expert Simon Sinek has argued for starting with "why" rather than with "what." As Sinek relates, neuroscience supports starting with "why," since purpose-oriented messages activate parts of the human brain that control emotions, behavior, and decision making. For more information, please consult https://startwithwhy.com/.

2. Leon F. Seltzer, "Anger—How We Transfer Feelings of Guilt, Hurt, and Fear," *Psychology Today,* June 14, 2013, https://www.psychologytoday.com/blog/evolution-the-self/201306/anger-how-we-transfer-feelings-guilt-hurt-and-fear.

3. Kristopher H. Morgan, Bradley Fulton, and Louis Ayala, "Only Angry Patients Return Surveys Right . .?" Press Ganey, p. 3, http://www.pressganey.com.au/snapshots/Only%20Angry%20Patients%20Return%20Surveys%20-%20Right.pdf.

4. Ami Schattner, Alexander Bronstein, and Navah Hellin, "Information and Shared Decision-Making Are Top Patients' Priorities," *BMC Health Services Research* 6 (February 2006), doi:10.1186/1472-6963-6-21. As the authors conclude, "Patients most frequently selected information and increased autonomy as their *most* desirable change, i.e. that physicians would provide them with full information about their illness and treatment and involve them in decisions. This option was chosen by 75/274 patients (27.4%) as their first priority and an *additional* 36 patients wished for more autonomy as their second choice. Altogether, 111 patients wished they had more information from their physicians and more participation in decisions as their first or second priority (111/548, 20.2%). Easier access to more sophisticated medical services or a shorter

queue for tests were the next most wanted improvements (18% and 16%, respectively). Continuity of care came next. Interestingly, the time their physician could spare for them or the cost of medications, were least likely to be among patient's chief concerns."

5. Ibid.

6. Patricia H. Berry et al., "Pain: Current Understanding of Assessment, Management, and Treatment," *American Pain Society*, http://american painsociety.org/uploads/education/npc.pdf. According to an American Pain Society study, "Pain is common. About 9 in 10 Americans regularly suffer from pain, and pain is the most common reason individuals seek health care. Each year, an estimated 25 million Americans experience acute pain due to injury or surgery and another 50 million suffer chronic pain. Chronic pain is the most common cause of long-term disability, and almost one third of all Americans will experience severe chronic pain at some point in their lives."

7. David W. Baker, "The Joint Commission's Pain Standards: Origins and Evolution," Joint Commission, May 5, 2017, p. 6, https://www.joint commission.org/assets/1/6/Pain_Std_History_Web_Version_05122017 .pdf.

8. "Inspiring Innovation: Patient Report of Hourly Rounding," Institute for Innovation, 2014, http://www.theinstituteforinnovation.org/docs/default -source/innovation-stories/inspiring-innovation-stories_patient-report -of-hourly-rounding_final.pdf?sfvrsn=2.

9. C. M. Meade, A. L. Bursell, and L. Ketelsen, "Effects of Nursing Rounds: On Patients' Call Light Use, Satisfaction, and Safety," *American Journal of Nursing* 106 (September 2006).

10. A. Barbieri et al., "Effects of Clinical Pathways in the Joint Replacement: A Meta-analysis," *BMC Medicine* 7 (July 2009), doi:10.1186/1741-7015 -7-32.

11. Roger Benjamin et al., "The Case for Critical-Thinking Skills and Performance Assessment," cae.org, May 2013, p, 6, http://cae.org/ images/uploads/pdf/The_Case_for_Critical_Thinking_Skills.pdf.

12. M. Gaie Rubenfeld and Barbara K Scheffer, *Critical Thinking Tactics for Nurses: Achieving the IOM Competencies* (Massachusetts: Jones & Bartlett Learning, 2015), pp. xii, 7.

13. These bullet points are taken directly from "The Core Competencies Needed for Health Care Professionals," Institute of Medicine, 2003, https://www.ncbi.nlm.nih.gov/books/NBK221519/. They also appear in Chapter 3 of A. C. Greiner and E. Knebel, eds., *Health Professions Education: A Bridge to Quality* (Washington, DC: National Academies Press, 2003).

14. "The Conscious Competence Ladder: Keeping Going When Learning Gets Tough," *Mind Tools*, https://www.mindtools.com/pages/article/newISS_96.htm.

15. Patricia Benner, Ronda G. Hughes, and Molly Sutphen, "Clinical Reasoning, Decisionmaking, and Action: Thinking Critically and Clinically," in *Patient Safety and Quality: An Evidence-Based Handbook for Nurses*, Ronda G. Hughes, ed. (Maryland: Agency for Healthcare Research and Quality, 2008), p. 95.

16. Ibid.

17. Rubenfeld and Scheffer, *Critical Thinking Tactics for Nurses*, p. 120.

18. "Resilience," *Psychology Today*, https://www.psychologytoday.com/basics/resilience.

19. Daphne M. Davis and Jeffrey A. Hayes, "What Are the Benefits of Mindfulness?" *American Psychological Association* 43 (July/August 2012): 2.

20. Ibid., pp. 2–4.

21. Bret Stetka, "Changing Our DNA Through Mind Control?" *Scientific American*, December 16, 2014, https://www.scientificamerican.com/article/changing-our-dna-through-mind-control/.

22. "25 Best Tactics for Building Personal Resilience," Brandon Gaille, September 12, 2016, http://brandongaille.com/25-best-tactics-for-building-personal-resilience/.

23. Bryan Roth, "Three Easy Ways to Find Your Resilience," *Duke Today*, February 23, 2016, https://today.duke.edu/2016/02/resilience.

24. "25 Best Tactics," Brandon Gaille.

25. "Healthy Nurse, Healthy Nation," American Nursing Association, accessed July 7, 2017, http://www.nursingworld.org/HealthyNurse.

26. "Mindful Eating: 5 Easy Tips to Get Started," *Huffington Post*, November 12, 2013, http://www.huffingtonpost.com/2013/11/12/mindful-eating-tips_n_3941528.html.

Chapter 6

1. As an *American Academy of Family Physicians Journal* article reminds us, several parallels exist between current healthcare debates and those of the 1990s. Today, "hospitals and other entities are buying practices and employing physicians as a way to achieve efficiencies associated with system-wide integration, manage large population groups, and better position themselves for value-based or bundled payments. Although the integration in the '90s often ended in disintegration, with many hospitals later selling off the practices they had bought, this latest effort appears to have some differences. For example, there is now a greater emphasis on reaching quality goals and expanding information technology to support the work" (Travis Singleton and Phillip Miller, "The Physician Employment Trend: What You Need to Know," *Family Practice Management* 22 [July/

August 2015]: 11–12, http://www.aafp.org/fpm/2015/0700/p11.pdf. See also Geri Aston, "Hospitals Wise Up When Adding Physician Practices," *Hospitals & Health Networks*, March 1, 2013, http://www.hhnmag.com/articles/5993-hospitals-wise-up-when-adding-physician-practices.)

2. Diana Henderson, Christy Dempsey, and Debra Appleby, "A Case Study of Successful Patient Flow Methods: St. John's Hospital," *Frontiers of Health Services Management*, Summer 2004, pp. 28, 30, http://journals.lww.com/frontiersonline/Abstract/2004/04000/A_Case_Study_of_Successful_Patient_Flow_Methods_.4.aspx.

3. Pamela Mitchell et al., "Core Principles & Values of Effective Team-Based Health Care," Institute of Medicine, Discussion Paper, 2012, p. 5, https://www.nationalahec.org/pdfs/vsrt-team-based-care-principles-values.pdf.

4. Ibid., p. 2.

5. Danielle D'Amour et al., "The Conceptual Basis for Interprofessional Collaboration: Core Concepts and Theoretical Frameworks," *Journal of Interprofessional Care* 19 (May 2005), doi:10.1080/13561820500082529; François Chiocchio, Paule Lebel, and Jean-Nicolas Dubé, "Informational Role Self-Efficacy: A Validation in Interprofessional Collaboration Contexts Involving Healthcare Service and Project Teams," *BMC Health Services Research* 16 (April 2016), doi:10.1186/s12913-016-1382-x.

6. Cathal Doyle, Laura Lennox, and Derek Bell, "A Systematic Review of Evidence on the Links Between Patient Experience and Clinical Safety and Effectiveness," *BMJ Open* 3, no. 1 (2013), doi:10.1136/bmjopen-2012-001570.

7. P. D. Cleary, "A Hospitalization from Hell: A Patient's Perspective on Quality," *Annals of Internal Medicine* 138, no. 1 (2003).

8. "Competing on Patient-Driven Value: The New Health Care Marketplace," Press Ganey, March 24, 2016, p. 13.

9. Anna T. Mayo and Anita Williams Woolley, "Teamwork in Health Care: Maximizing Collective Intelligence via Inclusive Collaboration and Open Communication," *American Medical Association Journal of Ethics* 18 (September 2016), doi:10.1001/journalofethics.2016.18.09.stas2-1609.

10. "Developing and Sustaining High-Performance Work Teams," Society for Human Resource Management, July 23, 2015, https://www.shrm.org/resourcesandtools/tools-and-samples/toolkits/pages/developingandsustaininghigh-performanceworkteams.aspx.

11. Aída Ortega et al., "The Influence of Change-Oriented Leadership and Psychological Safety on Team Learning in Healthcare Teams," *Journal of Business and Psychology* 29 (June 2014), doi:10.1007/s10869-013-9315-8.

12. Anthony J. Perry et al., "Enhanced Discharge Planning Program at Rush University Medical Center," in *Comprehensive Care Coordination for*

Chronically Ill Adults, Cheryl Schraeder and Paul S. Shelton, eds. (West Sussex, UK: Wiley-Blackwell, 2011).

13. Lyle Nelson, "Lessons from Medicare's Demonstration Projects on Disease Management and Care Coordination," Congressional Budget Office, working paper, January 2012, https://www.cbo.gov/sites/default/files/112th-congress-2011-2012/workingpaper/WP2012-01_Nelson _Medicare_DMCC_Demonstrations_1.pdf.

14. S. M. Shortell et al., "The Role of Perceived Team Effectiveness in Improving Chronic Illness Care," *Medical Care* 42 (November 2004).

15. Susan Wheelan concluded that small groups show better development and performance than larger ones ("Group Size, Group Development, and Group Productivity," *Small Group Research* 40 [January 2009], doi:https://doi.org/10.1177/1046496408328703).

16. This account was drawn from Roger Resar et al., "Using Real-Time Demand Capacity Management to Improve Hospitalwide Patient Flow," *Joint Commission Journal on Quality and Patient Safety* 37 (May 2011), doi:http://dx.doi.org/10.1016/S1553-7250(11)37029-8.

17. Verne Harnish, *Mastering the Rockefeller Habits: What You Must Do to Increase the Value of Your Growing Firm* (Virginia: Gazelles Inc., 2011).

18. Manoj Jain, "Huddles: In Football, Business and Hospitals," *Huffington Post*, January 22, 2015, http://www.huffingtonpost.com/manoj-jain-md -mph/huddles-in-football-busin_b_6528402.html.

19. Susan Ashcraft et al., "Interprofessional Clinical Rounding: Effects on Processes and Outcomes of Care," *Journal for Healthcare Quality* 39 (March/April 2017), doi:10.1097/JHQ.0000000000000039; A. Begue et al., "Retrospective Study of Multidisciplinary Rounding on a Thoracic Surgical Oncology Unit," *Clinical Journal of Oncology Nursing* 16 (December 2012), doi:10.1188/12.CJON.E198-E202.

20. For more advice on how to conduct interdisciplinary rounding, see the Institute for Healthcare Improvement's "How-to Guide: Multidisciplinary Rounds," Massachusetts Institute for Healthcare Improvements, updated February 2015 (available for download at http://www.ihi.org).

21. Andrew D. Auerbach et al., "Preventability and Causes of Readmissions in a National Cohort of General Medicine Patients," *Journal of the American Medical Association* 176, no. 4 (2016), doi:10.1001/ jamainternmed.2015.7863.

22. Heidi Godman, "Medication Errors a Big Problem After Hospital Discharge," Harvard Medical School, July 9, 2012, http://www.health .harvard.edu/blog/medication-errors-a-big-problem-after-hospital -discharge-201207095012.

23. Michael E. Porter and Sachin H. Jain, "The University of Texas MD Anderson Cancer Center: Interdisciplinary Cancer Care," *Harvard Business School Case*, pp. 9, 14 passim.

24. Michael E. Porter and Thomas H. Lee, "The Strategy That Will Fix Health Care," *Harvard Business Review*, October 2013, https://hbr.org/2013/10/the-strategy-that-will-fix-health-care.

25. Ibid.

Chapter 7

1. For this account, I rely on Amy Cowperthwait, conversation with the author, June 4, 12, 2017. See also Amy Cowperthwait et al., "Healthcare Theatre and Simulation: Maximizing Interprofessional Partnerships," *Clinical Simulation in Nursing* 11 (September 2015), doi:http://dx.doi.org/10.1016/j.ecns.2015.05.005.

2. Dudley Adams, "Selective Referral to High-Volume Hospitals Estimating Potentially Avoidable Deaths," *Journal of the American Medical Association* 283 (March 2000), doi:10.1001/jama.283.9.1159; Michael West, "Building Successful Teams: Sparkling Fountains of Innovation" *Midwives Magazine*, September 2004, https://www.rcm.org.uk/news-views-and-analysis/analysis/building-successful-teams-sparkling-fountains-of-innovation.

3. Ronda G. Hughes, "Nurses at the 'Sharp End' of Patient Care," in *Patient Safety and Quality: An Evidence-Based Handbook for Nurses*, Ronda G. Hughes, ed. (Maryland: Agency for Healthcare Research and Quality, 2008). See also L. Hall McGillis, "Nurses Perceptions of Hospital Work Environments," *Journal of Nursing Management* 15, no. 3 (2007), doi:10.1111/j.1365-2834.2007.00676.x; Claudia Schmalenberg and Marlene Kramer, "Types of Intensive Care Units with the Healthiest, Most Productive Work Environments," *American Journal of Critical Care* 16 (September 2007), http://ajcc.aacnjournals.org/content/16/5/458.long.

4. Hughes, "Nurses at the 'Sharp End' of Patient Care," p. 5. See also West, "Building Successful Teams"; Michael A. West, David A. Shapiro, and Bob Haward, "Leadership Clarity and Team Innovation in Health Care," *Leadership Quarterly* 14 (2003), http://www.astonod.com/wp-content/uploads/2015/01/Leadership-Clarity-and-Team-Innovation-in-Health-Care.pdf; Howard Giles et al., *The Handbook of Intergroup Communication* (New York: Routledge, 2012), pp. 21–42; H. K. Laschinger, J. A. Sabiston, and L. Kutszcher, "Empowerment and Staff Nurse Decision Involvement in Nursing Work Environments: Testing Kanter's Theory of Structural Power in Organizations," *Research in Nursing and Health* 20 (August 1997).

5. Michelle O'Daniel and Alan H. Rosenstein, "Professional Communication and Team Collaboration," in *Patient Safety and Quality*, p. 3. See also Alan H. Rosenstein, Mark R. Chassin, and Elise C. Becher, "The Wrong Patient," *Annals of Internal Medicine* 136, no. 11 (2002), doi:10.7326/0003-4819-136-11-200206040-00012.

6. Mark Keroack et al., "Organizational Factors Associated with High Performance in Quality and Safety in Academic Medical Centers," *Academic Medicine* 82 (December 2007): 1182.

7. Ibid.

8. Carrie Gibson, "Getting the Most Out of Your Mission: Organizational Missions as a Key to Employee Engagement," Northwestern School of Education and Social Policy, March 2013, http://www.sesp.northwestern .edu/masters-learning-and-organizational-change/knowledge-lens/ stories/2013/getting-the-most-out-of-your-mission.html.

9. Warren G. Bennis and Burt Nanus, *Leaders: Strategies for Taking Charge* (New York: Harper & Row, 1985), p. 82. Jim Collins and Jerry Porras further proposed that vision statements reflect the organization's core ideology and envisioned future, defining the envisioned future as "Big, Hairy, Audacious Goals" (BHAGs) created by senior leaders that direct the organization's efforts. As they argue, vision helps preserve the core purpose and values of the organization while also helping it look toward the future (Jim Collins and Jerry I. Porras, "Building Your Company's Vision," *Harvard Business Review*, September–October 1996, https:// hbr.org/1996/09/building-your-companys-vision). See also R. Gulati et al., "Vision Statement Quality and Organizational Performance in U.S. Hospitals," *Journal of Healthcare Management* 61 (September/October 2016).

10. Fenwick Feng Jing, Gayle C. Avery, and Harald Bergsteiner, "Enhancing Performance in Small Professional Firms Through Vision Communication and Sharing," *Asia Pacific Journal of Management* 21 (June 2014), doi:10.1007/s10490-013-9345-9.

11. Jacqueline Mayfield, Milton Mayfield, and William C. Sharbrough, "Strategic Vision and Values in Top Leaders' Communications Motivating Language at a Higher Level," *International Journal of Business Communication* 52, no. 1 (2015).

12. See Peter F. Drucker, *Management: Tasks, Responsibilities, Practices* (New York: E. P. Dutton, 1986), p. 115.

13. Krista Jaakson, "Engagement of Organizational Stakeholders in the Process of Formulating Values Statements," *Atlantic Journal of Communication* 18, no. 3 (2010); R. Bhattacharya, T. M. Devinney, and M. M. Pillutla, "A Formal Model of Trust Based on Outcomes," *Academy of Management Review* 23 (July 1998).

14. C. Neal, "A Conscious Change in the Workplace," *Journal of Quality and Participation* 22, no. 2 (1999).

15. Ibid. See also Peggy Simcic Brønn, Andreas Engell, and Håvard Martinsen, "A Reflective Approach to Uncovering Actual Identity," *European Journal of Marketing* 40, no. 7/8 (2000), https://doi.org/ 10.1108/03090560610670043; Joan E. Finegan, "The Impact of

Person and Organizational Values on Organizational Commitment," *Journal of Occupational and Organizational Psychology*, 73 (June 2000), doi:10.1348/096317900166958; Glynis A. Fitzgerald and Nancy M. Desjardins, "Organizational Values and Their Relation to Organizational Performance Outcomes," *Atlantic Journal of Communication* 12, no. 3 (2004); Richard Barrett, "Why the Future Belongs to Values Added Companies," *Journal for Quality and Participation* 22 (January/February 1999); Carol C. Bocchino, Bruce W. Hartman, and Pamela F. Foley, "The Relationship Between Person-Organization Congruence, Perceived Violations of the Psychological Contract, and Occupational Stress Symptoms," *Consulting Psychology Journal: Practice and Research* 55, no. 4 (2003); Joel E. Urbany, "Inspiration and Cynicism in Values Statements," *Journal of Business Ethics* 62 (December 2005), doi:10.1007/s10551-005-0188-2.

16. D. R. Graber and A. O. Kilpatrick, "Establishing Values-Based Leadership and Value Systems in Healthcare Organizations," *Journal of Health and Human Services Administration* 21 (Fall 2008).

17. James MacGregor Burns, *Leadership* (New York: Harper & Row, 1978), pp. 43–44.

18. Graber and Kilpatrick, "Establishing Values-Based Leadership," p. 184.

19. "High Reliability," Agency for Healthcare Research and Quality, updated July 2016, https://psnet.ahrq.gov/primers/primer/31/high-reliability.

20. "Achieving Excellence: The Convergence of Safety, Quality, Experience and Caregiver Engagement," Press Ganey, 2017.

21. Ibid., pp. 6–7.

22. Shaurya Taran, "An Examination of the Factors Contributing to Poor Communication Outside the Physician-Patient Sphere," *McGill Journal of Medicine* 13 (June 2011).

23. "Managing Organizational Communication," *Society for Human Resource Management*, December 11, 2015.

24. "Transparency Strategies: Online Physician Reviews for Improving Care and Reducing Suffering," Press Ganey.

25. Ibid.

26. Christy Dempsey and Deirdre Mylod, "Addressing Patient and Caregiver Suffering: Learn About a Framework for Mitigating Inherent Suffering and Preventing Avoidable Suffering," *American Nurse Today* 11 (November 2016).

27. H. K. Laschinger, J. Finegan, and P. Wilk, "New Graduate Burnout: The Impact of Professional Practice Environment, Workplace Civility, and Empowerment," *Nursing Economic$* 27 (November–December 2009).

28. "Nursing Special Report: The Influence of Nurse Work Environment on Patient, Payment and Nurse Outcomes in Acute Care Settings," Press Ganey, p. 12.

29. V. Gokenbach and K. Drenkard, "The Outcomes of Magnet Environments and Nursing Staff Engagement: A Case Study," *Nursing Clinics of North American* 46 (March 2011), doi:10.1016/j.cnur.2010 .10.008.

30. J. Cho, H. K. Laschinger, and C. Wong, "Workplace Empowerment, Work Engagement and Organizational Commitment of New Graduate Nurses," *Nursing Leadership* 19 (September 2006); M. A. Halm, "Hourly Rounds: What Does the Evidence Indicate?" *American Journal of Critical Care* 18 (November 2009), doi:10.4037/ajcc2009350.

31. *Safe Patient Handling and Mobility: Interprofessional National Standards* (Maryland: Nursesbooks.org, 2013), http://nursingworld.org/ DocumentVault/OccupationalEnvironment/SPHM-Standards -Resources/Sample-of-the-SPHM-book.pdf.

32. "Nursing Special Report: The Influence of Nurse Work Environment on Patient, Payment and Nurse Outcomes in Acute Care Settings," Press Ganey, 2015.

33. Amy Cowperthwait, conversation with the author.

Chapter 8

1. David Squires and Chloe Anderson, "U.S. Health Care from a Global Perspective: Spending, Use of Services, Prices, and Health in 13 Countries," Commonwealth Fund, October 2015, http:// www.commonwealthfund.org/publications/issue-briefs/2015/oct/ us-health-care-from-a-global-perspective.

2. Liyan Chen, "The Most Profitable Industries in 2016," *Forbes*, December 21, 2015, https://www.forbes.com/sites/liyanchen/2015/12/21/ the-most-profitable-industries-in-2016/#17befa3b5716.

3. Jerry W. Taylor, "A Brief History on the Road to Healthcare Reform: From Truman to Obama," *Hospital Review*, February 11, 2014, http://www.beckershospitalreview.com/news-analysis/a-brief-history-on -the-road-to-healthcare-reform-from-truman-to-obama.html.

4. Ibid.

5. Ibid.

6. Kyle Feldscher, "CBO Set to Release Analysis of Senate Healthcare Bill Monday," *Washington Examiner*, June 25, 2017, http://www.washington examiner.com/cbo-set-to-release-analysis-of-senate-healthcare-bill -monday/article/2627049.

7. Craig Clapper, e-mail to the author, June 28, 2017.

8. "Traits of a Healthy Nuclear Safety Culture," Institute of Nuclear Power Operations, April 2013, http://nuclearsafety.info/wp-content/ uploads/2010/07/Traits-of-a-Healthy-Nuclear-Safety-Culture-INPO -12-012-rev.1-Apr2013.pdf.

9. Clapper, e-mail to the author.

10. Donald M. Berwick and Andrew D. Hackbarth, "Eliminating Waste in US Health Care," *Journal of the American Medical Association* 307, no. 14 (2012): 1513 and abstract, doi:10.1001/jama.2012.362.

11. For more on this topic, please consult Mark D. Smith, *Best Care at Lower Cost: The Path to Continuously Learning Health Care in America* (Washington, DC: National Academies Press, 2013), pp. 1–3 passim.

12. Ibid., p. 334.

13. Kristin N. Ray et al., "Opportunity Costs of Ambulatory Medical Care in the United States," *American Journal of Managed Care* 21, no. 8 (2015).

14. Mattie Quinn, "To Many's Surprise, Obamacare Barely Budged ER Wait Times," governing.com, November 17, 2015, http://www .governing.com/topics/health-human-services/gov-emergency-room -wait-times.html.

15. This story originally appeared in Diana Mahoney, "Breaking New Ground in the Era of Health Care Consumerism," Press Ganey, April 21, 2016, http://www.pressganey.com/resources/articles/breaking-new -ground-in-the-era-of-health-care-cosnumerism.

16. Ibid.

17. Ibid.

18. Jonathan R. Slotkin, "Why GE, Boeing, Lowe's, and Walmart Are Directly Buying Health Care for Employees," *Harvard Business Review*, June 8, 2017, https://hbr.org/2017/06/why-ge-boeing-lowes-and -walmart-are-directly-buying-health-care-for-employees.

19. Ibid.

20. Melinda K. Abrams et al., "Delivery System Reforms: A Progress Report at Five Years," Commonwealth Fund, May 7, 2015, http:// www.commonwealthfund.org/publications/issue-briefs/2015/may/ aca-payment-and-delivery-system-reforms-at-5-years.

21. Ibid.

22. Michael E. Porter and Robert S. Kaplan, "How to Pay for Health Care," *Harvard Business Review*, July–August 2016, https://hbr.org/2016/07/ how-to-pay-for-health-care.

23. Ibid.

24. Jessica Schubel and Judith Solomon, "States Can Improve Health Outcomes and Lower Costs in Medicaid Using Existing Flexibility," Center on Budget and Policy Priorities, April 9, 2015, https://www .cbpp.org/research/health/states-can-improve-health-outcomes-and -lower-costs-in-medicaid-using-existing.

25. David Muhelstein, "Growth and Dispersion of Accountable Care Organizations in 2015," *Health Affairs Blog*, March 31, 2015, http:// healthaffairs.org/blog/2015/03/31/growth-and-dispersion-of -accountable-care-organizations-in-2015-2/.

26. Sylvia Matthews Burwell, "Better, Smarter, Healthier: In Historic Announcement, HHS Sets Clear Goals and Timeline for Shifting Medicare Reimbursements from Volume to Value," Vote Smart, January 26, 2015, https://votesmart.org/public-statement/947573/better-smarter-healthier-in-historic-announcement-hhs-sets-clear-goals-and-timeline-for-shifting-medicare-reimbursements-from-volume-to-value#.WWofhYjyvIU.

27. Kyra Bobinet and John Petito, "Designing the Consumer-Centered Telehealth & eVisit Experience," Office of National Coordinator for Health Information Technology, U.S. Department of Health and Human Services, https://www.healthit.gov/sites/default/files/Designing ConsumerCenteredTelehealtheVisit-ONC-WHITEPAPER-2015 V2edits.pdf.

28. "What Is Telehealth?" HealthIT.gov, https://www.healthit.gov/telehealth. See also "E-health and Telemedicine," U.S. Department of Health and Human Services, August 12, 2016, https://aspe.hhs.gov/system/files/pdf/206751/TelemedicineE-HealthReport.pdf.

29. Thomas Bodenheimer and Laurie Bauer, "Rethinking the Primary Care Workforce—An Expanded Role for Nurses," *New England Journal of Medicine* 375 (September 2016), doi:10.1056/NEJMp1606869.

30. Thomas Bodenheimer and Mark D. Smith, "Primary Care: Proposed Solutions to the Physician Shortage Without Training More Physicians," *Health Affairs* 32 (November 2013), doi:10.1377/hlthaff.2013.0234.

31. Ibid.

32. Ibid. See also M. P. Nowalk et al., "Evaluation of a Toolkit to Introduce Standing Orders for Influenza and Pneumococcal Vaccination in Adults: A Multimodal Pilot Project," *Vaccine* 7, no. 30 (2012), doi:10.1016/j.vaccine.2012.07.023.

33. For current figures, please consult the Bureau of Labor Statistics, http://www.bls.gov.

34. Nathan A. Boucher et al., "Agents for Change: Nonphysician Medical Providers and Health Care Quality," *Permanente Journal* 19 (Winter 2015): 91, doi:https://doi.org/10.7812/TPP/14-095. See also Marc Moote, Cathleen Krsek, and Ruth Kleinpell, "Physician Assistant and Nurse Practitioner Utilization in Academic Medical Centers," *American Journal of Medical Quality* 26, no. 6 (2011), doi:10.1177/1062860611402984; Robert H. Lohr et al., "Comparison of the Quality of Patient Referrals from Physicians, Physician Assistants, and Nurse Practitioners," *Mayo Clinic Proceedings* 88 (November 2013), doi:http://dx.doi.org/10.1016/j.mayocp.2013.08.013; Christine Everett et al., "Physician Assistants and Nurse Practitioners Perform Effective Roles on Teams Caring for Medicare Patients with Diabetes," *Health Affairs* 32 (November 2013), doi:10.1377/hlthaff.2013.0506.

35. Bodenheimer and Smith, "Primary Care."

36. Ibid. See also Rachel Williard and Thomas Bodenheimer, "The Building Blocks of High-Performing Primary Care: Lessons from the Field," California HealthCare Foundation, April 2012, http://www.chcf.org/~/media/MEDIA%20LIBRARY%20Files/PDF/PDF%20B/PDF%20BuildingBlocksPrimaryCare.pdf.

37. Annette M. Boyle, "VA: Expanded Role for Advanced Practice Nurses Will Improve Care Access Physician Group Claims That Will 'Significantly Undermine' Quality," *U.S. Medicine*, July 2016, http://www.usmedicine.com/agencies/department-of-veterans-affairs/va-expanded-role-for-advanced-practice-nurses-will-improve-care-access-physician-group-claims-that-will-significantly-undermine-quality/.

38. Mary D. Naylor and Ellen T. Kurtzman, "The Role of Nurse Practitioners in Reinventing Primary Care," *Health Affairs* 29 (May 2010), doi:10.1377/hlthaff.2010.0440.

Epilogue

1. Christina Prignano, "Widower thanks hospital staff for care after wife's death," *Boston Globe*, October 7, 2016, https://www.bostonglobe.com/metro/2016/10/07/widowed-husband-writes-thank-you-letter-hospital-that-cared-for-his-wife/tE4yzhEc2NjRENEDaMJOoM/story.html and Peter DeMarco, "A Letter to the Doctors and Nurses Who Cared for My Wife," *New York Times*, October 6, 2016, https://www.nytimes.com/2016/10/06/well/live/a-letter-to-the-doctors-and-nurses-who-cared-for-my-wife.html?_r=0.

2. Ibid.

3. Ibid.

4. "Health Care Improvement: Raising the Bar on the Patient Experience," Agency for Healthcare Research and Quality (forthcoming publication, July 25, 2017).

5. Ibid.

Index

About the Author

CHRISTINA (CHRISTY) DEMPSEY, RN, is Chief Nursing Officer at Press Ganey. She is responsible for providing clinical guidance to help clients transform the patient experience, and leads Press Ganey's efforts to reduce patient suffering and develop compassionate and connected care across the continuum. In addition, she works to increase employee and physician engagement, improve the flow of patients through organizations, boost quality and efficiency, and prepare organizations for healthcare reform.

Before becoming Chief Nursing Officer, Christy served as leader of clinical and operational consulting services at Press Ganey, helping clients embrace the clinical components of the patient experience by both redefining and redesigning the way patients flow and care is delivered in organizations. Her work led to 70 percent reductions in waiting time, double digit percentile improvements in patient satisfaction, enhanced teamwork and leadership, and operational improvements in scheduling, staffing, and data integration.

Since 2008, Christy has served as a faculty member at the Missouri State University Department of Nursing. She is a member of the American Nurses Association (ANA), Sigma Theta Tau, American Organization of Nurse Executives (AONE), Association of periOperative Nurses (AORN), American College of Healthcare Executives (ACHE), and Missouri Organization of Nurse Leaders (MONL). She serves as an ANCC Pathway to Excellence Appraiser and as an editorial board member of the *Journal of Nursing Administration (JONA)* and the *Journal of Patient Experience (JPE)*. She serves on the board of the Missouri Organization of Nurse Leaders (MONL), and is a Fellow of the American Academy of Nursing.

Christy frequently speaks and publishes nationally and internationally on patient experience, nursing, patient flow, physician-hospital collaborations, and the balancing of cost and quality.

A registered nurse with over three decades of healthcare experience in nursing, perioperative and emergency services management, medical practice, supply chain and materials management, and physician-hospital collaboration, she holds master's degrees in business and nursing and is certified in perioperative nursing and executive nursing practice.

Christy resides in Springfield, Missouri, with her husband, Tom.

About Press Ganey

Press Ganey was founded more than 30 years ago, based on a passion to help improve the way in which healthcare is delivered. Today, that principle remains a core element of Press Ganey's mission to help healthcare organizations across the continuum reduce suffering and enhance caregiver resilience to improve the safety, quality, and experience of care.

Press Ganey partners with providers to capture the voices of patients, physicians, nurses, and employees to gain insights to address unmet needs. Through the use of integrated data, advanced analytics, and strategic advisory services, Press Ganey helps clients transform their organizations to deliver safer, high-quality, patient- and family-focused care.

Press Ganey is recognized as a pioneer and thought leader in patient experience measurement and performance improvement solutions. As a strategic business partner to more than 26,000 healthcare organizations, Press Ganey leads the industry in helping clients transform the patient experience and create continuous sustainable improvement to healthcare delivery.

For more information, please visit pressganey.com.